Women
in Career
& Life
Transitions

Sandy Anderson, MBA, PhD

jist
Publishing

Women in Career and Life Transitions
© 2000 by *Sandy Anderson, MBA, PhD*

Published by JIST Works, Inc.
8902 Otis Avenue
Indianapolis, IN 46216
Phone: 317-264-3720   Fax: 317-264-3709   E-mail: jistworks@aol.com
Visit our Web site for information on other JIST Works products: www.jist.com

Edited by Kitty Jarrett
Proofread by Becca York
Interior design by Debbie Berman
Cover design by Honeymoon Image & Design Incorporated

Printed in the United States of America.

03   02   01   00   9   8   7   6   5   4   3   2   1

ISBN: 1-56370-670-9

To my loving husband, Bob, and my beautiful daughter, Alexandra.
Your constant support and inspiration mean the world to me.
Thank you for encouraging me to pursue my dreams.

ACKNOWLEDGMENTS

I'd like to express my appreciation to all the individuals—family, friends, colleagues, and the JIST Works, Inc., staff—who believed in this book long before it became one. Also, a special thank you to the many women who freely shared their career and life experiences so that others may benefit. Your touching stories are the heart and soul of this book. Finally, a *big* thank you to my wonderful husband, Bob, for watching Ali in the wee hours of the morning so that I could write this book, and to Ali for being my little angel throughout this process. I couldn't have done it without your support.

Contents

CHAPTER 3

Choosing a Suitable Work Arrangement 41

CHAPTER 4

Evaluating Your Training and Educational Needs 61

PART II: GETTING READY

CHAPTER 5

Expanding Your Comfort Zone 79

CHAPTER 6
Getting Your Support Systems in Place 93

PART III: GOING FOR IT

CHAPTER 9
Finding the Work You Love 155

Preface

I knew that having a baby would change my life, but I never could have imagined the powerful feelings that would come over me when my eyes met Ali's, seconds after she was born. In the 7 weeks she's been with us, those feelings intensify and the love grows stronger every day. She has rocked my world in a way that I find difficult to put into words.

When I was pregnant, I visualized carrying on with my work as a writer and consultant after my baby was born. No problem. I'd have the baby in December and take the rest of the month off to be with her and my husband, Bob. We'd have a good amount of quality time to adjust and get to know each other in this wonderful new relationship. In January I'd be able to work around her napping schedule and on weekends when my husband Bob could be home to watch her. It would all fall into place beautifully.

December came and went so quickly that it seemed nonexistent. We had the holiday hustle and bustle, family was here to visit and see the baby, and we were slowly adjusting to the new world of parenthood and being a threesome (after 12 years of being a couple). What happened to our quality time with Ali? Where did it go?

Now here it is, mid-January, and I'm faced with a dilemma. I made a commitment to write a book on mastering change. I also have a brand new baby, whom I want to sit and stare at all day. I long to talk to her, hold her, and see her smile. She is my priority. I don't want to hire child care. I want to care for her myself. I want to know her like the back of my hand and I want her to know me. I want to be here to encourage and support her development. But I've also made a commitment to write this book in record time.

I had no idea that my feelings for this baby would be so strong, that they could overpower my previous desire to continue working after she was born. As long as I stay on the fence, I'm miserable, I'm not giving my best to Ali and Bob, and I'm not focused on writing this book.

I'm lucky to have options, but isn't it sometimes easier when things are decided for us or they magically fall into place like the pieces of a puzzle? The truth is, I'm no different from anyone else. Change is scary. So are the risk and commitment that come with making a decision and following through. When I make a choice, I must act on that choice and say good-bye to the road not taken.

If I decline this book offer and opt to spend all my time with Ali, then I'll be giving up the opportunity to publish the career book for women I've longed to write for 2 years. If I choose to write the book, then I must commit a huge chunk of focused time each week to achieve my goal of completing the book quickly. And because I don't wish to use child care, these are hours I must squeeze out of every day while Ali is (hopefully) napping.

Can I do it? Dare I do it? Am I crazy, or what? Can someone please tell me what to do? What is the best thing? Is it possible to have my cake and eat it, too? Why must I be faced with such difficult decisions? My inner voice repeats these questions over and over until I do something, until I arrive at a solution to this emotional tug-of-war.

I ask myself what I would do given only a split second to make the choice. I say, "Write the book! You can do it! Somehow you'll find a way. And your time with Ali and Bob *will* be quality when you make this commitment and get on a schedule that allows you to achieve your desires. But first you must *get off the fence!*"

When I sit down to write, I'm distracted. I want to stare at Ali (even while she's sleeping). I keep thinking, "This *is* a balancing act, and I must give myself time to advance and adjust, and get past the learning curve. I know I can do it, but growing pains are tiring, frustrating, and as the expression suggests, *down-right painful.*"

Welcome to the world of change. I myself face all the fears and obstacles I address in this book. Approaching new situations can provoke a mixture of emotions, including elation, excitement, anxiety, self-doubt, and depression. These feelings tire us out, create stress, and often zap our motivation and forward momentum.

Part of the change process involves working through the tearing emotions that cloud your thinking so much that making a decision is nearly impossible. These emotional struggles are important to taking the first step in a new direction—much the way a baby crawls before walking.

I finally come to the conclusion that I need to write this book for me as much as I need to write it for other women facing similar dilemmas. Life changes have a dramatic impact on our career choices, and I've yet to find a career book that addresses this reality.

If you find yourself at a crossroads because of a dramatic change that "rocks your world," then please read this book. I wrote it to successfully coach you through this process. You deserve this time-out to explore and ultimately define the best next step for you. We're all here for a reason. Let's get closer to finding your reason for being.

Amazing Facts About Women

Women across the country are jumping on new career opportunities at an accelerated pace. According to the U.S. Department of Labor Women's Bureau, the following are some amazing facts about women in the workforce:

◆ There were 105 million women age 16 and over in the United States in 1997. Of that total, 63 million were in the civilian labor force.

◆ Between 1996 and 2006, women will account for 59% of total labor force growth.

◆ The number of working women doubled between 1970 and 1997, from 30 million to 60 million.

◆ The majority of women workers remain in the labor force during their childbearing years. As of 1996, this included 70% of mothers with children under age 18, 77% of mothers with children ages 6 through 17, 62% of mothers with children under age 6, and 59% of mothers with children under age 3.

◆ Women-owned businesses represent one-third of all domestic firms and 40% of all retail and service firms.

◆ The number of firms owned by women grew 78% between 1987 and 1996—nearly twice the rate of increase in all U.S. firms (47%).

◆ Women-owned firms employ 26% of the U.S. labor force. In fact, 18.5 million people owe their jobs to a woman business owner.

◆ Women-owned firms contributed $2.3 trillion in sales to the U.S. economy in 1996, an increase of 236% since 1987. Revenues generated by women-owned businesses have more than tripled in 9 years.

◆ Women-owned businesses lead the way in providing employee benefits. They share business profits with employees at an earlier stage. They are also more likely than other businesses to offer flextime, tuition reimbursement, and job sharing.

◆ Working wives contribute substantially to family income. In 1996 the median income for married-couple families with the wife in the paid workforce was $58,381, compared with $33,748 for those without the wife in the paid workforce.

◆ Since the mid-1980s, women have outnumbered men in graduate school.

◆ By the year 2050, 1 in 12 people will be 80 years old or older, and it's predicted that 2 out of 3 of them will be women.

INTRODUCTION

Do you realize that work and life are inseparable? Think about how changes in your personal life affect your work life, and vice versa. I have yet to find a career book that takes this reality into account. There's no question that preparing a good résumé and landing job interviews are important, but what about the impact of life changes that take place in unison with career changes?

How can you look for a job when your marriage is falling apart? What do you do when you've invested 20 years in your career, and at age 40 your first baby is on the way? How do you react when your boss tells you that companywide changes are being implemented, and your position has been cut? How do you decide what to do with yourself when your husband dies? What is your purpose when your children leave home and you've spent 20 years raising them to become responsible, well-rounded adults? What do you do when your company offers a generous incentive to retire, but you still want to work?

These changes are by no means exclusive to women; however, many "typical" circumstances dramatically affect the career and life choices women make. Let's explore this further. We all know that women physically have babies. Career-committed women are more likely to forgo or postpone childbirth, which triggers a continual reexamination of values and priorities. At the other end of the spectrum are women who forgo or postpone their careers (and income-earning potential) to stay home and care for their children, spouses, and/or aging parents. Women over 65 are five times more likely to lose their spouses to death than are men that age. Such a loss can result in feelings of emptiness, as many of these women have devoted their lives to caring for their families.

According to a recent survey conducted by the Families and Work Institute, a nonprofit research group based in New York, women also invest 4 hours into household responsibilities to every 1 hour that their partners invest. Single and divorced women with children must somehow care for their children and home, *and* earn a living in a world where women earn 75% of what men earn and hold less than 5% of the top executive positions (Source: U.S. Department of Labor Women's Bureau).

In order to make suitable career choices, it's imperative that our life circumstances be taken into account. In the world of work, it has long been established that men tend to mentally and physically separate their work and personal lives. For the most part, women have had to conform to this approach or put their careers at risk in an effort to handle personal commitments (for example, "the mommy track"), with little or no support.

Research reveals that most women have an automatic tendency to integrate their work and personal lives, and that those who do have less stress and are more content with all areas of their lives. It is because of this that I've realized a dire need for a career book that integrates our work and personal lives as women so naturally do.

Employers are just beginning to realize the value of this concept with their employees by offering benefits and programs to help individuals achieve work/ life balance. They're learning that the end result will be happier, more productive employees and an improved bottom line for the company. If *your* ultimate goal is to achieve maximum work/life satisfaction and balance, read on!

According to the U.S. Department of Labor, women comprise 46% of the workforce. By the year 2005, twice as many women will join the workforce as men. The average woman will have 7 different careers in her lifetime and hold 15 jobs. Eighty percent of women are not happy in their current positions. What is the underlying message here?

The message is all about *change*. Change is constant. Change is inevitable. It comes in all shapes and forms, and it's here to stay. Our personal lives are continually changing, and so is the world around us. Just think of all the changes that have occurred in the latter part of the 20th century: personal computers, the Internet, electronic banking, fast-food restaurants, microwave cooking, cellular/digital telephones, computerized supermarkets, two-income families, and day care centers. Let's not forget to mention the tremendous progress that's been made in the aerospace, media, and medical industries. These changes affect all aspects of our personal lives, from the kinds of foods we eat to where and how we work.

Change can overwhelm us or open up opportunities we never dreamed possible. Large organizations, for instance, are breaking down into small self-managed units. Many full-time employees are being replaced by a contingent workforce. About 20% of all professionals now work as temporary workers, including lawyers, doctors, and executives. As technology continues to advance at a rapid pace, and corporations increasingly hire independent contractors to work on a per-project basis, temporary, part-time, and self-employment opportunities will continue to flourish.

Hence, another source of motivation for writing this book was to empower women with the tools to overcome personal obstacles during times of career and life transition, and offer insight and inspiration on how to define and pursue a desirable work/life path in the ever-changing world.

On a personal level, you'll learn how to handle emotions that are running rampant (such as fear, anger, depression, loneliness), create support systems (including fostering support from family and friends), expand your comfort zone, manage stress, set goals, develop a financial plan, and welcome change.

On a professional level, you'll learn how to master career change in the 21st century. The world of work is in a constant state of flux. In this book you'll get all the guidance you need to pursue your new direction, including information on how to

◆ Align your career choice(s) with your values, interests, and abilities
◆ Choose a suitable work arrangement (for example, traditional 9-to-5 job, part-time work, temporary work, job sharing, telecommuting, self-employment, home business, independent contracting, portfolio career, volunteer work)
◆ Decide whether to gain experience and/or go back to school
◆ Survive college
◆ Create great résumés and cover letters
◆ Conduct hands-on research
◆ Use networking to achieve your goals quickly
◆ Experiment with new careers
◆ Step through a career decision process
◆ Find the work you love in an arrangement that suits you
◆ Master the art of interviewing for jobs and negotiating offers

This book provides all the personal and professional support you need to step through your work/life transition. Whether your career choice involves going back to school, pursuing your dream to become a doctor, starting your own business, doing volunteer work, or putting your work on the back burner to become a mom first, you'll find valuable insight to help you achieve your goals.

PART I

Self-Evaluation

CHAPTER 1

WHERE ARE YOU NOW?

"You have many gifts that you've never opened.
These are gifts of talent, ability, and 'reach' that
are yours for the taking."

PRICE PRITCHETT, PhD

T hink of this chapter as an opportunity to open your "gifts," your unrealized desires, talents, and abilities. You will learn about yourself by taking part in a brief self-evaluation. You'll check in with yourself to see where you are emotionally, personally, and financially. By doing so, you'll establish a starting point for your time of transition in each of these areas. When you know where you stand, you'll be in a better position to determine precisely what your needs are. When your needs are determined, we'll be able to address how best to meet them in Chapter 6, "Getting Your Support Systems in Place."

Most of this chapter is devoted to information and exercises designed to target your needs, values, interests, and abilities. My goal is to assist you in bringing out the real *you* so that you'll be armed with the self-knowledge you need to pursue a direction you're passionate about, which we'll start to discuss in Chapter 2, "Where Do You Want to Be?" At the same time, I want you to relax, be honest in your answers, and have fun. After all, a gift isn't much of a gift if there's no element of fun to it.

This is a perfect opportunity for journaling. If you keep a notebook handy, you can write down your thoughts while you read. You might want to separate your journaling by chapters so that you can go back and review particular areas or see how you've progressed.

Julia Bauer, founder and owner of Résumé Resources, a résumé and career coaching business in Northern California, says that many job seekers would rather skip the self-discovery phase and jump to putting together a résumé and starting a job hunt. Julia says

> *Often people are in a hurry to get on with their new career, and*
> *they don't want to "waste time" going through the investigative*

process. The problem with this is that it often backfires. In their haste to start their new career, they don't have enough information to decide whether they'll like it (and whether it pays enough, has job openings, and whether they have the right education and qualifications). This makes it difficult to create a convincing résumé highlighting their relevant experience. In order to know what experience is relevant, they first need to know a lot about themselves and their new career.

Emotional Check-in

In this section you'll do an emotional check-in to get in touch with how you're currently feeling. Take this time to be honest with yourself about how the impact of change has affected your morale. Are extreme emotions paralyzing you—stopping you in your tracks—so that you're afraid to take a step in any direction? The way to get around this is to identify and focus on your immediate goal. In the questions and exercises that follow, you'll have the opportunity to formulate your definition of success so that you can set goals to realize it. An important part of this process involves targeting vulnerable areas in need of emotional support.

Leslie, Age 47

Leslie's heart ached when her second child left home for college. Leslie was left alone with the dog and cats, and she felt lifeless. She and her husband, Jeff, had worked hard together, building a life that included saving for retirement and setting aside money so their children could go to college. Then one horrible day, Jeff died of a heart attack, leaving Leslie to fend for herself and the children.

"I remember trying to remain strong for the kids," Leslie says. "The pressure on me was tremendous. I was so stricken with grief that I didn't realize how much I was holding inside. It was such a shock. Thank God my close friend Dana was there for me. She was not only my shoulder to cry on, but she insisted on watching the kids for short periods of time to give me a chance to mourn the loss of Jeff. That time-out was just what I needed. I was able to be introspective and decide what to do next with my life."

At another turning point, with the last of her kids leaving home, Leslie realized that the difficult experience of losing her husband unexpectedly taught her the importance of checking in with herself and taking a much-needed time-out to regroup and refocus.

The Impact of Change

Everything new that ever happens to us—whether it's getting married, moving, going on a diet, learning to ski, or losing a loved one—results in change. Unfortunately, we're not taught how to deal with change. It's as if we're expected to grow up automatically knowing how to gracefully seek out, accept, and respond to change.

Why is learning how to deal with change so important? We feel insecure when we don't know what lies ahead. We become anxious and worried. In short, change brings on stress. In his book *You Can Excel in Times of Change* (Pocket Books), Shad Helmstetter reflects

> *What is at the root of insecurity?* Change. *What is always found close to any problem of deep anxiety?* Change—*or something that* should *change but isn't changing. What is one of the basics of human life that all people want* most, *fear* most, *and* need *most?* Change. *What is the only absolutely certain human condition that will exist from the moment of birth throughout an entire lifetime to the moment of death?* Change.

Negative emotions resulting from the fear of change cause stress that can lead to physical symptoms. We all know the toll that continued stress can take on our health. Stress is one of the biggest contributors to emotional and physical illness in the United States today. Needless to say, change—the most predictable and feared aspect of our existence—is certainly worthy of learning how to manage, and we will talk about this crucial issue in Chapter 11, "Mastering Change." In learning how to master change, we'll learn how to manage stress so that we can lead happier, healthier, more balanced lives.

How's Your Morale?

Let's do a quick check to see where your morale is during your time (or anticipated time) of transition. How do you feel emotionally? Are you happy? sad? angry? depressed? indifferent? lonely? fearful? anxious? stressed? many or all of the above? During times of transition, it's normal to experience turbulent emotions (although this need not be the case, if you learn how to manage change properly).

After all, we're brought up thriving on routine and predictability. Get up in the morning, go to school, come home, do homework, go out and play (or the reverse of the latter two, if you're a true procrastinator). Most of us aren't accustomed to change. We haven't learned how to deal and roll with it as it comes along—and come along it does, in a steady flowing stream, ready or not.

Change can drastically affect a person's satisfaction with life. If you're uneasy during a transition and are anxious to steer your ship to the nearest port (or any port, just to feel like you belong somewhere), you risk your long-term happiness by selling out to ease your short-term discomfort. Remember that uneasiness is a natural part of the change process, so don't confuse it with thinking you're permanently unhappy. Being in a state of flux can be difficult at best because people are creatures of habit.

We're not taught how to deal with change in our growing years, or even to think of it as a normal part of everyday life. So what do we do? We run from change. We avoid it. Instead, we need to learn how to make change work *for* us instead of *against* us.

Your Definition of Success

We can start by identifying our own unique definition of success. Society tends to honor the workaholic—the individual striving to be number one—as the ultimate picture of success. The influence of this portrayal, however, can unfortunately encourage us to behave in a self-destructive fashion. It robs us of time and energy. As we work harder, we make more money. The more money we make, the more we spend. The more we spend, the more we need to make, and so forth. We are caught in an endless loop, trying to keep up with our needs, not to mention those of others, and of course the image of success we bought into to begin with. Such a scenario can be vicious, exhausting, and meaningless.

That's why it's so important to define success on your own terms. You may view success as your ability to simplify your life and live with less, while doing so in a life pursuit you thoroughly enjoy. You may experience success in terms of your capacity to influence and help others, or be the best parent or partner. You may see it as your ability to lead a balanced life. In its most basic form, success may equate to finding happiness.

What is your definition of success? Without regard for what others think, do, and feel, go from your gut and write down your thoughts about success in your journal. It might help to think of yourself in your rocking chair at age 95, reminiscing over the years. What successes would touch you most, make you feel content, proud, and glowing inside?

Time for an Emotional Time-out?

Taking the time to define success on your own terms is a way of stepping out of your daily routine to introspect on what it's all about—this life we were born to live. During a time of transition, it's healthy and necessary to take an emotional time-out, to heal, reflect, and search for new directions. In their book *LifeLaunch* (Hudson Institute Press), Frederic Hudson and Pamela McLean refer to this phase of life as "cocooning," a period we travel in and out of throughout our lives:

> When you cocoon, you take stock of your life, talk to yourself, and get in touch
> with your core values and feelings. Just as a caterpillar cannot anticipate
> becoming a butterfly when it enters its cocoon, adults feel awkward and lost at
> the beginning of a transition, but when they come out of the cocoon they feel
> transformed with new life direction.

In whatever way you can take a time-out to regroup and redirect—whether it be during regular small chunks of time or all at once—do it. You deserve the opportunity to discover (or rediscover) yourself. In fact, you've already started cocooning by buying this book. In essence, you're saying good-bye to the old you and welcoming the new you—strong, confident, focused, and ready to take on the next phase of life.

Emotional Areas in Need of Support

The last part of your emotional check-in involves a quick evaluation of your support systems. Do you feel isolated? lonely? Do your emotions run hot and cold? Do you desperately need to take brief time-outs periodically? Jot down what you feel you're lacking in the way of emotional support or healing. This could be support from yourself, family, friends, a good therapist, associates, a support group, or others you can relate to who are going through a similar situation. This self-knowledge will allow you to concentrate on the areas in need of improvement in Chapter 6.

Personal Check-in

When I'm about to make a major transition, I find it essential to look at where my time is being spent. I do this because I don't want to overcommit myself, and I want to see how much time I can squeeze out of my schedule to make a healthy and smooth transition. In short, I look for time to step back and get in touch with myself and where I am in my cocoon.

Granted, some changes in life, such as a sudden downturn in health or the death of a loved one, are not predictable (at least at the moment in which they happen). But for the most part, we can see major changes coming. Even in the case of failing health or death, we are often given a heads-up and can take measures to adjust our lifestyles or prepare and plan for the change accordingly. In this section you'll complete an exercise that encourages you to look at your current commitments and think about how you'd ideally like to spend your time.

Teri, Age 34

Teri found herself ready to get back into the working world after 12 years away. Until now, her days had been dictated by the kids' needs and functions. With Katie starting "big kid" school, Teri realized she had 20 or 30 hours to commit to a career of her own—or did she?

When Teri sat down one morning to list her commitments and figure out where her time was spent, she was amazed. She says, "I actually thought I deserved a 3-week cruise when I saw how much time went to the kids and their activities, and how little was left over for my pursuits. Even with my youngest daughter in school a good portion of the day, my weeks were filled." Teri had fooled herself into thinking that she had time for a part-time career, when in truth she didn't.

"The more time I have, the more I find myself committing to others and neglecting myself," Teri says. This reality check was helpful to Teri because it made her aware of the fact that she needed to lighten her load by delegating or saying no more often in order to pursue a part-time career of her own.

Current Commitments

As a simple exercise, jot down the amount of time you spend on your current commitments in an average week. Next to your estimates, put the amount of time you *desire* to spend on each commitment. Exercise 1.1 is a list to help you get started.

Exercise 1.1

Time Commitments

Commitment	Current Time Spent	Desired Time Spent
Job	_____	_____
Volunteer work	_____	_____
School/continuing education	_____	_____
Caretaking (e.g., kids, elders, spouse, pets)	_____	_____
Household responsibilities	_____	_____
Family relationships (e.g., kids, spouse, extended family)	_____	_____
Social/professional relationships (e.g., friends, business affiliations)	_____	_____
Personal (e.g., exercise, diet, spiritual, self-improvement)	_____	_____
Leisure	_____	_____
Sleep	_____	_____
Other	_____	_____
Total Hours Spent	_____	_____

After you write down your estimates (both actual and desired), total them and divide by 7 to find the time spent on your average daily commitments. (I bet you never thought you'd need a calculator while reading this book!) Hopefully, both columns average close to 24 hours. If the averages are way off the mark, take a closer look at your figures to see where you're under- or over-estimating time spent. Don't worry about being exact. A rough idea will do. But if your 24-hour day is more like 36 hours, you might want to consider taking that 3-week cruise with Teri.

Personal Areas in Need of Support

This might seem like a lesson in mathematics, but it can be very helpful to see where your life is out of sync in relation to where you want it to be. Are you spending more time in the caregiver mode than you care to? Are you paying enough attention to your overall physical and mental well-being? Are you eating properly? getting enough sleep? Do you get consumed in household responsibilities, leaving little time for yourself? Are you currently working? If so, you might have reflected that you desire to work fewer hours than you actually do (at least in your current position).

As a result of your findings from Exercise 1.1, "Time Commitments," put an × next to the commitments you feel are so out of line with what you desire that they need attention as soon as possible. We'll need to work on these, so keep this valuable information handy. It's crucial to establishing support systems, which we'll discuss in Chapter 6.

Financial Check-in

Knowing where you stand financially is a critical aspect of making a smooth and successful transition to your new direction. It's also imperative to conducting any kind of financial planning. In the sections that follow, you'll do some simple exercises to help establish your current financial situation and identify areas in need of improvement.

Denise, Age 40

After her divorce Denise felt like her entire life had been turned upside-down. For so many years she wantingly put her schooling and career on the back burner for her husband and kids. Now, financially, she had no choice. "Issues I had never concerned myself with were suddenly brought to the forefront—my health insurance, car insurance, credit card debt, and even my fitness club dues. My list of expenses seemed overwhelming." Denise continues, "I knew I couldn't run away from reality any longer. The divorce settlement was negligible, and what little savings I had was shrinking rapidly."

Denise needed a working budget or financial plan to determine her present and future happiness. But first she had to know where everything stood. "I finally took a long weekend when Bernie had the kids and wrote down all my financial commitments and income sources," Denise says. "It was a rude awakening, but a necessary step that eventually led to a plan I'm very proud of." She admits that if she hadn't sat down and looked at where things stood, she wouldn't be where she is today—self-sufficient, with no credit card debt. "I'm even able to set some money aside for the future," says Denise. "The future was something Bernie and I constantly put off, thinking we were too young to worry."

Financial Status

In your journal, write down your monthly expenses. Next to that, write down your monthly income sources. Total each column. Exercise 1.2 is a list to help you get started.

Exercise 1.2

Financial Position

Monthly Expenses	Amount Spent	Monthly Income	Amount Spent
Rent/house payment	_____	Employment	_____
Food	_____	Investments	_____
Utilities	_____	Pension	_____
Health insurance	_____	Social Security	_____
Car insurance	_____	Child support	_____
Life insurance	_____	Alimony	_____
Entertainment	_____	Unemployment benefits	_____
Car payments	_____	Severance pay	_____
School payments	_____	Other	_____
Child care	_____	_____	_____
Household upkeep	_____	_____	_____
Credit card payments	_____	_____	_____
Investment expense/ payments	_____	_____	_____
Miscellaneous (e.g., job hunting expenses)	_____		
Other	_____		
_____	_____		
_____	_____		
_____	_____		
Total	_____	*Total*	_____

Financial Areas in Need of Improvement

Just as you did in the previous sections, aimed at targeting your emotional and personal needs, take a close look at your financial status. Does your income meet your expenses? Are any areas off balance and in need of improvement?

In Exercise 1.2, "Financial Position," write down your goals for the income and expense areas you want to change (next to the actual amounts). For instance, say your monthly (household) employment income is $4,000, and you want to increase that to $4,500. Or maybe you spend $500 per month on entertainment, and you would like to decrease that to $400. Or maybe your utilities run $200, and you'd like to lower them to $150. Or perhaps you want to increase your monthly contribution to investments, such as a retirement account, from $500 to $650.

After writing down your desired income and expense amounts, total both columns. Does your income-to-expense ratio from the desired amounts look substantially better than that resulting from the actual amounts? What steps can you take to create and stick to a budget that allows you to achieve your goals, much as Denise did in the opening scenario of this section? Can you eat out less often? take fewer or less expensive vacations? shop for bargains? This information will be helpful when we discuss financial planning and surviving unemployment in Chapter 6.

All About You

The last step in the check-in process involves defining your needs, values, interests, abilities, and skills. You should take advantage of this opportunity to delve into your personality and identify the things you feel passionate about. This will put you in a prime position to choose a suitable career. You can do this quickly and painlessly by completing the exercises in the following sections.

Mary, Age 55

Mary, an administrative assistant, was restless in her job of 13 years. The work no longer challenged her. The people had grown stale. The party was over. "It was getting to the point where I hated Sundays because I knew I had to go to work on Monday," Mary says. "Even my days off seemed like work because I was so preoccupied with it. What really depleted my enthusiasm was hearing my coworkers constantly talk about 'living for retirement.' I've been single all my life, and I don't ever see myself retiring unless I'm not physically or mentally able to work. Until recently, I loved my job and sang all the way to work. Then I went to a seminar that forced me to take a good look at where my life was headed. I realized that I'll only pass this way once, and I want to make the most of my time left on earth."

Mary went through the self-evaluation exercises described in the following sections, and found that she'd be happier working for herself. In Chapter 3, "Choosing a Suitable Work Arrangement," you'll be amazed to learn how this revelation led Mary to leave her "miserably safe" administrative position to take on an exciting, creative, and adventurous challenge.

Needs and Values

What do you want most out of life? What really matters to you? Psychologist Abraham Maslow, in *Motivation and Personality* (Harper & Row), said that people are restless until they're doing what they're suited for. A writer must write, a singer must sing, and a teacher must teach in order to find inner tranquillity. "What a person can be, he must be," said Maslow. "This need we call self-actualization."

Maslow spent several years studying the relationship between needs and self-actualization, and came up with a hierarchy of needs. He believed that our needs motivate us to grow and develop on five different levels:

- ◆ *Level 1—Survival:* This level includes our most basic needs to stay alive, such as the need for food, water, air, sex, warmth, clothing, and shelter.
- ◆ *Level 2—Safety:* At this level we strive for security and stability by creating safe living and working environments, creating safe communities, and setting aside money for the future.
- ◆ *Level 3—Love and belonging:* Care and acceptance from others are a vital part of our growth and development. Positive relationships with others give us joy, courage, and a sense of belonging.
- ◆ *Level 4—Esteem:* At this level we seek recognition and respect in our life's work and in the community at large. We may strive for more autonomy by scheduling our own time or taking on more responsibility.
- ◆ *Level 5—Self-actualization:* At this level we need to be in touch with the resources that lie deep within us. These include making total use of our potential by fulfilling personal goals, achieving personal freedom, and experiencing joy. Our accomplishments are valued not only by ourselves, but by our family, friends, and community. We have a definite mission in life.

What Do You Need?

According to Maslow, unless our basic physical needs (survival and safety) are met, we're unable to fulfill our potential. Work can produce the income to satisfy our basic needs. In addition, it can provide affiliation with others (Level 3 needs), recognition (Level 4 needs) and a personal life mission that's valued by ourselves and others (Level 5 needs). Hence, work plays a powerful role in our lives. Therefore, choosing a career path that fits your life path is paramount.

At this turning point in your life, what need level motivates you most? In what way might you satisfy your needs? Jot down one or two thoughts next to each level listed in Exercise 1.3.

What Do You Value?

We talked about your definition of success in the section "Emotional Check-in" earlier in this chapter. What we were really discussing is your values. Your idea of success represents what's important to you. Knowing what you value (even in the broadest sense) is the first step toward finding your new direction.

The toughest part of value definition is distinguishing what's important to you from what you or others think you *should* do. Every time you use the word *should* when you speak or think, recognize it as a signal that what you're referring to is something you don't truly want, or that you are not behind (at least for

Exercise 1.3

Your Position in Maslow's Hierarchy of Needs

Level	Thoughts
Level 1 (Survival)	
Level 2 (Safety)	
Level 3 (Love and belonging)	
Level 4 (Esteem)	
Level 5 (Self-actualization)	

the moment). Shoulds confuse us and impede our progress. They're generally tied to some kind of guilt, fear, anger, or frustration that we buy into.

When I worked as a software engineer for a number of years, I came to a point where I hated my job. I had reached a dead end, but felt that I *should* stick with my career because the money was good. In my heart, I wanted to pursue something creative on my own. I was caught in a mental and emotional tug-of-war; my heart and mind were at battle for some time. I drove myself nuts over all the shoulds for staying and continued to neglect my gut reasons for leaving. I was a mass of guilt, anger, and confusion.

Finally, it dawned on me that I really wasn't confused. Like Mary, I had created my own miserably safe prison with walls made up of fears and shoulds. Those walls kept me from venturing out to do what I longed to do. When I realized I was holding myself back, I was able to work through my fears and shoulds, and go on to define and pursue my life mission. The moral of the story is that shoulds are time-wasters and energy-drainers.

What shoulds are prevalent in your life? Do they hold you back, or are they really disguising wants that are tied to your values? How can you eliminate the shoulds in your life, or change them to genuine desires? (Take a moment to reflect, and write down your responses to these questions in your journal.)

Before you define your career direction, it's crucial that you visualize the kind of lifestyle that's desirable to you. I want to clarify at this point that throughout this book I use the term *career* to mean a *life pursuit* that doesn't necessarily equate to getting paid. Therefore, women participating in volunteer work or raising a family would consider these passions as all or part of their careers. In this broad sense, *career* references all work and life pursuits.

Focus on each of the areas listed in Exercise 1.4 (or others of importance that aren't listed), and then write down what you consider to be your ideal scenario. This is your opportunity to fantasize and let your imagination soar, keeping in mind that what you can conceive, you can achieve.

After you identify your ideals in these areas, write down steps you can take (no matter how small) to get closer to where you want to be (if you're not already there). These steps will become your short- and long-term goals that will lead you to fulfill your needs and desires, and live an existence that mirrors your values.

You can establish your short-range goals from your long-range goals by paying attention to Maslow's hierarchy of needs. The unmet needs that are lowest on the hierarchy are more urgent than the higher-level needs. Oftentimes during a time of transition (e.g., divorce, death of a spouse), your entire life is turned upside-down and your most basic needs (e.g., income, security, shelter, health) are threatened. It's imperative that you address these needs immediately as your short-term goals. Your capacity for seeking higher needs, such as love, esteem, and self-actualization are restricted until your lower-order needs are met. Hence, the unmet higher-order needs on your list become your long-range goals.

Interests and Personality

Besides knowing your values, knowing what interests you is important to finding the career you love and are suited for.

Mining for Ore—The Search Within

While attending graduate school, I had to turn in a 25-page paper filled with potential ideas for research that might eventually develop into my dissertation. The only requirement was that I had to allow my thoughts and ideas to flow freely on paper, with no regard for how I was presenting the material.

This exercise was extremely fruitful, as it not only turned up my eventual dissertation topic, but it also provided ideas for the topics of several papers I submitted throughout the remainder of my educational journey. Even more important, I learned that creative expression is a fun, easy, and nonthreatening way to explore interests.

Much like the research ideas I carried around in my head that were part of my motivation for enrolling in graduate school, you carry ideas in your head that motivate you to find a fitting career. Now is the time to explore those ideas on paper. Pick up your journal and write down anything that interests or excites

Exercise 1.4

Career and Life Planning

Area of Focus	Ideal Scenario	Possible Steps
Living environment		
Physical well-being		
Work environment		
Income		
Children		
Diet/exercise		
Love relationships		
Physical appearance		
Extended family		
Personal achievements		
Friends		
Confidence/self-image		
Pets		
Emotional well-being		
Privacy		
Amount of leisure time		
Freedom		
Education		
Intellectual ability		
Hobbies and recreation		
Creativity		
Personal habits		
Material possessions		
Spiritual well-being		
Investments		
Personal development		
Other		

you. This could be anything from your passion for teaching your child something new to a specific occupation you might want to pursue. The object is to allow your mind to relax. Dismiss your internal judge. Don't think, "I can't do this because of this, this, and this." Pretend you can do anything, and allow yourself the luxury of free creative expression. Exercise 1.5 lists some questions to help you get started. The goal of this exercise is to tap into the activities that excite you and make you feel enthusiastic. We'll be using the "ore" you turn up in other activities throughout the book.

It's Party Time!

Imagine yourself boarding a large ship, filled with happy passengers. They're all having a party, and you're invited. Of course you're more than willing to don your party hat and join them. The ship is filled with the aroma of exotic foods, festive music, and laughter. You don't know anyone, but the people are warm and receptive.

You spot six distinct groups with people huddled close, completely engaged in one another. You stand back in awe, wanting to join one of the groups. The atmosphere on the ship is so magnetic you can hardly stand it. You feel the pull and long to be a part of the buzz.

As you stand there, lost in thought and admiration of the dynamic picture before you, a friendly face approaches. The captain of the ship invites you to join one of the groups. He explains that each of the six groups is filled with people who have the same interests and personality types, and who work in similar capacities. You look at your watch and realize you only have time to mingle with two of the groups. Which of the following would be your first choice? Your second choice?

Physical people (also referred to as *realistic personalities*) enjoy activities that involve working with their hands and/or bodies. They work with objects, machines, plants, or animals and tend to love the outdoors. They also explore, fix, or make things with their hands. They may teach fitness or dance classes, build houses, play on professional sports teams, or train animals at the zoo.

Orderly/detail people (also referred to as *conventional personalities*) lead organized and structured lives. They often work with numbers and/or clerical tasks. They're good at following rules and routines. They attend to every detail and ensure that a job gets done. Preferring to work for someone of power, they may be employed in banking, bookkeeping, data processing, or accounting.

Service-oriented people (also referred to as *social personalities*) are sensitive to the needs of others. Primarily living in their feelings, they enjoy closeness and sharing, and being a part of groups in unstructured settings. They may teach, heal, or help people in their work at schools, hospitals, or social service agencies. They might also be hairdressers, bartenders, or tour guides.

Exercise 1.5

Identifying Your Passion

Probing Questions	Thoughts
What do you enjoy doing with your personal time?	
What are your talents?	
What are your hobbies?	
What do you love to talk about?	
What do people say you're good at?	
What do you enjoy doing around the house?	
What do you like doing in your current line of work?	
What have you enjoyed doing in previous work capacities?	
As a child, what did you have the most fun doing?	
As a child, what did you dream of becoming?	
How do you visualize yourself in the future?	

Persuasive people (also referred to as *enterprising personalities*) are self-motivated leaders who are talented at organizing, persuading, and managing. They become thoroughly involved in their work. They enjoy dealing with people and projects. They thrive on money, power, status, and taking risks. Quick decision makers, they're confident and like being in charge. They may work in sales, management, or law, or run their own businesses.

Curious people (also referred to as *investigative personalities*) are independent thinkers, intellectually curious, logical, and insightful. Primarily living in their minds, they like to ask Why? and How? in their work. They enjoy complex mental challenges and exploring ideas through reading and discussing. They may work in scientific research, in hospital laboratories, or in the design and analysis of computer programs.

Creative people (also referred to as *artistic personalities*) express themselves through their creative endeavors in music, dance, drama, writing, or art. They tend to lead unstructured lives, preferring to work independently, rather than with others. They are perceptive to color, form, sound, and texture. They're intuitive visionaries, who enjoy solving problems by creating something new. They may be actors, musicians, artists, composers, authors, or sculptors.

Jot down in your journal the two groups you desire to mingle with. This information tells a lot about your interests and personality. In fact, there's a good chance that your ideal career will fall into one or both of the groups you choose. We'll be plugging the results of these exercises in to finding your passion and purpose in the next chapter, so be sure to keep them close at hand.

Abilities and Skills

Did you notice in the party exercise that the interests of each of the groups were aimed at data, people, or things? Data is involved in every activity we take part in because it conveys ideas and information. We transfer data through words or music (reading or listening), facial gestures, and colors, as well as numbers, letters, and symbols. In fact, anything that's not a person or concrete thing is considered data.

Data is conveyed when we work with people and things, when we research, instruct, learn, manage, speak, coordinate, update, observe, monitor, plan, write, read, and sell. We may have minimal interaction with people (e.g., a letter carrier) or complex interaction (e.g., a counselor). In working with things, we might operate machines or tinker with tools and gadgets to make or repair items. Our body may be the primary thing we work with, as in teaching aerobics.

Regardless of whether our work emphasizes data, people, or things (or a combination thereof), some form of data is always exchanged. We have become an information-intensive society. As a result, the "knowledge entrepreneur" who works well with data will increasingly replace service and factory workers in coming years as more and more jobs become automated.

Data, People, and Things

Turn to your responses to the questions posed in Exercise 1.5, "Identifying Your Passion," which revealed the interests and activities you enjoy. Jot down the steps you took to accomplish each activity in your journal. Next to each step write a *D* for data, a *P* for people, or a *T* for things to reflect the area the task emphasizes. For instance, if one of my favorite activities is planning a backpacking trip, the steps I might take to accomplish this would be think about what I need to bring and write it down (*D*), call the clerk at the camping store to inquire about purchasing some necessary items for the trip (*P*), and drive or carry the items home after purchasing them (*T*). If one of my favorite interests or pastimes is reading, I would consider that a one-step activity that emphasizes data, and I'd place a *D* next to that item.

Be aware of how you deal with data, people, and things in the steps you take to accomplish each activity. The following is a list of skills, organized by their area of emphasis, to assist you. Keep in mind that most tasks require a combination of areas, but you're concerned with the area that's most prevalent in the steps you took to accomplish the interests and activities you listed in your journal:

◆ *Skills related to working with data:* Read, write, edit, remember, speak, translate, report, summarize, describe, interview, imagine, invent, compose, improvise, design, conceive ideas, create symbols or images, combine colors, convey emotions and ideas, use words imaginatively, inventory, count, calculate, compute, manage money, budget, work with numbers, estimate, collect, measure, use statistics, classify, follow instructions, record, file, retrieve, transcribe

◆ *Skills related to working with people:* Assist, be sensitive to feelings, listen, understand, build rapport, encourage, heal, advise, draw out people, reconcile, serve, raise others' self-concepts, initiate relationships, organize people, direct others, manage, instruct people, converse, entertain, consult, work as a team, cooperate, share credit and appreciation, help, raise funds, stimulate, sell, negotiate, persuade, lead, supervise, motivate, arbitrate, divert

◆ *Skills related to working with things:* Assemble, build, install, operate tools, shape, type, play a musical instrument, sew, cut, photograph, paint, draw, cook, wash, feed, press, repair, drive, perform on a stage, carry, lift, deliver, operate machines, use muscular or eye–hand coordination, care for animals

When you've finished coding your steps in the columns under your activities and interests, tally up all the D's, P's, and T's. Do you tend to emphasize one area over the others? Are your totals close in two areas, or even all three? Whether your interests and activities emphasize one, two, or all three areas, be assured that there's a fitting career waiting for you. Because the majority of people have average skills, and average skills are what most jobs require, most people (including you) can do many jobs.

Knowing what you know now, it's easy to see which area the groups at the party emphasize—data, people, or things. The physical people (who work with their hands and/or bodies) emphasize things. The service-oriented people (who are sensitive to the needs of others) emphasize people, as do the persuasive people (self-motivated leaders). The orderly/detail individuals (who work with numbers and/or clerical tasks) emphasize data. Finally, the investigative people (independent thinkers, intellectually curious) and artistic people (creative expressionists) tend to emphasize data as well.

Just for fun, compare the results of the preceding exercise—where you broke down your interests and activities into steps emphasizing data, people, and things—against the two groups you chose to mingle with at the party. Do you see a pattern developing?

Summing It All Up

In this chapter you have participated in an information-gathering process. With each step taken, you've gained self-knowledge and awareness. In essence, you're laying the foundation for making a well-informed decision on where to go from here with your life. Now it's time to plug the results from this chapter in to finding a work/life direction you feel passionate about. That's the primary goal of Chapter 2.

WHERE DO YOU
WANT TO BE?

*"Forget about your age! Do what you want,
regardless of how old you'll be when you accomplish
it. Time will pass anyway, so why not take advantage of this opportunity to achieve your dreams?"*

SANDY ANDERSON, PhD

ow that you've uncovered all sorts of information about yourself, let's start plugging it in to potential directions you'd like to
pursue. The wonderful thing about this process is that your choices
are wide open. You might decide to change jobs, explore a new career
direction altogether, be a full-time stay-at-home mom, or go back to
school. This chapter is about finding your passion—a life mission
that really excites you today—whatever that may be. Your primary
goal in this chapter is to narrow down all the information you're gathering to one to three directions you'd like to explore further.

Stacey, Age 28

Stacey experienced a life change that literally "rocked her world."
She and her husband, Tom, and their two kids survived the disastrous
earthquake that occurred in California in the early 1990s. "Even
though the earthquake lasted just a couple minutes," Stacey says, "it
seemed like ages to me. All I could think of was getting to the kids
and making sure they were okay. I had to work my way down the
hall, through the maze of wall hangings and furniture that were
collapsing all around me. I felt pieces of glass slicing through my

(continued)

(continued)

legs every step of the way, but I was determined to get to my babies."

It took this earth-shaking experience for Stacey to reevaluate her priorities in life. She says, "When my life and the lives of the ones I hold so dear were severely threatened and I saw how quickly I could lose everything in a matter of minutes, I decided to really live each day as if it were my last. I asked myself, 'What is important to me right now?' The answer was clear—quit my 10-year career as a management executive, stay home, and enjoy raising my kids—in a rural area and in a different state, of course." The aftershocks that followed reinforced Stacey's decision to relocate and stay home with her children. It took a natural disaster for her to get her priorities in order, but she grew from the experience and has never felt happier.

Types of Major Changes

Some of the major changes that occur in a woman's life include

- ◆ Pregnancy
- ◆ Birth of a baby
- ◆ Career burnout
- ◆ Job layoff
- ◆ Kids leaving home
- ◆ Divorce/separation
- ◆ Return to school
- ◆ Moving
- ◆ Becoming a caretaker for elderly parents
- ◆ Retirement
- ◆ Change in health
- ◆ Loss of a loved one
- ◆ Natural disaster
- ◆ Personal/spiritual growth

Do you ever notice how major changes seem to spark even more change? A tragic earthquake made Stacey realize that she was complacent in her career and that her heart longed to be home to raise her 3-year-old twin girls. In the aftershocks that followed, Stacey and her husband, Tom, became convinced that they'd be happiest if they moved east, to a small rural town with more intimacy and less crime and congestion. A major quake caused a ripple of changes to occur, all for the better.

Without even realizing it, the most difficult part of the change that Stacey endured was what led up to the earthquake. She was miserable in her job. The earthquake literally shook her up and pushed her to take action and relieve the stress and dissatisfaction she'd been experiencing in her job since her twin girls had been born.

Finding Your Passion

We hear this statement all the time: "Find your passion." What is passion anyway, and how do we know when we have it? The dictionary defines passion as "boundless enthusiasm." Isn't that enthusiasm without limits? Imagine waking up in the morning to pursue your chosen life mission with boundless enthusiasm. This could be you, and you'll know you're on the right path when you feel *in the flow*.

Living in the Flow

Flow is that feeling when things are moving along in an automatic, effortless fashion—with a highly focused state of consciousness. Author Mihaly Csikszentimihalyi offers some characteristics to help you recognize when you're in the flow:

1. *You have clear goals every step of the way. You know how to proceed, and know what needs to be done.*
2. *Your actions produce immediate feedback letting you know that what you're doing feels right.*
3. *Your abilities are well matched for your actions, and you experience a balance between the challenges you partake and your skills.*
4. *You have total focus on what you're doing—your actions and awareness are merged.*
5. *You have intense concentration on the present. You aren't easily distracted.*
6. *You have no worry of failure. Your skills are adequate for the job.*
7. *All self-consciousness disappears. Your actions make you feel stronger and "at one with the universe."*
8. *Your sense of time becomes distorted. Clock time is irrelevant.*
9. *Activity becomes "autotelict" which is Greek for "something that is an end in itself."*

Dana, Age 30

When her husband, Peter, got a job transfer to Dallas, Dana was not only eager to start fresh in her new home, but she wanted a new career, too. She had been working in the banking industry for 5 years, "feeling like a square peg in a round hole," she says. "I was never really happy in the banking field, and this was a chance to start over with everything in my life. With the big move coming, I was motivated to clear out the clutter in my house. I pictured moving to a new home with a clean garage and closets—and a brand new wardrobe! How could I continue in a stale career? That vision did it for me. I knew that I'd have to go back to school or get some training, but I was willing to do whatever it took to land a position in the health field."

Peter's job transfer ended up being a blessing in disguise for Dana. She was afraid of the new challenges that lay ahead, but her excitement over her new start gave her the courage to continue opening doors on her path of self-discovery.

The secret to leading a happy life is to get flow from as many things as possible. If everything we pursue in our work and personal lives is an end in itself, then nothing is wasted, and everything is worth doing for its own sake.

Throughout this chapter we'll step through the process of finding a balance between your abilities and the challenges you desire to take on so that you can live in the flow.

Choosing an Environment for Your Work/Life Mission

Choosing an environment for your work/life mission will help you narrow down your job choices. Each environment category has hundreds—and some even thousands—of jobs, many of which have similar characteristics. Review the following environment descriptions and make a note in your journal of those that appeal to you most. Where do you see yourself fitting in and feeling in the flow? If you're in doubt, talk to people who work in the settings that interest you the most, and see if you can follow them around for a day to get an idea of what you can expect.

Business

Business includes any setting where two or more people get together to trade goods and services. This could be an office in a corporation, the desk in the back of an auto body shop, a retail jewelry outlet, or a secretarial service run out of your home. The world of business is composed of many facets, such as marketing, finance, personnel, accounting, purchasing, and consulting. Business primarily involves working with data. This could mean using paper data such as writing, reading, typing, data/word processing, and filing. It could also mean using mind data such as researching, organizing, and analyzing.

Industry

Industry is basically concerned with products. Painting buildings, driving buses, constructing homes, and growing tomatoes would fall into this category, as would jobs related to the testing and quality control of products. Industry in this sense primarily involves working with things.

Education

The education arena includes teaching careers in schools, colleges, community centers, and privately owned learning facilities, as well as training in business and industry. Education primarily involves working with people.

Communication/Entertainment

Communication and entertainment settings can range from working as a clown for hire to producing in a TV studio to writing magazine articles. Because these "glamour" fields are highly competitive, opportunities are limited. A good amount of talent, luck, and perseverance are necessary to land jobs in this area. Connections with people in the field are also helpful. Communication and entertainment usually involve working with data and people.

Health

Health care workers may find employment in any setting. The settings that typically come to mind are hospitals and doctor's offices. However, employment in the health field can be found in all the work environments listed here. The health profession is expanding rapidly because of the increase in specialization and technological advances. This field primarily involves working with people.

Government/Military

The government and military employ people of all types in every setting—from agricultural fields to hospitals, and from prisons to the outdoors. Written, oral, and/or physical exams are generally required to qualify for most positions. The pay for these positions has increased over the past years, but so has the job insecurity. With some persistence, any personality type can find opportunities in the government or military.

Home/Family

I'm including the home as a separate environment because more and more women are opting to work from home and many are deciding to ditch their careers to stay home and raise children.

These two trends are steadily increasing at a rapid pace. About 30% of women are choosing to forgo careers altogether to stay home with their kids. Changing values and a lack of flexibility in the workplace are two big reasons for this occurrence. The work-at-home population is rising by 15% annually, with two women jumping aboard for every man. This is not surprising, given that working from home gives women tremendous flexibility to have a career and care for their kids, too.

Women without kids or whose kids have left the nest are also finding home businesses to be a great opportunity to take control of their lives and have the kind of personal freedom they never found working for someone else. The home is a perfect environment for work in the business arena. In particular, service-oriented occupations are most suitable for the home.

Plugging In Your Personality Type

Now that you've begun to look at the environments you'd like to focus on in pursuing your work/life mission, it's time to plug in your personality type. Remember the party exercise in Chapter 1, "Where Are You Now?"? What two groups of people did you want to associate with most at the party? Did you lean more toward data, people, or things? How do these groups compare to the environment(s) you prefer to work in? Is there an overlap?

A New Mom's Dilemma: Should I Stay Home with My Baby or Go Back to Work?

If you're a new mom trying to decide whether to stay home with your baby or go back to work, here are five questions to help you make the decision. The first answer that strikes you is likely to be your true feeling:

1. Do you dread spending long periods of time on your own without adult interaction?
2. Do you have support from others that will help with child care, or are you willing to seek the support or pay for help from others while you're working?
3. Do you thrive in environments where you're constantly learning and seeking new information?
4. Will your employer work with you in creating a flexible work arrangement to help you meet your new demands (e.g., job sharing, part-time work, telecommuting)?
5. Which would you rather have more of—time or money?

If you answered no to at least two of questions 1 through 4 and you answered "time" to question 5, you'll probably be happier if you stay home with your baby. You might have to scale back financially to pull it off, but the rewards in terms of coos, smiles, and seeing developmental milestones will be well worth the tradeoff.

If you answered yes to at least two of questions 1 through 4, and answered "money" to question 5, you'll probably be happier if you continue to work after having your baby. If you don't want to work full time, talk to your employer about establishing a flexible work arrangement, or consider starting a home business where you have complete control over your schedule.

Business environments tend to attract all personalities, especially the enterprising (persuasive leaders) who make great managers and conventional (orderly/detail) types who enjoy an organized, structured position working with numbers and/or clerical tasks. The social (people) person might also find this a desirable setting in dealing with people and their problems. The artistic (creative) person might enjoy work in advertising, layout and design, or multimedia. The realistic (physical) type might enjoy managing products and production, and the investigative (curious) personality might gravitate to research and problem solving—think tank–type stuff.

Industry primarily attracts the realistic type because the focus is usually on product development. This typically involves work with machines and tools; however, this could take on an artistic slant, as in the case of the creative type who paints pictures or invents something new. Those on the investigative side might enjoy the engineering and scientific research involved in product development. The conventional types might see that each detail is tended to and that the job is done correctly.

All personality types can be found in education. If you like to "wear multiple hats," education might be a good choice for you. Enterprising and social personalities thrive on the task- or people-oriented interactions involved in teaching, leading, and motivating others. Those with a realistic slant might focus on teaching subjects such as physical education, military, fire science, and shop, whereas the artistic types might gravitate to the humanities and fine arts, crafts, and design classes. Investigative types are needed for scholarship and research and for teaching liberal arts and sciences. Conventional types are great at teaching the basics.

Artistic personalities are naturally attracted to the communications/entertainment work environments. Those with a slant toward the enterprising, conventional, realistic, or investigative can find positions in the marketing, business administration, clerical, engineering, and research areas of media. Realistic types who are creative might enjoy industrial design, whereas conventional creative types might gravitate to computer-aided design. Artistic people with an enterprising side might open their own galleries or become book publishers. Many opportunities are popping up daily for artistic folk who are technically savvy.

In health care settings, the investigative "people" person might enjoy helping others solve their health care problems. The conventional person who is good with people would likely take to the routine systems found in this field. The realistic person can find interesting work that's challenging, such as physical therapy. Enterprising and social people enjoy interacting with others, as caretakers, leaders, motivators, and inspirational guides.

The government and military attract all personality types because of the variety of jobs available. And if you're setting up shop at home, you have infinite opportunities to work with data, people, and/or things in a variety of career paths, regardless of your personality type.

Establishing Your Motivation for Working

Everyone works for a reason, and it's important to clearly define your reasons. Is making money your top priority? Does work provide a source of identity? self-esteem? self-confidence? Is being recognized in your work important? Perhaps you want to work to keep busy. Is your goal to have adult interaction? Are you interested in new learning opportunities? Are you looking for a challenge? intellectual stimulation? Do you want to work so you can contribute to society at large?

In your journal, establish a list of reasons for working. Jot down what automatically comes to mind as your true burning desire. Put your number-one goal at the top of the list, then number two, number three, and so on. You might have one goal or a dozen.

As much as possible, elaborate on each goal so your reasons are clear and precise. If your number-one reason for wanting to work is to make money, write

Nancy, Age 45

Nancy retired after a 22-year career as a computer technician in the military. She took off for a few months to introspect and decide what she wanted to do with her life. She was recently divorced after her 20-year marriage broke up because of irreconcilable differences, and her two kids had left home for college. Aside from caring for her cat, Chloe, Nancy's responsibilities were minimal. "I was in the military for so long and was used to routines and regimens," Nancy says. "When all that was over, I felt completely lost. I wanted someone to tell me what to do and how to do it. I even felt like I needed someone to tell me what to wear, after dressing in uniforms for so long. My pension wasn't enough to live a comfortable lifestyle, so I thought I'd supplement that with part-time work."

Nancy learned from checking in with herself and attending a career coaching session that she loved the physical training required in the military and the interaction with people—opportunities she didn't get in her position as a computer technician. Some career exercises revealed that she enjoyed working with data, people, and things equally. She thrived on variety and was bored with her computer career.

After much thought, Nancy decided to pursue a part-time position as a fitness instructor, where she could enjoy the physical movements and coordination required, the opportunity to teach people about health and fitness, the ability to create new aerobic routines, and the time to interact with students by helping and guiding them. This turned out to be the perfect career for Nancy to supplement her pension, provide the variety she longed for, and challenge her desires to work with data, people, and things.

down how much you want to make and what you plan to do with it. Perhaps you're the sole breadwinner in your family and you need money to pay the bills. Or you might want money to supplement your spouse's income so you can take more vacations, put away more money for retirement, or have more "fun money."

After you've elaborated on each goal, go back over your list and put a star next to the goals that are an absolute must for you to accomplish in your work. These are your necessities. Any goals that you don't set off with a star are considered nice to have, but not necessary. If you have prioritized your list according to your true desires, your necessities should all be at the top.

Ralene Friend and Karen Friend, a mother-and-daughter team who founded Friend Communications, a firm devoted to understanding today's female consumer, offer a powerful strategy to help you stay focused on achieving your career goals. Ralene says

> One of the most helpful tools we have used to keep us on track is a list of "must-be's." In the very beginning, we formulated a list of six things that must

be true in our lives and in our business. The general rule of thumb is that anything we decide to do must meet at least three of our criteria. For example, one of the things on our list is that our work must be fun and enjoyable. If it isn't, we say no. Once in a while we do something that meets all six criteria— and have an incredible experience. The list helps us focus on what's most important to us so we can continue to create careers we both enjoy and are truly passionate about.

Pursuing Your Interests

Now turn to your responses to the questions posed in the mining-for-ore exercise (Exercise 1.5, "Identifying Your Passion") in Chapter 1 that revealed the interests and activities you enjoy. It's time to take the next step and brainstorm about possible careers that might be suitable based on the activities you noted in that exercise. Keep your talents and desired work patterns in mind. "One of the reasons I'm doing magazine publishing is my personality type," says Chris, an entrepreneur. "I'm very good at starting businesses and getting them going. I like short-term projects with deadlines. That's why magazine publishing is perfect for me."

When I did Exercise 1.5, I performed a task called *clustering*. If you're a visual person, I highly recommend clustering for this brainstorming task. Start with a big blank sheet of paper—the bigger, the better. Transfer your interests from the exercise sheet to this cluster sheet, allowing lots of space in between each interest. Put a circle around each interest.

Write down ideas for any related opportunities at the end of a line extended from each circle of interest. For example, if my interest is "working with computers," I would write that on my big sheet and draw a circle around it. I would then draw lines to possible careers such as computer programmer, computer trainer, and Web site developer.

Another one of my circled interests might be something I did as a child, such as "playing with dolls." I can draw lines to directions such as stay-at-home mom, child care provider, health care provider, and teacher.

If another one of my circled interests is "investing money and watching it grow," I can branch off from there to financial planner, stockbroker, personal investment counselor, and so on. These financial careers also satisfy my desire to work with computers, so I would draw lines from these careers to that circle of interest as well.

You can have a lot of fun with this exercise. It's even more productive when you get ideas for potential directions from a friend. The number of possibilities listed can be mind-boggling. Instead of trying to narrow down your choice, start with a few hunches and target occupations that satisfy what interests or excites you. Look at the environments you visualized being happy in. What kind of jobs would you find in these settings that satisfy the interests and activities you turned up in the Exercise 1.5 questions? You might turn up ideas you hadn't thought of.

OUACHITA TECHNICAL COLLEGE

Comparing Your Results with Your Reasons

When you've exhausted all your ideas on paper, highlight or put a star next to the careers that stand out as your top choices. Look for careers that satisfy multiple interests. In a previous section, I asked you to prioritize your goals (or reasons for working) in your journal. Now is a good time to glance over your goals and bounce them against your top career choices. Do your top career choices satisfy your necessary goals? How about the goals that would be nice to have? You might want to put two or three stars next to the career choices that satisfy the most goals.

Incorporating Your Abilities and Skills

As I said earlier, your primary goal in this chapter should be to narrow down all the information you're gathering to one or several directions you'd like to explore. The final step in this process is to incorporate your abilities and skills. In the party exercise in Chapter 1, you chose two groups to mingle with. Here again are the personality types that comprise the groups you chose from, along with brief descriptions:

- *Realistic:* Physical people who enjoy working with their bodies and hands.
- *Investigative:* Curious thinkers who enjoy solving problems by thinking and analyzing.
- *Artistic:* People who see new possibilities and want to express them in creative ways.
- *Social:* People who live primarily in their feelings and enjoy helping others.
- *Enterprising:* Energetic leaders who are talented at persuading and managing.
- *Conventional:* Orderly, detailed people who enjoy following the guidelines of others to get work done.

Doing Your Research

Now it's time to hit the library and do some research. Before you go, I want to make sure you're armed with the information you'll need to make the trip quick and painless. First, run through Table 2.1, which is a list of jobs from *The Guide for Occupational Exploration* (published by JIST Works) that are grouped by the personality types listed above. For ease of reference, the decimal numbers at the beginning of each job area correspond to the numbers in *The Guide for Occupational Exploration.* Put a check mark next to any of the 66 groups and their corresponding tasks that spark your interest immediately. Don't put much thought into it, but quickly review the list.

Table 2.1

Job Groups, Listed by Personality Type

Job	Description

Realistic Job Groups

Mechanical

❑ 05.01 Engineering	Applying research of science and math to the design of new products and systems
❑ 05.02 Managerial Work—Mechanical	Managing technical plants or systems
❑ 05.03 Engineering Technology	Collecting, recording, and coordinating technical information
❑ 05.04 Air and Water Vehicle Operations	Operating planes/ships to carry freight/passengers
❑ 05.05 Craft Technology	Doing highly skilled hand/machine custom work
❑ 05.06 Systems Operation	Caring for large, complicated mechanical systems such as heating and power
❑ 05.07 Quality Control	Checking/testing materials/products in nonfactory situations
❑ 05.08 Land Vehicle Operation	Operating/driving vehicles that haul freight
❑ 05.09 Materials Control	Keeping records of flow/storage of materials and products
❑ 05.10 Skilled Hand and Machine Work	Doing moderately skilled hand/machine work
❑ 05.11 Equipment Operation	Operating/driving heavy equipment such as in construction and mining
❑ 05.12 Manual Labor—Mechanical	Doing nonfactory manual labor with machines and tools

Industrial

❑ 06.01 Production Technology	Setting up/operating machines to produce goods in specific ways
❑ 06.02 Production Work	Doing hand/machine work to make a product, or supervising/inspecting this work
❑ 06.03 Quality Control	Testing, weighing, inspecting, and measuring products to meet standards
❑ 06.04 Manual Labor—Industrial	Basic manual labor in production requiring little training

(continued)

Table 2.1 *(continued)*

Job	Description
Nature	
☐ 03.01 Managerial Work—Nature	Planning work for farming, fisheries, logging, and horticulture
☐ 03.02 General Supervision—Nature	Supervising on farms or in forests, fisheries, nurseries, and parks
☐ 03.03 Animal Training/Care	Training, breeding, raising, showing, and caring for nonfarm animals
☐ 03.04 Manual Labor—Nature	Doing basic physical labor related to farming, fishing, and gardening
Protective	
☐ 04.01 Safety/Law Enforcement	Administration and enforcement of laws and regulations
☐ 04.02 Security Services	Protecting people and property from crime, fire, and other hazards
Physical Performance	
☐ 12.01 Sports	Participating in sports of all sorts, including playing, training, coaching, and officiating
☐ 12.02 Physical Feats	Amusing/entertaining people with special physical skills and strengths
Investigative Job Groups	
Scientific/Analytic	
☐ 02.01 Physical Sciences	Research/development in physics, chemistry, geology, and computer science
☐ 02.02 Life Sciences	Studying functions of living things/ways they relate to environments
☐ 02.03 Medical Sciences	Practicing medicine to prevent, diagnose, and cure illness in people or animals
☐ 02.04 Laboratory Technology	Doing laboratory work to carry out studies of various researchers
☐ 11.01 Mathematics/Statistics	Using numbers and computers to analyze and solve problems
Artistic Job Groups	
Artistic/Creative	
☐ 01.01 Literary Arts	Producing creative pieces from writing to publishing, for print, TV, and films
☐ 01.02 Visual Arts	Doing artistic work (paintings, design, and photographs) for sale or for media

(continued)

Table 2.1 *(continued)*

Job	Description
❑ 01.03 Performing Arts—Drama	Performing, directing, teaching for stage, radio, TV, and film
❑ 01.04 Performing Arts—Music	Playing an instrument, singing, arranging, composing, and conducting music
❑ 01.05 Performing Arts—Dance	Performing, teaching, and choreographing dance routines
❑ 01.06 Craft Arts	Producing handcrafts, graphics, and decorative products
❑ 01.07 Amusement Arts	Entertaining/doing novel routines at carnivals, circuses, and fairs
❑ 01.08 Modeling	Posing for artists and displaying clothing, accessories, and other products

Social Job Groups

Human Services

❑ 10.01 Social Services	Helping people deal with personal, vocational, educational, and religious concerns
❑ 10.02 Nursing/Therapy Services	Providing diagnosis and therapy to help people get well
❑ 10.03 Child/Adult Care	Assisting with medical/physical care/services

Accommodating

❑ 09.01 Hospitality Services	Touring, guiding, greeting, and serving people to help them feel comfortable
❑ 09.02 Barber/Beauty Services	Hair/skin care to help people with personal appearance
❑ 09.03 Passenger Services	Transporting people by vehicle, and instructing/supervising
❑ 09.04 Customer Services	Waiting on people in a routine way in business settings
❑ 09.05 Attendant Services	Providing personal services to people at home or when traveling

Social/Enterprising Job Groups

Leading/Influencing

❑ 11.02 Educational/Library Services	Teaching and providing library services
❑ 11.03 Social Research	Studying people of various backgrounds, both past and present

(continued)

Table 2.1 *(continued)*

Job	Description
☐ 11.04 Law Counseling	Advising and representing people and businesses regarding legal matters
☐ 11.05 Business Administration	Designing procedures, solving problems, and supervising people in business
☐ 11.06 Finance	Setting up financial systems, controlling, and analyzing financial records
☐ 11.07 Services Administration	Designing procedures, solving problems, and supervising people in business
☐ 11.08 Communications	Writing, editing, translating information for media, including radio, print, and TV
☐ 11.09 Promotion	Advertising, fund raising, sales, and public relations
☐ 11.10 Regulations Enforcement	Checking/enforcing government regulations, company policies, and procedures
☐ 11.11 Business Management	Taking responsibility for operation and supervision of a business
☐ 11.12 Contracts and Claims	Negotiating contracts and investigating claims

Enterprising Job Groups

☐ 08.01 Sales Technology	Selling technical equipment or services, including insurance
☐ 08.02 General Sales	Selling goods and services, wholesale/retail to individuals, business, or industry
☐ 08.03 Vending	Peddling and promoting items in public settings

Conventional Job Groups

☐ 07.01 Administrative Detail	Doing secretarial or technical clerical work
☐ 07.02 Mathematical Detail	Keeping numeric records, doing basic figuring
☐ 07.03 Financial Detail	Keeping track of money flow to and from the public
☐ 07.04 Oral Communications	Giving information in person or by communication systems
☐ 07.05 Records Processing	Putting together records and keeping them up-to-date
☐ 07.06 Clerical Machine Operation	Using various machines to record, process, and compute data
☐ 07.07 Clerical Handling	Keeping data in order by filing, copying, sorting, and delivering

After you've checked the job groups that interest you, take the list to your local library and ask for *The Guide for Occupational Exploration* (published by JIST Works) from the reference desk. This is a great resource that lists the occupations that belong to the groups listed in Table 2.1. To get a general idea of the skills, education, and experience that are preferred or required for occupations that interest you, see the *Occupational Outlook Handbook* (published by JIST Works). From aerospace engineer to water treatment plant operator, this reference covers approximately 250 occupations, encompassing a vast amount of data on opportunities, training, qualifications, salaries, working conditions, career advancement, and job outlook.

Did you check off the job groups that listed the top career choices you turned up in Exercise 1.5? How do your favorite occupations fit with the work environments you chose earlier? The results of these exercises provide valuable clues to help clarify the work/life path that's best for you.

Patty, Age 39

Patty was laid off from her job as a word processor for a Department of Defense contractor. "I hadn't been on the job long when they gave me a pink slip one morning," Patty says. "The contract was up on the job I'd been working on, and without a moment's notice, I was out of work. With four kids to feed, I knew we couldn't get by on my husband's postal worker's salary. My dad has always asked me to help out in the family restaurant. I thought that this might be the time to jump on board."

But Patty was nervous about working for her dad. After a few sessions of talking and doing some revealing exercises, we learned that she's a social/enterprising person by nature and would rather be starting a business of her own. As it turned out, her ultimate goal was to start a newspaper publishing business where her four children could eventually have jobs if they decided to. "But only if they decide that's what they want," she says. "I don't want to push them to be in the business like my dad has pushed me. Ironically, I have a creative child who loves to explore new things (artistic personality), one who loves working with numbers (conventional personality), one who is curious and would be good at research (investigative personality), and one who enjoys tinkering with things (realistic personality). In the publishing business, there would be a job for everyone. After talking about this, I think I'd be crazy not to do it. It's something I've always imagined, and now that my job is history, I might as well go for it!"

Hot Careers for the 21st Century

By 2005, employment will rise to 144.7 million jobs, representing an increase of 14%, or 17.7 million jobs, according to the U.S. Department of Labor Women's Bureau. Many of these new jobs will be in areas we wouldn't have anticipated even

10 years ago. With the job market rapidly changing, careers that used to offer solid positions are in decline, whereas occupations once unheard of are now among the fastest growing. That's why it's critical to plan your work/life path with all the information available about where the jobs are and where they'll be in the future.

Education and Training

Women have a giant stake in the current and future job market, as their labor force growth is expected to increase at a faster rate than men's—16.6% for women, compared with 8.5% for men through 2005. Education and training are critical elements in preparing for our employment futures. As the following list reveals, many high-paying, fast-growing occupations require at least a bachelor's degree:

Jobs Requiring a Bachelor's Degree or More

Occupation	Weekly Wages (Full-Time Position)
Lawyer	$1,131
Physician	$1,040
Systems analyst	$845
Computer engineer	$845
Marketing manager	$845
Management analyst	$789
Financial manager	$715
Residential counselor	$694
Teacher, secondary	$690
Teacher, specialty education	$647
Physical therapist	$640
Writer or editor	$633
Accountant	$615
Personnel specialist	$611
Product designer	$590
Artist	$575
Social worker	$506

Jobs that require a bachelor's degree or more education are concentrated in the professional specialty group where median weekly earnings are higher than the average for all full-time wage and salary workers ($467). Other fast-growing, high-paying jobs that may not require a bachelor's degree but do require postsecondary education or training include those in the following list:

Jobs Requiring Postsecondary Education or Training

Occupation	Weekly Wages (Full-Time Position)
Registered nurse	$685
Police officer	$632
Instructor, sport	$530
Instructor, nonvocational	$530
Instructor, vocational education	$530
Paralegal	$497
Mechanic, AC/heating	$497
Correctional officer	$485
Licensed practical nurse	$450

Unfortunately, fast-growing jobs that don't require postsecondary education also don't offer higher than median pay. These include occupations such as home health aides, human service workers, retail salespersons, cashiers, and truck drivers.

Future Growth

Most of the jobs with the fastest projected growth are concentrated in the rapidly growing services, retail trade, and government industries.

Health Services Occupations

Within the service-producing industries, a large number of the fastest growing jobs fall in the health services sector, which is expected to expand more than twice as fast as the economy as a whole. It's predicted that 7 of every 10 new jobs for technicians will be for health-related positions. Fast-growing health services occupations include personal/home care aides and home health aides, dental hygienists, radiologic technologists, registered nurses, and physical/corrective/occupational therapists.

Health services occupations will continue to grow because of

- ◆ The growing population of elderly persons
- ◆ The discovery of new therapies for life-threatening and disabling conditions
- ◆ Medical advances that extend the lives of more patients with critical problems
- ◆ The need to maintain records for an increasing number of medical tests, treatments, and procedures
- ◆ Continued recognition of the need for preventive medical care by the population, physicians, and health organizations

Computer-Related Occupations

Computer-related jobs will grow at a fast rate in the coming years because of the continuing advances in computer technology. The expanding need for scientific research, productivity gains, and demand for cost reductions will fuel the need for computer engineers/programmers, systems analysts, and computer repairers.

Retail Trade

Salespersons, cashiers, waiters and waitresses, food preparation workers, marketing/sales worker supervisors, and food services and lodging managers can expect substantial job growth. Many of these jobs don't require postsecondary education or training. As a group, they offer lower than average median earnings. They also have a history of high employee turnover and few fringe benefits, and much of this work is short term in nature.

Employment in Education

The elementary school population is expected to rise by 2.2 million, the secondary school population by 2.6 million, and the postsecondary school population by 3.1 million, creating a need for more teachers. The number of needed special education teachers will also increase, reflecting greater awareness of the abilities and potential contributions of people with disabilities.

Nontraditional Occupations for Women

Nontraditional occupations include any jobs in which women comprise 25% or less of total employment. These fast-growing jobs offer higher wages than many of the occupations where women are in the majority:

High-Paying, Fast-Growing Nontraditional Occupations for Women

Occupation	Weekly Wages (Full-Time Position)
Engineer	$897
Architect	$702
Construction inspector	$648
Firefighter	$629
Police officer and detective	$582
Mechanic and repairer	$519
Insulation worker	$485

Declining Occupations

Although many jobs and job areas are growing rapidly, others are experiencing significant declines. This is a result of technological advances, organizational changes, shifts in consumer demand for certain goods and services, foreign trade, and changes in the geographic location of the production of certain goods and services.

Declining occupational positions include farmers, sewing machine operators, electrical/electronic assemblers, private household cleaners/servants, office machine operators, service station attendants, and bank tellers. Although state and local government employment are projected to increase by 2.2 million through 2005, federal government employment is projected to decrease by as much as 235,000.

Hot Job Spots for the 21st Century

Here's a listing of the U.S. regions and industries where the demand for workers remains red hot. If you're contemplating a career move, you might just want to pull up stakes and relocate altogether:

Hottest Places to Work

Region	Industry
Las Vegas, Nevada	Casinos
Phoenix, Arizona	High-tech, small manufacturing
Austin, Texas	High-tech, manufacturing
Salt Lake City, Utah	Bio-tech, construction
Boise, Idaho	High-tech, retail
Atlanta, Georgia	Business services, retail
Portland, Oregon	Semiconductors
Albuquerque, New Mexico	High-tech, services
San Jose, California	High-tech
Dallas, Texas	Financial services, communications
Fort Lauderdale, Florida	Data processing
Mobile, Alabama	Telemarketing, financial services
Orlando, Florida	Software design, entertainment
Seattle, Washington	Aviation, high-tech
Raleigh, North Carolina	Pharmaceuticals, high-tech
Indianapolis, Indiana	Pharmaceuticals, publishing

Targeting Top Career Choices

Based on all the research you've done so far, make a list of your top career choices. Your list may have as few as 1 or 2 choices and as many as 15. If you generate a list with more than 15 career directions, it can be a bit overwhelming. We have more research to do, so if it turns out that you exhaust all 15 directions and don't find your new direction, you can always create a list of your secondary choices.

Take a close look at your list of primary career alternatives. Prioritize them in the order in which you're interested in pursuing them further. Look for the top one, two, or three careers that satisfy your necessary goals (reasons for working) and incorporate your personality, interests, and desired work environment. If you're having trouble deciding how to prioritize the list, try focusing on your top three choices. The best way to do this is to listen to your intuition. At some level, you usually know which choices feel right for you.

Getting Into the Driver's Seat

Now that you've narrowed down your career choices to the few that you'd like to pursue further, it's time to talk about the different work arrangements available. Once again, you have many options to choose from, and we'll discuss them in depth in Chapter 3, "Choosing a Suitable Work Arrangement." The beauty of having options is that you can create a work/life path that suits your desires and needs. You can set things up so that you're in control, and as research suggests, people who feel in control are the happiest people.

CHAPTER 3

CHOOSING A SUITABLE WORK ARRANGEMENT

"The average person is only capable of four productive hours of work a day. The rest is spent filling time."

TONY SHIVELY

T he world of work is ever-changing. Not only are new careers popping up daily, but the capacity in which people work is also evolving. Working the traditional 9-to-5 schedule for an employer is quickly becoming an unpreferred work arrangement, especially for women with families and various other personal desires and commitments. Work styles with flextime are "in," and they are here to stay.

We're all familiar with the traditional 9-to-5 work routine that typically involves working for an employer 50 weeks per year. For many, this work arrangement is best. Then there are those who get burned out having work as the central focus of their lives. They want more time to devote to being with their families, pursuing their interests, and giving back to the community.

Just think of all the benefits that could occur if more people began working fewer hours per week. We'd all have ample time to enjoy an enriched life. More people would be employed. Those with special needs such as parents, the elderly, and the disabled would be able to work a shorter schedule. As more people work from home or in "virtual offices," the air will be cleaner and the roads less congested, and far fewer deaths will occur as a result of car accidents. Companies and the environment will experience tremendous savings of energy and resources.

In this chapter we'll discuss a variety of flexible work arrangements, including reduced work schedules, rearranged work schedules, and independent work. We'll also touch on two work arrangements that are growing in popularity—portfolio careers and volunteer work. Some of these work options are really taking off, and others are barely past the starting gate. Take a look, and decide on the best fit for you.

Reduced Work Schedules

Do you really want to work full time? If the answer is no, a reduced work schedule might be just the thing for you. Reduced work schedules involve working fewer hours per week than the traditional 40-hour workweek requires. Better known as "part-time work," the popularity of this option has jumped 50% in recent years, with more than 6 million part-time professionals comprising the entire U.S. workforce. In fact, part-time professional opportunities are growing 25 times faster than other full-time or nonprofessional part-time jobs.

One exciting part about this increase is that part-time professional positions are paying well. According to Catalyst, a New York research firm specializing in women in the workforce, one-third of corporate part-timers earn salaries ranging from $35,000 to over $100,000 per year. Lawyers and accountants earn even more, with two-thirds in the $80,000 to over $100,000 salary range.

Women are on the forefront of the part-time movement. A whopping 97% of people in the part-timer category are moms who want to spend more time with their families. Others are jumping aboard as well. What are their reasons? Approximately 7% to 10% want more personal time to care for aging parents. Many who are retired want part-time work to keep busy and/or supplement their savings. And many child-free workers are deciding to step off the career ladder—with many changing career directions altogether—in order to have a life, too.

The most popular reduced work schedules are part-time work requiring fewer hours than the standard full-time work schedule, temporary work involving work schedules arranged on a call-in or as-needed basis, and job sharing, where two or more employees share the responsibilities, pay, and benefits of one position.

Part-Time Work

Standard part-time work is increasingly common, with 57% of all employees working this schedule. The reasons that part-time opportunities in the workplace will continue to increase are numerous. The following are the top 10 reasons part-time work opportunities are expected to explode:

- ◆ The lack of professionalism once associated with part-time work is decreasing.
- ◆ The growing number of women with children is changing workplace mindsets and values.

- Because the pool of skilled workers is diminishing, the negotiation power of those that remain is increasing.
- This is the age of the contingent workforce, whereby employers are offering short-term, freelance work opportunities.
- As international business increases, so does the demand for a nonstandard workday.
- Technology supports a reduced workweek by computerizing administrative tasks.
- Companies are becoming more "family friendly," and offering part-time professional positions enables them to compete for qualified workers.
- Twenty- and thirty-somethings want a life of their own making and are willing to sacrifice money and to work fewer hours in exchange for more personal time.
- Research confirms that offering part-time work improves worker morale and productivity, allowing companies to retain valued employees.
- The focus on returning to the family is perceived as one cure for societal ills such as the increase of teenage gangs and violent crime.

It's important for you to assess the advantages and disadvantages of part-time work to see if it's for you.

The following are some of the advantages of part-time work:

- You have more time for family and personal interests.
- It allows for a wider range of flexible scheduling possibilities.
- You might receive prorated pay and benefits.
- This option is easy to start, especially if you're already established and have a good track record with a company.

The following are some of the disadvantages of part-time work:

- Your job might require full-time effort and might not be suitable.
- Your pay and promotions might be less frequent.
- Managers and coworkers might view you as being less committed.
- You might be one of the first to get laid off if layoffs occur.
- Working fewer hours reduces your income.
- You might have less time to interact with coworkers.
- You might miss out on critical information if you're not present full time.

Temporary Work

According to the National Association of Temporary Staffing Services (NATSS), there are 1.3 million temporary workers today, a population that has tripled over the past 10 years. Since 1982 the temporary worker population has risen 250%, while the nation's total workforce has increased by only 20%.

Just what is temporary work? Temporary work is found through temporary employment agencies. Temporary employment agencies work by recruiting a pool of workers, or *temps*, whom they can send out on jobs, or assignments, when a company, or client, has a position to fill.

Temps sign up with a particular agency and register their requests in the agency's database. The beauty of this is that it's possible to specify that you want a position for certain days or hours, or that you want to work full time during certain times of the year.

Generally, the company you work for pays a fee to the agency in addition to the temp's salary. Companies like this because when they have a short-term need for a worker, hiring a temp is cheaper than hiring a full-time employee and giving that person benefits.

Temporary agencies such as Kelly have specialized in clerical and administrative positions—where about half the temporary workforce resides. However, larger cities have temp agencies for almost every type of professional, such as accountants, engineers, lawyers, management executives, computer programmers, and financial and insurance services workers.

The following are some of the advantages of temporary work:

- You have more time for family and personal interests.
- You can pick and choose your job assignments.
- You can make a gradual transition back to the workforce if you've been away for a while.
- You can experiment with different jobs and work environments.
- You can try out different employers to find a good fit.
- You can get on-the-job training.
- The work comes to you, so you don't have to spend time looking for a job.
- You don't have to deal with the paperwork involved with billing and taxes that self-employed people face.

The following are some of the disadvantages of temporary work:

- It might be difficult to get child care if your schedule isn't consistent.
- Your job is only as secure as your last paycheck.
- You sometimes work at a lower rate than other employees doing the same work.
- You might not feel like part of the team.
- You probably won't receive any employee benefits from the companies you work for. (However, some of the biggest national temp agencies such as Kelly, Interim, Manpower, Olsten, Tiger, and Winston offer basic benefits such as health coverage, a sign-up bonus, referrals, and even paid vacation days.)
- You might end up doing the work that no one else desires.
- You might miss out on employee training, rewards, and recognition from your employer.
- You usually have to arrange your schedule in accordance with the client's business hours.

◆ Your paychecks will be cyclical, and you'll experience periods of feast or famine.

◆ You probably won't be able to work from home.

Job Sharing

Across the United States, more than one-third of corporations polled by human resource consultants Hewitt and Associates offer job sharing—an arrangement between two part-time employees to fill one full-time position. A growing number of workers, the majority of whom are mothers, are discovering the advantages of job sharing. By splitting the workweek and the workload in half, job sharing moms have increased their time for hobbies, volunteering, and family activities.

Ruth, Age 45

Ruth's 75-year-old mother was dying of cancer, and Ruth wanted time away from her job as an accountant for a large corporation to care for her at home. Ruth's dad had passed away 5 years previously, so she was the only close family her mom had now. It tugged at her heart to see her mom deteriorate. She was committed to doing whatever it took to be there for her mom in her time of need. In her current work arrangement, Ruth consistently put in 60-hour weeks, leaving little time for a personal life, which she had given up long ago.

The solution Ruth arrived at involved a creative combination of flexible work arrangements. "Setting something up to satisfy my need to be home to care for my mom and please my manager took a tremendous amount of research and planning up front," Ruth says, "but the outcome was well worth the effort. I set up a job sharing arrangement with another company employee, and on the days that I was scheduled to work, I was able to telecommute. All my work can be done from home anyway, and because my manager knows the quality of my work and trusts me, it wasn't difficult to sell the idea. The job sharing portion of the arrangement took some doing to convince management—mainly because it's new to our company and has never been tried before. I had to cut back my hours to part time in order to care for my mom, so job sharing was the perfect answer. Although I'd still be working part time, at least I could work from home."

This arrangement proved to be a blessing. Ruth was able to give her mom the love and care she deserved in her last 6 months of life. "We were never closer," Ruth says. "And when mom died, I carried on with the job sharing and telecommuting arrangements because everything was working out so beautifully. But more importantly, during my time away from work, I did a lot of soul-searching. I realized how short life is and how lonely it can be if you don't have people to share it with. I wanted to take the extra time to focus on me and having a relationship—something I've avoided most of my life by burying myself in my work."

Usually both partners in a job sharing situation split one full-time salary. They also split company fringe benefits according to the hours worked, or select from cafeteria plans based on individual needs. If one partner already has health care coverage, for instance, she might choose vision care coverage instead. The majority of job sharers work in the clerical/administrative fields, but job sharing arrangements for professional positions are becoming increasingly common.

The following are some of the advantages of job sharing:

◆ You have more time for family and personal interests.
◆ You can work part time without sacrificing your full-time career.
◆ Management positions requiring a full-time presence might be available to those who want to work part time.
◆ If you're returning to work, job sharing allows you to phase back in.
◆ You can focus on the portions of the job that you like and do best.
◆ You have a built-in partner to share ideas and solve problems with—and celebrate successes with, too.
◆ You have someone to cover for you in case of sickness or emergency.
◆ You can relax on days off, knowing that someone reliable is covering for you.

The following are some of the disadvantages of job sharing:

◆ Working fewer hours reduces your income.
◆ You might have to convince your employer, who might be reluctant to allow certain higher-level or management jobs to be shared.
◆ Participating in job sharing arrangements might affect your promotion prospects.
◆ Communication might be a problem if job sharers don't overlap their schedules.
◆ Your performance depends on the performance of someone else.
◆ You might have difficulty sharing the authority, decision making, and credit of a high-status position.
◆ One partner might feel that the other has more interesting work, works less overtime, or does not perform at an acceptable level.
◆ You and your partner might not be compatible. If the partnership breaks up, your job might be at risk.
◆ You might have to share a workspace with someone else.
◆ It might be difficult to find someone with complementary skills to share a job with you.
◆ If your partner moves or quits, your job is at risk.
◆ You won't be able to attend the same meetings or appointments as your partner.
◆ You might have to work full time if your partner is sick or goes on vacation or leave.
◆ It might be difficult to climb the corporate ladder if you can't find a job sharing partner with suitable experience and skills for a particular position.

Rearranged Work Schedules

If you're sick of working 9 to 5, but still want to put in a minimum of 40 hours per week, you can be sitting at home reading the paper and drinking coffee while others are on the road during rush-hour traffic. With a rearranged work schedule, you can spend less time on the road and enjoy more personal time as a result. The following are some examples of rearranged work schedules:

◆ *Flextime:* Flextime involves working a schedule with unspecified starting and ending times set by each employee. However, most companies designate specific times, generally called *core hours*, that all employees must be present.

◆ *Compressed workweek:* A compressed workweek involves condensing the typical 5-day workweek into fewer days. For example, you could work 4-day weeks of 10-hour days or 3-day weeks of 12-hour days.

◆ *Modified worktime:* Modified worktime involves schedules that vary from the norm for an occupation, an industry, a workplace, or a locale. These schedules might differ daily, weekly, or seasonally.

◆ *Staggered worktime:* Staggered worktime involves schedules assigned at intervals so that workers don't all arrive and leave together.

Independent Work Arrangements

Independent work arrangements offer a great degree of control over work environment, workhours, and workload. Many people are taking the plunge in this direction, especially women.

Julia, Age 40

When Julia's son was born in 1989, the company she worked for at the time was in the process of laying off several employees, including her boss, who, as Julia says, "happened to be female in a predominately male company and culture." Julia suspected that she'd be next, if it weren't for the fact that she was 9 months pregnant and "a lawsuit waiting to happen."

Before she left for maternity leave, Julia had a meeting with her new (male) manager. "I explained to him in no uncertain terms that I would definitely be returning to work after my maternity leave," Julie says, "especially since we had just bought a house in a very expensive housing market. I also mentioned several times that if a manager was going to be chosen to replace the woman who had just been laid off while I was on maternity leave, I wanted to be considered and interviewed for the position. At the time I was a senior project

(continued)

(continued)

manager, with no real career path except into that management position. I had a bachelor's degree in communications and had also completed graduate coursework in business, psychology, and education. Well, the big surprise came while I was on maternity leave. The replacement manager was hired—a man with no college degree and no experience in project management. I was never interviewed for the job! I probably could have sued, but I didn't have the energy or interest at that point."

"My experience emphasizes how real the 'mommy track' is," Julia says. "Some things have changed in the past 10 years, but the bottom line is that companies want employees they can count on, and mothers are often 'distracted' by things like sick children, doctor's appointments, and teachers conferences. Even if women don't actually let these things affect their jobs, the corporate attitude (or fear) is that they might. No wonder career-committed women downplay the mommy thing. The business world for the most part doesn't care about our families. Unless it's good for their business, what they care about are profits and the bottom line. Women have learned to compartmentalize their lives and keep the kids sort of hidden away at home so as not to jeopardize their careers. This is one of the reasons I went into semi-retirement after my daughter was born in 1993. It was no longer worth it for me to try to do it all. Fortunately, in 1995 I founded my own business and can now play by my own rules."

Entrepreneurship

Women are starting small businesses at twice the rate of men. Most of these businesses are small, service-oriented businesses that can be run out of the home. For this reason, we'll discuss home business in detail in the next section, but first let's talk about entrepreneurship in general and establish whether it's for you.

An entrepreneur can be someone who has an idea for a service or product and then creates a business to sell that service or product. An entrepreneur can also be someone who buys an existing business, a franchise, or a distributorship in a network marketing company.

The following are some of the advantages of small business ownership:

◆ You are your own boss.
◆ The profits are yours.
◆ You have pride of ownership.
◆ There is no red tape involved in making decisions.
◆ You can put your dreams and ideas to work.
◆ You hire your own people.
◆ You know your customers.

The following are some of the disadvantages of small business ownership:

◆ There is financial risk.
◆ It generally requires very long hours, especially in the beginning.
◆ It can be a strain on family and friends.
◆ You get few days off for vacations.
◆ You must pay for your own benefits (e.g., health insurance—if you're not covered on a spouse's plan—vacation, sick leave) and those of your employees.
◆ Businesses run in cycles of highs and lows, which creates sporadic cash flow.
◆ You might lack the skills needed to run various aspects of the business.
◆ You might have insufficient capital to start and run the business.

Rating Yourself as a Small Business Owner

Exercise 3.1 lists some questions to ask yourself to help you decide whether to start your own business. Rate yourself on a scale of 1 to 5, with 1 indicating that you don't believe you possess the trait, and 5 indicating that you strongly believe you possess the trait.

If you score 41 or higher, you're a shoo-in as a business owner. A score of 31 to 40 indicates that you have qualities associated with being an entrepreneur. A score of 18 to 30 is borderline, but you might make it in your own business. If you score 17 or lower, you're probably better off working for someone else.

Tips for Getting Started

In order to get a business started, you have to satisfy the following minimum requirements:

◆ *Financing:* Will you need to raise startup or investment capital to launch your business?
◆ *Legal matters:* What types of licenses and zoning matters will pertain to your business?
◆ *Taxes:* How will you track income, Social Security, state, and local taxes?
◆ *Insurance:* What types of insurance will you need (e.g., liability, health)?
◆ *Accounting:* How will you keep the books and financial records for your business?
◆ *Business structure:* What type of business structure will you choose? (e.g., sole proprietorship, partnership, corporation)?
◆ *Business name:* Will you work under your personal name or do business as some trade name?
◆ *Marketing:* How will you attract customers? This is the most vital aspect of running a business. A business won't survive without customers.

Exercise 3.1

Personality Inventory—Small Business

Trait	Description	Score (1–5)
Good organizer	I plan my activities before I start them, usually writing them down so I can refer to them later.	_____
Relate well with people	I like people and find it easy to get along with most personality types.	_____
Independent worker	I like doing things on my own and don't need someone telling me what to do.	_____
Take responsibility	I always take charge of things and follow through with projects.	_____
Leader	I can convince most people of the merit of my ideas.	_____
Hard worker	I don't mind working hard if it's for something I want and believe in.	_____
High energy level	I have an abundance of energy to do what I want to do.	_____
Decision maker	I make decisions quickly when I have to, and most of my decisions turn out fine.	_____
Persevering	When my mind is made up to do something, I don't stop until I'm finished.	_____
People can trust me	I'm a person of my word, and I don't say things I don't intend to follow through on.	_____
Total score		_____

Home Business

As mentioned previously, women are starting businesses at an explosive rate, and most of these businesses are run out of the home. More than 40 million Americans, the majority of whom are women, own and operate home businesses, generating annual revenues of $500 billion. Home businesses are the fastest growing segment of the U.S. workforce.

The following are some of the top home businesses:

◆ Business consulting and services
◆ Computer services and programming
◆ Financial consulting and services
◆ Marketing and advertising
◆ Medical practice and services
◆ Graphics and visual arts
◆ Public relations and publicity
◆ Real estate
◆ Writing

Mary, Age 55

Remember Mary, the administrative assistant from Chapter 1, "Where Are You Now?" who was burned out in her job of 13 years? She didn't see herself retiring "unless she wasn't physically or mentally able to work." After a long self-evaluation process, Mary decided to start a secretarial service from home. "It was a big step, giving up my 'job security' and steady paycheck," she says, "but I was ready for a change, and had always had a longing to strike out on my own to see if I could do it. What a growth experience this has been."

Mary had made many contacts in her administrative assistant position. Her job involved constant interaction with managers from client companies, with whom she forged solid relationships. When she left to start a business of her own, many of these managers found a need for her services. Mary says, "The connections I made on my job didn't provide enough business to pay the rent, but it sure beat having to start from scratch. I'd suggest to anyone starting a business that you get a few clients to begin with. Getting that first customer or two is the toughest challenge of all. Once you get two established clients, if you do a good job, they'll tell others, and your business will grow through word-of-mouth. There's no better way to get business than from referrals because you don't have to spend time and money on advertising. The key is to consistently do high-quality, timely work, and your clients will automatically tell others about your services."

The following are some of the advantages of home business:

◆ You have control over the following:
  — Scheduling of your time (e.g., personal, family, and work roles)
  — Your income level
  — Job security
  — How you dress
  — Your level of stress
  — Whom you work with
  — Your environment
  — Your career destiny

◆ You get the following additional benefits:
  — You have no commute.
  — You don't have to purchase an expensive wardrobe.
  — You can create a more balanced existence.
  — You can spend more time with family and friends.
  — You can be a good role model and socialize your kids for the world of work.

— You have more personal time because you don't have to commute to an office.
— You can be your own boss.
— You can take advantage of tax breaks such as the home office deduction.
— You have low overhead because you don't have to rent an outside office.

The following are some of the disadvantages of home business:

◆ Isolation
◆ Lack of self-discipline
◆ Distractions
◆ Interruptions
◆ Lack of support from family and friends
◆ No physical separation of work and family
◆ Self-imposed stress
◆ Concern about business image (e.g., lack of professionalism)
◆ Difficulty getting loans for startup
◆ Difficulty finding good in-home child care
◆ Weight gain and decline in physical appearance

Hot Work-at-Home Careers for 2000 and Beyond

Financial Services
◆ Personal investment planner
◆ Expense-reduction consultant

Personal Services
◆ Gift buying/gift baskets
◆ Party coordinator
◆ Personal coach/instructor

Caregiving Services
◆ Child care
◆ Elder care
◆ Speech pathologist

Specialized Services
◆ Web site developer
◆ Computer consultant
◆ Client-prospecting marketer
◆ Desktop publisher
◆ Copywriter
◆ Interior designer
◆ Paralegal
◆ Detailed vacation arranger

Rate Yourself for a Work-at-Home Arrangement

Exercise 3.2 is a brief personality inventory adapted from *The Work-at-Home Balancing Act* by Sandy Anderson (published by Avon Books) that you can take to see if you're suited for working from home. Rate yourself on a scale of 1 to 5, with 1 indicating that you don't believe you possess the trait, and 5 indicating that you strongly believe you possess the trait.

If you score 48 or above, you are definitely well suited for working at home. A score of 30 to 47 suggests that you're likely to succeed, but might have some struggles. If you score less than 30, a home business might not be for you, but if you really have the desire and are willing to do whatever it takes to make the situation work, you might not want to close the door on this option just yet.

If you're not ready to start a home business but still want to work from home, you might consider telecommuting, whereby you can continue to work for someone, stay connected to a company, and satisfy your desire to work at home. This is a great option because it gives you an opportunity to see if working at home is for you, while keeping a steady paycheck and benefits rolling in. Telecommuting could be just the launching pad you need to ultimately start a home business; it's a popular independent work arrangement that we'll discuss in more depth in the next section.

Avoiding the Scams

"Assemble our products from home. Earn $300 per week." Unfortunately, there are a lot of scams out there—everything from companies offering big bucks for envelope stuffing and product assembly to franchises and network marketing companies promising huge profits for selling gumball machines and facial creams. I'm always leery of companies promising hefty incomes in short periods of time and those asking you to pay them money up front. If a business opportunity sounds too good to be true, it probably is, and it might be best to steer clear.

Thoroughly research the business you choose. Call your local Better Business Bureau (BBB) or the BBB located in the state where the company selling the opportunity resides. Also, call the National Fraud Information Center Consumer Assistance Hotline (800-876-7060). Always look for a money-back guarantee with any opportunity you purchase. Any company offering a desirable commodity will offer a guarantee. Gaining awareness will lower your risk factor.

Exercise 3.2

Personality Inventory—Work-at-Home Business

Trait	Description	Score (1–5)
Self-motivated	I'm a self-starter and I enjoy launching new projects.	_____
Self-disciplined	I'm good at sticking to tasks and seeing them through.	_____
Enjoy solitude	I enjoy spending long periods of time by myself.	_____
Thrive on control	I thrive on having control over every aspect of my work and personal lives.	_____
Strive for perfection	I have a tendency to strive for perfection in my work.	_____
Committed	I will be committed to doing the best job possible in my work, and will do whatever it takes to get new business and satisfy my clients.	_____
Self-confident	I am a self-confident person. I generally have a positive attitude and try to keep my sense of humor when the going gets tough.	_____
Risk taker	I'm willing to take a risk as long as I feel that the outcome of the risk is worth my investment of money, time, and emotions.	_____
Knowledge seeker	I thrive on learning new things, seeking information, and "wearing multiple hats" because variety excites me.	_____
Support elicitor	When I need help, I'm not afraid to admit it or ask for it. I'm willing to pay for help with child care, house cleaning, and certain aspects of my business that would be more cost-effective or make more sense to delegate.	_____
Good communicator	I have good communication skills, both oral and written.	_____
Creative	I'm a creative person by nature and am always thinking of new ideas or ways to solve problems. I'm open-minded and am able to overcome challenges by using my creativity.	_____
Total score		_____

Best Work-at-Home Careers for Moms

Whether you can work at home with kids present depends on the ages of your children (Do they require close supervision?), their personalities (Are they fussy or clingy?), and your line of work (Will your business require a lot of phone work or client visits?). The best businesses for moms are those that allow you to work a flexible schedule (while children are asleep, occupied, napping, or at school). The following business positions involve work that can be done during the wee hours of the morning or late at night, while children are asleep:

- Bill auditor
- Bookkeeper
- Child care provider
- Computer programmer
- Copywriter
- Desktop publisher
- Editorial services provider
- Freelance writer
- Gift basket maker
- In-home tutor
- Information broker
- Mailing list service provider

- Mail-order businessperson
- Medical biller
- Medical transcriber
- Newsletter publisher
- Proposal and grant writer
- Public relations specialist
- Résumé writer
- Reunion planner
- Tax preparer
- Technical writer
- Transcript digester
- Word processor

Telecommuting

Telecommuting allows company employees to work all or a portion of their workhours from home or at a satellite facility. They "commute" or stay in touch with the office via telephone, e-mail, and fax machines. Currently, about 15 million workers telecommute on a part- or full-time basis. Because of the tremendous advancements in technology, it's easy and inexpensive to equip a high-powered office at home. As the number of "knowledge workers" such as writers, graphic designers, and computer specialists continue to increase, the opportunities for telecommuting have never been greater.

You reviewed the pros and cons of starting a home business in a previous section. Most of these apply to telecommuting as well. In addition, if you want to telecommute, there are upsides and downsides you can stress to your employer. The first thing your employer will want to know is the impact your proposed telecommuting arrangement will have on the company, and it's critical that you've examined it from all angles and are able to overcome any objections.

Many companies offer telecommuting to selected employees. Small businesses, which can be greatly affected by the loss of even one worker, are leading the trend. In her book *Telecommute!* (published by John Wiley & Sons), Lisa Shaw stresses the upside and downside to the employer of having employees who telecommute.

The following are some of the upsides of telecommuting:

◆   It decreases office expenses, including rent, utilities, and equipment.
◆   It increases productivity.
◆   It decreases employee turnover.
◆   It increases the ability to self-manage, thus relieving management of the entire supervision responsibility.
◆   It meets Clean Air Act requirements.
◆   It sets up an automatic disaster-recovery program (e.g., after a fire, earth-quake, or flood).
◆   It fosters a more content workforce.
◆   It creates jobs and equipment to meet the needs of telecommuters.
◆   It offers a company the ability to be more competitive in the marketplace.
◆   It shows workers that the employer cares about them.
◆   It teaches supervisors to exercise a more flexible management style.
◆   It fosters more focused, concise communication with colleagues and managers.
◆   It enhances computer literacy.

The following are some of the downsides of telecommuting:

◆   Some managers don't trust employees they can't see, and are used to basing performance on attendance rather than on output or results.
◆   Telecommuters can be less able to meet customer needs.
◆   Work teams can deteriorate when members are scattered.
◆   Telecommuting can appear to favor some employees over others.
◆   Meetings must be coordinated in advance.
◆   Future promotions might be affected; however, the effect of telecommuting can be positive (if work performance goes up) or nega-tive (if management overlooks you because you're not physically present in the office).
◆   Managers must adapt to using different methods of supervision.

Is Your Job Right for Telecommuting?

Do you currently work in a job that lends itself to telecommuting? Service-oriented work such as computer programming, bookkeeping, and writing is ideal for telecommuting. The work that's best suited for home is that which requires independent actions and large blocks of concentration: reading, writing, plan-ning, budgeting, and so forth. These activities take up varying percentages of time for different employees. It all depends on your job. A lawyer would prob-ably be able to use at least one day at home per week to conduct research and write briefs. For some positions, it would be difficult to justify telecommuting.

Top Job Positions for Telecommuting

- Computer programmer
- Computer systems analyst
- Data-entry clerk
- Desktop publisher
- Lawyer
- Legal assistant
- News reporter
- Public relations professional
- Sales representative
- Software engineer
- Sportswriter
- Technical writer
- Translator

These might include upper-level managers, retail sales positions, customer-service workers, manufacturing employees, and health care professionals.

To determine whether your job is appropriate for telecommuting, write down your regular and irregular job responsibilities. From that list, estimate what percentage of the work can be done just as easily from home as in your office. If you work a 5-day workweek and at least 25% of your work can be done at home, then you could probably justify telecommuting one day each week. Use this exercise to help create a list of the duties you'll perform on the day(s) you work at home in your proposal to your employer.

Outsourcing

A new corporate trend called *outsourcing* takes place when a company contracts an outside party (an independent contractor) to take on the responsibilities of a certain task or department in order to cut costs. This involves a variety of work activities such as payroll, accounting, secretarial, or maintenance service.

Basically, as an independent contractor, you're self-employed and have all the responsibilities of any business owner. However, independent contracting offers a way to work with the same company over the length of time that the contract specifies. If you have a solid contract with a company that requires full-time work indefinitely, you'll have more "job security" and you won't have to continually look for new business, which is essential for the survival of all businesses.

Consulting and brokering offer a wide range of opportunities for independent contractors. The following are the top jobs and fields for work as an independent contractor, many of which can be done from home:

- Script, newsletter, résumé, and other types of writing
- Manuscript editing and proofreading for writers and publishers
- Training program delivery
- Training system development
- Word processing

Part-Time Work, Job Sharing, and Telecommuting: Taking the First Step

If you decide to approach your employer about turning your full-time job into a part-time position, or one that involves job sharing or telecommuting, be sure to do your homework first. What possible objections will your employer have? Be prepared to overcome these objections both verbally and in writing.

Put together a one- or two-page detailed proposal that includes your company's mission statement near the top. In the body of the proposal, list all the advantages your chosen work arrangement will provide for your employer. Explain your rationale for desiring this flexible work option and why you're the best person to work in this capacity. List all job duties that will be performed, by whom and when they will be performed, and the procedure for performance evaluations. Explain how and when you'll communicate with your office and coworkers when you're absent. Mention whether this work arrangement will be temporary or permanent. Will you need special equipment? If so, who will pay for it and who will be responsible for it? Head off any and all objections (see the disadvantages for the given arrangement, mentioned previously in this chapter) by formulating your responses beforehand. This will assure your manager that you mean business and that you are the best person for this new work arrangement.

- Real estate appraisal
- Engineering support
- Office organization and design
- Market research
- General research analysis
- Meeting planning and management
- Social event planning and management
- Graphic art and illustration creation
- Computer programming
- Marketing management and services
- Interior design and decorating
- Consulting and brokerage services
- Financial services

Portfolio Careers

What if you're the kind of person who enjoys work that involves a lot of interaction with people, but you also thrive on working alone? How about creating a career that suits both needs? I worked at home as a writer for some time and found that I needed to balance my writing with another activity that provided more interaction with people. Also, I thrive on variety and tend to get bored doing one thing.

The solution I came up with is one that many people are adopting: a *portfolio career*. Much like a financial portfolio, a portfolio career consists of two or more income-earning pursuits. In my career portfolio, I can earn a living from writing, consulting, public speaking, and conducting workshops.

The beauty of this arrangement is the ability to diversify. If you put all your energies into one career pursuit, you're in trouble when that pursuit hits a financial low point or disappears altogether. With multiple income sources, you're better able to combat the high and low cycles characteristic of working on your own. This is emphasized when your multiple careers complement each other. If I conduct a workshop or give a talk, I can also sell books or pick up new clients. My marketing efforts produce synergy when I'm able to sell more than one product or service at a time. This is an exciting phenomenon, especially when you see the positive results in your bank account.

Volunteer Work

Doing volunteer work for a cause or community that you're behind can be intrinsically rewarding. If you're in search of a life mission that doesn't require earning income, there are many opportunities to share your talents and gifts in places such as hospitals, libraries, pet adoption agencies, and school districts.

For information on getting started, you can contact the United Way Volunteer Center in your area. The United Way provides a variety of services, from the American Heart Association to People for Trees to the YMCA. Volunteer opportunities are as diverse as the myriad of United Way agencies, and you're sure to find something to suit your needs and interests.

Volunteering offers a way to overcome the age-old dilemma: "You've got to have experience to get hired, but you can't get hired without experience." Volunteering allows you to test a particular job you're interested in to see if it's right for you. We'll discuss volunteering further in Chapter 8, "Exploring Your Options ," where you'll have the opportunity to investigate your options by doing hands-on research.

The Best Option for You

Now that you've had a basic overview of the advantages and disadvantages of various work arrangements, you can determine which option is best for you. Do you want to work part time or full time? Do you want to work for someone else or for yourself? Do you want to work from your home or in an outside setting? Do you want flexibility and freedom, or do you prefer a structured, routine schedule? Do you thrive on variety and "newness" in your work, or do you prefer predictability? Do you need an income, or are you able to volunteer your time? Answering these questions will help you decide which work arrangement to go with. Don't be afraid to try different work styles until you find the best fit.

CHAPTER 4

EVALUATING YOUR TRAINING AND EDUCATIONAL NEEDS

"Go confidently in the direction of your dreams."

HENRY DAVID THOREAU

Midlife women are going back to school in droves. They realize that learning is a lifelong experience that can open up directions for personal growth. Jobs that require higher levels of skills and education will continue to be the high-growth occupations in the coming decade. Higher education and training are the principal means by which women attain career advancement and greater employment status. You may be pondering the possibility of returning to school. You can take courses to improve your basic skills, explore various areas of specialty to prepare for a new career, or foster your own enrichment and growth.

In this chapter we'll take a look at your current skills in relation to your top three career choices and evaluate what you need to do to prepare for each career. We'll explore several available educational and training options, from vocational programs offering free classes to distance learning on the Internet. This chapter gives tips for surviving college as an adult learner, as well as financial resources to help you achieve your goals.

Never Too Old

Women of all ages who have worked very little or not at all for pay outside their homes are going to college in record numbers. Between 1980 and 1989, women 25 years and older enrolled in college at a rate four times greater than that of women younger than 25. As women's life span continues to increase, there's plenty of time to accomplish goals such as going back to school in our later years. The average age of adults going back to school is above 30, and there's no maximum in sight. In fact, I recently read about a 92-year-old woman who just received her associate's degree.

Studies show that the great majority of women are fearful about returning to school. They wonder, "Am I too old to learn, too old to compete with younger college students?" Whatever your age, it might reassure you to know that with few exceptions, women returning to school report growth in confidence along with newfound goals. Many women who had previous school records that qualify as disasters return and become outstanding students because they've matured and have a solid direction to aim for. The bottom line is that you're never too old to return to school, so put on your backpack, grab a cup of coffee, and let's discuss your educational and training options as they relate to your top three career choices.

Identifying Your Transferable Knowledge and Background

Back in Chapter 2, "Where Do You Want to Be?" when you went to the library to research your top three career choices in the *Occupational Outlook Handbook* (published by JIST Works), you wrote down the skills, education, training, and experience that were preferred or required for each job. To get a hands-on feel for the necessary background to do each job, you should talk to people who work in the field and add to your list anything new that they tell you. If you don't know anyone in that career, ask people in your circle of influence who they know that works in the job you're interested in pursuing. (For more details on conducting informational interviews, see Chapter 8, "Exploring Your Options.")

The nature of today's workplace is different from that of the past. It's characterized by global competition, cultural diversity, new technologies, and new management processes that require workers to have critical thinking, problem-solving, and communication skills, as well as advanced levels of job skills. Employers are looking for people who are teachable and flexible—committed to lifelong learning that permits them to change and grow on many levels on an as-needed basis.

In your journal, draw three vertical lines down a page, making four equal columns. Put the following labels at the top of the four columns: Required, Preferred, Satisfied, and Needed. At the top of the page, put your number-one job choice. Now take all the skills, education, and experience applicable to your number-one job choice and write each one in the appropriate Required or Preferred columns. You might want to put two or three spaces between each qualification so that you have room to write in the Needed column.

Now, put a check mark in the Satisfied column for each qualification you already possess. In the Needed column, write down the skills, education, and experience you need in order to do the job. Go through this exercise for each of your top three job choices so that you know what qualifications you're lacking. After you've done this, we can move on to explore education and training options to satisfy any areas that are lacking.

Education and Training Options

To gain the skills, education, and experience needed for your top three career choices, you have many options to choose from, depending on what's required for the job. You can start by taking personal enrichment courses or a certificate program at a local college, or you can get started on an academic degree program. You might want to get training on a particular job at a vocational school. Or you might decide to bypass school altogether and do an internship or volunteer work to get some experience first. Consider the knowledge and skills you'll need for each of your top career choices as you review educational and training options described in the following sections.

Continuing Education

Many colleges and private institutions offer certificate programs and individual courses in a variety of fields, generally focusing on the most up-to-date trends. You'll also find personal enrichment courses. A community college in my area offers a vast array of courses on subjects such as stress management, improving relationships, creative writing, assertiveness training, public speaking, starting a home business, various arts and crafts, financial planning, and getting your life organized.

Certificate programs offer concentrated subject matter that can be completed in less time than an academic degree (usually within a year). Some offer college credits. The nice thing about these programs is that you walk away with skills you can use immediately. Completion of a certificate program demonstrates to employers that you're serious about your future and committed to professional advancement. It also conveys mastery of a specific body of knowledge or skill. This could provide the edge you need to get started in a new career.

Most certificate programs require no prerequisites (that is, prior courses taken). Here's a listing of certificate programs offered through the Extension Program at the University of California at San Diego, a college in my area. Oftentimes these programs focus on career preparation in budding fields where no academic degree programs exist:

- Alcohol and drug abuse counseling
- Business computing
- Career counseling
- Childbirth and perinatal educator training
- Community college instruction
- Copyediting
- Educational technologies
- Fitness instruction and exercise science

- Graphic design
- Lactation consulting
- Multimedia development
- Web publishing

Contact the local colleges in your area to inquire about continuing education (also known as extended studies, community service, or extension programs). You'll find certificate programs and individual courses you can take for personal enrichment or to explore a particular field of interest. You can also try private learning centers in your area that feature a wide variety of classes focusing on personal and professional development. The Learning Annex, for instance, offers classes in San Diego, Los Angeles, San Francisco, and New York. For more information, visit the Learning Annex Web site at www.learningannex.com.

Kinds of Colleges

In order to choose a college that meets your needs, it's important to know about the kinds of colleges that exist so you can make an informed decision. The following sections explore the major types of colleges.

Universities

Universities are large colleges, or clusters of colleges, that are often state supported, such as the University of California, with its several branch campuses. Some contain several colleges, such as the College of Law, the College of Sciences, or the College of Liberal Arts.

Universities offer 4-year degrees—either a bachelor of arts or a bachelor of science. They also offer master's degrees, which require 1 or 2 years of academic credit past the bachelor's level. About half of the universities offer doctoral programs (that is, PhD programs) in various fields of study. This requires a few more years of academic credit past the master's level.

If you have no prior college credits completed, you'll most likely need an excellent high school record to qualify for admission to a university. A popular alternative is to transfer to a university after you've completed 2 years of work at a community college (which is a lot less costly than a university). Generally, your 2 years of credits earned at a community college will be accepted for full credit toward a bachelor's degree, and you'll lose no time overall.

Four-Year Colleges

Four-year colleges grant bachelor's degrees. These institutions do not always offer higher degrees. Four-year colleges tend to be smaller than universities and usually have a more restricted, specialized range of offerings. Liberal arts colleges offer degrees with concentrations of study in such fields as psychology, history, politics, philosophy, literature, foreign languages, and fine arts.

Scientific or technical colleges offer degrees with concentrations of study in such fields as mathematics, physics, engineering, astronomy, and architecture. Liberal arts and scientific colleges often overlap, with similar offerings. Four-year colleges are either state supported or are private institutions supported by a combination of endowments, alumni contributions, investments, and tuition charges.

Vocational Colleges

Vocational colleges train students in highly specific career fields such as accounting, advertising, law, real estate, insurance, cosmetology, journalism, filmmaking, acting, and medical transcription. Most of these institutions are private and charge tuition. The programs offered are 2 years or less in length.

Marilyn, Age 30

Marilyn had a 3-year-old daughter, Tracey, and if all went well, she and her husband had plans to have a second child. When I talked with Marilyn, she wanted to start a medical transcription business from her home so that she could be there to care for her kids. "Medical transcription is something I can do from home in the wee hours of the morning or late at night, while Tracey is sleeping," Marilyn says. "During the day there are no guarantees that I can get any work done, but I have to work. My family needs the income to survive. If I choose something I can do day or night, I won't have to worry about paying for child care because my husband can cover for me while he's not working."

Marilyn didn't have any training as a medical transcriptionist. She was employed as a veterinary assistant and didn't like having to leave Tracey in child care each day to go to work. So she investigated her options and found a free vocational program through the local school district that offered certification courses in medical transcription. "That program was the best find," she says. "When I went to class the first day, it was filled. Most people would have given up, but I kept coming back until someone finally dropped and I took their place. Now I'm a certified medical transcriptionist, and I have the knowledge and experience to work in this new field. It satisfies all my needs, and I couldn't be happier."

First, you should try calling your local school district to see if it offers tuition-free vocational education or job training courses. California offers such a program, called Regional Occupational Program (ROP), and it's funded and run by local school districts. Local and state taxes pay for the program. ROP offers training for a variety of careers. Here's a list of tuition-free training programs that you might find in your area:

◆ Agriculture
◆ Animal care/veterinary assistant

- Auto technology
- Cabinetmaking/woodworking
- Commercial cleaning
- Computer technology
- Construction technology
- Cosmetology
- Diesel technology
- Drafting/computer-aided design
- Education/child care
- Electronics
- Engine repair
- Fashion design/production/upholstery
- Financial services
- Food services
- Graphic communication/commercial art
- Hospitality/tourism
- Interior design and sales
- International trade
- Manufacturing technology
- Marketing/management/real estate
- Medical/dental assistant/technician programs
- Office professions programs
- Photography
- Public safety/legal careers
- Telecommunications
- Truck driving

Oftentimes vocational colleges include instruction on self-directed job searching, such as filling out applications, interviewing techniques, and locating potential employers. Many offer job referral assistance. Although many vocational colleges are fine institutions with formal accreditation, others have been nicknamed "storefront schools" because other colleges don't recognize the degrees they offer.

If you find a vocational college you're interested in attending, thoroughly research its reputation. You can do this by contacting the admissions office at local colleges to see if they're familiar with the school. You might want to contact employers in your field of interest to get an opinion of the school and to see if these employers hire employees who have completed the program. You can also ask the vocational college for names and numbers of students who have completed the program so that you can contact them to see what they thought of the program and find out how it has helped them progress in their careers.

Finally, you should find out whether the college you're interested in attending is accredited. Accreditation is a means of voluntary, nongovernmental review by educators to ensure that colleges and universities attain a certain level of quality. Accredited institutions meet the standards of quality set by the agencies that accredit them, and this usually bestows more credibility on their programs and graduates. You don't want to spend your time and money on a program that awards degrees whose value and status are questionable.

Community Colleges

Community colleges are usually fully accredited institutions that offer 2-year programs leading to either an associate of arts or an associate of science degree. Students who earn such a degree can go on to complete a bachelor's degree in 2 more years of work at a 4-year institution. Community colleges are supported by a combination of state funds and local taxes. The cost of tuition is usually quite a bit lower than the tuition charged by universities and 4-year colleges.

If you're returning to college after the age of 25, a community college might be your best bet. It's the perfect stepping stone because it's inexpensive, the credits you earn are fully transferable to a 4-year college, and it offers tremendous flexibility—you can make your own hours and go part time, and it's probably closer to home than other types of schools.

Alternative Admissions Programs

If your high school record is shaky, you might want to look into an alternative admissions program, which helps applicants who don't meet the usual academic criteria to gain immediate admission to a 4-year college. As previously mentioned, the most popular alternative is attending community college to complete 2 years of lower-division credit and then transferring to a 4-year institution. However, 4-year colleges want to open the door to all interested applicants, so here are some conditions under which you might qualify for a particular school's alternative admissions program if your high school grades were average:

- ◆ You have high scores on the Scholastic Aptitude Test (SAT), which shows you have the capacity for college work.
- ◆ You have a history of stable employment, demonstrating your ability to stick to a task.
- ◆ You are a mom who wants to improve the quality of life for you and your child.
- ◆ You're a member of a racial or an ethnic minority.
- ◆ Your overall grade point average is not up to par because you had difficulty with certain subjects such as physics or calculus.
- ◆ You make a good impression during an interview for potential admission to the school.
- ◆ You can provide two letters of recommendation from former high school teachers or employers who were impressed with your abilities.
- ◆ You have an impressive record of extracurricular activities in high school, such as participation in student government, the school paper, or sports.

Distance Learning

Distance learning has opened all kinds of doors to gaining an education through home study. The Internet has made this possible like never before. If returning to school seems impossible because of distance or a lack of time, then this could be the perfect solution to allow you to achieve your educational goals.

Online degree programs are offered by traditional institutions such as Penn State and Indiana University, as well as nontraditional entities, such as University Online and the Global Network Academy. You can find listings of numerous institutions offering online instruction at the University of Wisconsin-Extension's Distance Education Clearinghouse at www.uwex. edu/disted/home.html. A thorough listing of institutions offering accredited degrees at the undergraduate and graduate levels can be found at www.accrediteddldegrees.com. Also, Chapter 13, "Recommended Resources," presents some great books on distance learning programs that you'll want to check into.

Beverly, Age 45

Everything was moving along fine in Beverly's life. She had a loving husband and two kids in high school, and she loved her work as a physical therapist. Then one day her life was changed dramatically by a single incident. Beverly lost the use of her legs in a car accident. "I had always been there to help accident victims recover, and now here I was, in need of my own services. It was almost more than I could handle," Beverly says.

Beverly searched high and low for a counselor who specialized in working with accident victims, to help her work through her anger and grief over her disability. "I ended up finding a great counselor," she says, "but she was a 2-hour drive away, which is not convenient for someone in my condition." This void eventually sparked her to enter a psychology program in counseling so that she could provide a service to people who suffered from debilitating injuries and illnesses. "I had already been working with this population," Beverly says, "but with the accident, I could genuinely relate from my own experience. It seemed only natural that I follow my overpowering urge to help others work through their loss and find their new purpose."

With the support of her husband and two children, Beverly enrolled in a distance learning program so that she could do home study to complete the education required to become a counselor. She set up a study room at home, with all the technological bells and whistles, and went to work. She eventually graduated and put in the internship hours required to get her license as a practicing therapist. She wound up with so many satisfied clients that she started her own practice from home and had people coming from all directions to benefit from her services.

Distance learning on the Internet usually takes one of the following forms:

◆ Electronic mail (delivering course materials, sending in assignments, getting/giving feedback, using a course listserv as an electronic discussion group)
◆ Bulletin boards/newsgroups for discussion of special topics
◆ Downloading of course materials or tutorials
◆ Interactive tutorials on the Web
◆ Real-time interactive conferencing
◆ Corporate Web sites (that is, *intranets*) protected from outside access, that distribute training for students
◆ Informatics, in which the student uses online databases, library catalogs, gopher, and Web sites to acquire information and pursue research related to study

A common belief is that learning at a distance is lonely. In reality, electronic connectedness offers a different kind of interaction than what takes place in traditional classrooms. Some learners aren't comfortable with it because of the lack of nonverbal cues. The advantage of it, however, is that it teaches students how to collaborate with distant colleagues and diverse individuals—skills that will be increasingly needed in the global workplace.

Research shows that adult learners found the following strategies critical to success in electronic learning: becoming comfortable with the technology, determining how often to go online, dealing with textual ambiguity, processing information online or offline, seeking and giving feedback, and using one's learning style to personalize the course.

Before you invest time and money into a distance learning program, check to see if it meets the following criteria:

◆ If it's a degree program, is it accredited?
◆ Does the program provide technical training and orientation?
◆ Is there a plan for technical failures as well as access to technical support when needed?
◆ Does the program foster learning-to-learn, self-directed learning, and critical thinking skills?
◆ Does the program help you develop information management skills?
◆ Does the program offer mixed modes of instruction—for example, combined e-mail discussion with audio/video methods to enhance the social aspect?
◆ Does the program offer learner-centered activities for both independent and group work that fosters interaction?

Alternative Routes to Educational Credit

If you're looking for ways to shorten your educational journey, you'll be happy to know that many options exist.

High School Credit

You can earn a high school equivalency certificate through the General Educational Development (GED) program. For more information, you can contact your local school district or

GED Testing Service
One Dupont Circle NW, Suite 20
Washington, DC 20036-1163
www.nald.ca/gedblue/default.htm

College Credit

Colleges and universities administer tests such as the College Level Examination Program (CLEP), which enable you to earn credit by examination. For more information call 215-750-8420.

Some colleges and universities give credit for work experience, which decreases the length of time you spend in school. You can get more information by writing to

Council for Adult and Experiential Learning (CAEL) National Headquarters
223 W. Jackson Boulevard, Suite 510
Chicago, IL 60606

How to Get Credit for What You Have Learned as a Homemaker or Volunteer is a helpful publication that's available for about $5 through Educational Testing Service:

Educational Testing Service
Publication Order Services (TO-1)
CN6736
Princeton, NJ 08541-6736
www.ets.org/index.html

Many colleges and universities offer degree programs with courses that can be taken in weekend sessions. If you're short on time, this might be a direction worth pursuing. Some offer TV courses and programs that can be completed at home.

The Center for Adult Learning and Educational Credentials at the American Council on Education evaluates courses given by private employers, community organizations, labor unions, government agencies, and military education programs. You can get more information from

American Council on Education
The Center for Adult Learning and Educational Credentials
One Dupont Circle NW, Suite 1B-20
Washington, DC 20036
www.acenet.edu

Cooperative Education

Cooperative education gives you the opportunity to work for pay in positions that complement your academic program. Alternating work and school takes somewhat longer than the traditional method of study with a summer break. However, by taking positions with increasing levels of responsibility, you'll have a solid résumé with which to approach the job market for a full-time position.

Internships

Internships are work assignments that are available through colleges and corporations in a variety of fields for little or no pay. Some offer educational credit. Through an internship program, you can gain practical, on-the-job experience, discover your strengths and weaknesses, and evaluate possible career paths. Work experience—even if you have to volunteer—is one of the best ways to beef up your résumé and gain skills and expertise in areas you're lacking.

Tuition, Fees, and Other Costs

Because what it costs to attend college varies widely from state to state, I'll give you some averages. These reflect full-time student status. If you attend on a part-time basis, your annual tuition will most likely be considerably less. Because vocational colleges range from free to a sizable amount of money, I won't include them here:

Educational Fees

Type of Fee	*Average Cost*
Community college tuition	$400 to $500 per year
Four-year state college tuition	$1,200 to $1,600 per year
State university tuition	$2,500 to $3,500 per year
Additional nonresident tuition (if you're an out-of-state student attending a state-supported institution)	$2,000 to $4,000 per year
Private four-year college tuition	$12,000 to $14,000 per year
Miscellaneous fees (e.g., student services, accident insurance, health services, parking, ID card, grade mailing)	$100 to $200 per year
Textbooks	$35 to $75 each, or $350 to $750 per year
Room and board	$4,000 to $6,000 per year

Financial Aid

The cost of education and training after high school can be costly, but don't allow money to hold you back from achieving your educational goals. Financial assistance is available, and it's imperative that you learn about the many federal and nonfederal sources of aid. I'll give you a general overview here; however, your best bet is to contact the Financial Aid Office at the college you're interested in attending.

Your college will have a financial aid officer who can provide accurate, up-to-date information to students in need of financial aid. You can also call the Federal Student Aid Information Center at 800-433-3243. Either of these sources can provide a free government booklet titled *The Student Guide: Financial Aid from the U.S. Department of Education.*

If you have access to the Internet, check www.swc.cc.ca.us/CampusResources/Library/aid.htm. This site, offered by Southwestern College Library, offers links to many resources and information on colleges and financial aid.

Financial aid falls into four broad categories, which are discussed in the following sections: scholarships, loans, grants, and work-study. You might qualify for any or all of these options.

Scholarships

Scholarships are various amounts of money given to students who have demonstrated above-average academic ability or who qualify for special categories (e.g., based on gender or race). The money doesn't have to be repaid. The idea behind scholarships is to encourage excellence and competence in learning. Some scholarships are based on financial need and some aren't. Because there are so many special categories of scholarships, you don't have to be a straight-A student to be eligible. Generally you need an academic track record reflecting that you've completed some college courses and letters of recommendation from instructors. If you're a reentering student, it might not make sense for you to apply for a scholarship of any kind until you've completed a semester of academic work, which will establish your grade point average (GPA) and give you the opportunity to request letters of recommendation from instructors you've had in classes.

Loans

Loans are sums of money that have to be repaid with interest over a long-term period. The two basic kinds of student loans available are private and government loans. Private loans are provided through banks and other commercial lending agencies, which offer relatively low interest rates compared to those of other loans. These loans are usually easier to qualify for than standard loans.

Government loans are provided primarily by the federal government, the state, or a combination of both. Like all loans, these must be repaid with interest; however, the interest rates are lower than those available through commercial organizations. The big plus of government loans is that they're easy to qualify for and are readily available to students who wouldn't otherwise be able to borrow money.

Another advantage of government loans is that they don't have to be repaid until you've completed your higher education. Some are subsidized by the government, and are interest deferred until after you graduate. Government loans also offer a grace period upon graduation, so payments don't begin for at least 6 months. You can defer the loan further if you continue going to school, become a volunteer, or are unable to find employment in your field.

Grants

A grant is an amount of money that doesn't have to be repaid. It's basically a gift. Unlike scholarships, grants aren't based primarily on academic ability; they're based on financial need. To find out whether you qualify for a particular grant, you must apply. The U.S. Department of Education has developed a plan that requires state participation. At the federal level, the plan is known as the State Student Incentive Grant Program. Your state has a specific name for its program. For more information, talk to the financial aid officer at the college of your choice.

Work-Study

Within an academic environment, there might be positions funded by the government, for up to 10 hours per week over the school term, to help students finance their education. These are called work-study positions. Carefully read the job notices in the Financial Aid Office of the school you're interested in attending. If the information is vague, phone the person who would be hiring for the position for more details. Work-study is a great way to supplement the financing of your education. In addition, it gives you the opportunity to apply your knowledge to different settings and pick up some new transferable skills, which can help you to further clarify your career goals and beef up your résumé.

Ten Tips for Surviving College

I went back to school in my 30s to get a master's degree and doctorate. I started preparing by taking classes at the local community college. I didn't know how I'd adjust to being a student again. When I attended school growing up and in my undergraduate college years, I was used to being among the youngest in my class. How would it be to return to school as a "mature" student? Would I fit in? Would I feel strange?

It was a relief and an inspiration to find that when I returned, I was surrounded by students of all ages. In fact, school is a place where age isn't an issue. All students are created equal, and the camaraderie and support I experienced among my fellow classmates made my return to school an exciting period of personal growth. I made mistakes here and there, and I did things I wish I hadn't. For this reason, I'll point out 10 ways to make your return to school a pleasant and fun experience. These are tips that I learned along the way, from others and on my own. I want to share them with you so that you can start your educational journey off on the right foot:

1. Create a plan with milestones and time frames to help you meet your educational goals. This is critical. While in graduate school I found that my quick progress was directly related to the fact that I set up milestones and time frames for the completion of my coursework for each class and for the completion of each course toward my degree. This was a big motivator for me. I didn't put anything in writing that I didn't fully expect to achieve, so I made sure that my goals were realistic. Chart your entire educational journey. Treat your classes like you're going to a job and you have deadlines you must meet. If you're in a distance learning program, create arbitrary deadlines for the completion of your work within each course and for the completion of the required courses for your degree or certificate. This will help you stay on track and give you a sense of achievement when you see yourself sticking to your plan.

2. Provide yourself with incentives and rewards, especially for achieving big milestones. After you complete that big term paper or class you've been working so hard in, reward yourself with a weekend getaway, or do something fun to take your mind off school (especially if you're returning to school full time). If your budget is slim, maybe you can take in an afternoon matinée with your kids, or go out to dinner with a friend. Find little ways to pamper yourself. School is hard work. It's like a job. But when you work hard at it, you need to allow yourself to take breaks and play hard, too.

3. Find a mentor you can trust and confide in. This could be a more advanced student, a graduate of the program you're in, or someone working in the career field you're pursuing—someone who has a genuine interest in supporting your efforts to succeed. A mentor is a role model you can follow. She or he can provide a boost when you're feeling down, or point you in the right direction when you feel lost. A mentor can help you brainstorm and troubleshoot problems. Briefly checking in over the phone or by e-mail or perhaps meeting for a cup of coffee from time to time can do wonders. It's always nice to have at least one person who has been there and can relate to what you're experiencing. Many schools now offer mentoring programs, so check this out at the school you're interested in attending.

4. Be flexible and learn to adapt to the wide range of different personality styles of your instructors. Sometimes you'll find that you clash with a particular style. You can talk to classmates to learn about their experiences with different instructors, but in my experience this can boggle your mind. You're likely to get conflicting feedback on every instructor. The only way to know whether you like an instructor's teaching style is

to take one of his or her classes and see for yourself. You might be surprised to find that you enjoy the instructors that other students don't. Sometimes it's difficult to tell how you feel until you've been in a class for a while. My advice is to be prepared to roll with the punches. You can learn to adapt to different personality styles. There's an art to this, and it's a talent you can use in future job positions, especially in the global marketplace, where you'll find a diversity of people.

5. Get comfortable with public speaking. If you have anxiety at the thought of talking before a group, then take a public speaking class. Usually a communications class is required for an undergraduate degree; however, you can ease into this by taking a brief noncredit class through continuing education at a local community college. Also, investigate Toastmasters, an organization that has groups that meet each week for the purpose of improving public speaking skills. When giving presentations in classes, use visual aids or handouts to relieve some of the pressure to convey all the information verbally. Research shows that visual aids increase the interest level and attention span of audiences. Add some humor to your presentations, too. Audiences—students or not—want to be entertained. If they see you having a good time, they'll have one, too.

6. Ask for support from your family and friends. Completing any kind of school program takes a lot of focus and hard work. Tell family and friends your goals and reasons for wanting to accomplish this educational mission. Let them know how they can best help you. And let them know that they're important to you and that their support really matters. Sometimes family and friends feel slighted because your focus is no longer on them. By keeping the lines of communication open, you can prevent hurt feelings and misunderstandings.

7. Consider working with a study group that meets in person or online. For some students, study groups offer a way to stay self-disciplined and on track with the completion of school projects and assignments. If you get burned out working on your own day in and day out, a study group might be the perfect motivator for you. Find a group of three or four students that you click with, and meet with them each week. You can set goals as a group on what you expect to accomplish from week to week. If you're in a distance learning program, take advantage of online discussion groups. One advantage of meeting with a group is that each person has different strengths and weaknesses that you can share and help each other with. Also, by working with a team on a regular basis, you learn a skill that is most valued by potential employers—being a good team player.

8. Do your schoolwork in brief time frames. I always found that I performed my schoolwork best when I worked in brief "power shifts" of about 3 hours. Allow yourself blocks of 2 or 3 solid hours to concentrate on your work, and you'll be amazed at what you'll accomplish. I

always found that I could do more in a concentrated, short period than I ever could when the work was spread out all over the day and night because I was constantly distracted or interrupted.

9. If you have excessive test, math, or other anxiety, talk to a school counselor. A certain amount of anxiety is normal and usually stems from bad experiences in early school years. Remind yourself that you're a different person today, with many life experiences behind you. By understanding your anxieties, you can use that energy to propel yourself beyond the fear. Think of your anxiety as the extra jolt of adrenaline that you need to take the test, do the math, or give the speech, and do a good job.

10. Become an optimist and only hang around positive people. I can't stress this enough. Keep a positive attitude in your approach to school and all its challenges, especially when the going gets tough. This is so much easier to do when you associate with optimistic people. You'll run across many students who are never happy with their instructors or their classes. They can drain you with their constant negativity. Everyone has problems, but these people get swallowed up in self-pity and seem to think that everyone else has it easy. My advice is to steer clear of these people and foster a supportive group of people in your school program that you can trust and confide in. It's refreshing to have people you relate with to help overcome challenges and celebrate accomplishments. Your educational journey will be much more rewarding if you have a group of like-minded peers to share it with.

Choosing the Best Path

Making the decision to go back to school or get training in a new field can fill you with a mixture of apprehension and excitement. When you make the plunge, however, you'll find that your fear gradually disappears and a newfound confidence takes over because you have made the decision and acted on it.

You can overcome most of your fears up front by creating a game plan with milestones you'll accomplish while achieving your educational and training goals. The milestones should ideally be the steps you need to take to get started, and you can begin by addressing the issues covered in this chapter.

Take time to research the various available schools and training options. Also, look into financial aid resources. You'll be investing time and money, so choose the program that will best allow you to achieve your career goals in a learning environment that complements your personality (e.g., classroom instruction, distance learning, online learning). To help you get started, the next two chapters address objections that might be stopping you in your tracks: the fear of taking the first step and a lack of support.

PART II

GETTING READY

CHAPTER 5

EXPANDING YOUR COMFORT ZONE

"Avoiding danger is no safer in the long run than outright exposure. Life is either a daring adventure or nothing."

HELEN KELLER

The comfort zone is that place where we perform well—practically on autopilot. When we move outside our comfort zone, we often feel anxious and stressed. These emotions result from the fear of doing something less than perfect or making a mistake. Our self-image feels threatened.

The reason we feel anxious and stressed outside our comfort zone is that our self-image works like a regulating mechanism. Just as a thermostat controls room temperature by sending electrical impulses to start or stop the heater whenever the room is below or above the temperature setting, we're controlled by tension when we move either above or below our comfort zone. Our self-image is the subconscious picture, or setting, of where we belong. It regulates our behavior by allowing us to move above or below our current comfort zone only slightly without experiencing stress and anxiety.

Hence, stepping out of our comfort zone to make a change involves risk, but with that risk comes opportunity—the opportunity for personal growth. During the process of change, it's normal to expect anxiety, stress, and old fears to be awakened. Unfortunately, the downside of living a "safe" life—resisting the scary emotions that come with change—is that it's like being in prison, and the boundaries get tighter and narrower as we get older.

In this chapter you'll be putting your top three career choices through the "barrier test" to find out how much you're willing to expand your comfort zone to make each choice a reality. We'll discuss how you can expand your comfort zone and take more risks to achieve your goals. The ultimate goal is to build increased self-belief and confidence so that you're ready and willing to take the first step.

The Barrier Test

You've done a lot of research on your top three career choices. You know what background and experience are required to do each job. Now comes the true test. Are you willing to do what it takes to achieve at least one of your career goals?

In the following sections you'll find five barriers that commonly stand in the way of taking that first step in a new direction. Run each of your top career choices through the barrier test to see what you're willing to do (or not willing to do) to achieve it. Take notes in your journal for each career choice.

This screening device is a great way to shed light on what stands in the way of your dreams. By looking at each barrier one at a time for each career choice, you can break down your fears into digestible bites that you can easily deal with.

Time

Have you ever noticed how much busywork you do on a day-to-day basis? We often think we don't have enough time to change directions because we're so caught up in the routine of our everyday lives. A lot of our time is spent caring for others and pursuing the current chapter we're on. We all have certain roles, responsibilities, and commitments. The desire for change is knocking on your door—now. Do you tend to say, "No. Go away. I'm too busy. I don't have time to make a change"?

In Chapter 1, "Where Are You Now?" you did an exercise (Exercise 1.1, "Time Commitments") to see how you spend your time. You wrote down estimates of your current commitments. You also projected the amount of time you want to spend on each commitment. Take a look at your estimates to see where you're spending your time. What areas are you willing to cut back on to free up time to move in a new direction? The projections you made about the time you want to spend on each commitment will probably give you some insight.

If you're not willing to take a look at how you spend your time, then you might question how much you genuinely want to pursue a new direction. Maybe you're not ready at this time. There's usually a lot more time available than you think, because much time is wasted doing things you don't enjoy or appreciate. Wouldn't you be happier spending your time working toward something you desire instead of muddling along in your current routine, where you feel miserably safe?

Money

Do you allow money, or the lack thereof, to stand in your way? The most popular "excuse" goes something like this: "I can't change careers because I'm making a good income in my current line of work—income that I (or we) need to get by. If I change course and start over from square one, I'll have to forgo my salary and I (or my family) won't survive."

Maybe you want to pursue a new direction that will make little or no money at first—maybe it will even cost money, if you want to start a business or go back to school, for instance—and you feel pressured to take a job just for the income.

Look back again at another exercise in Chapter 1 (Exercise 1.2, "Financial Position") on itemizing your current monthly income and expenses as well as your goals for the areas you want to change. You might find that, as with your time, there are places where you can cut back (e.g., take fewer or less expensive vacations, eat out less often and microwave instead, shop for bargains instead of paying full price at a department store).

If you have a partner who is earning income, can you forgo your income and live on your partner's for a year? I interviewed a number of home business owners—women and men—who did this in order to launch their business. They left well-paying jobs to start a business from home and be there to raise their children. They cut every corner possible to make their dream a reality. They made sacrifices and did without a lot of material things.

No matter what your situation—even if you're a divorced or single parent—don't allow money to stand in your way. Open the door and investigate your options. If you're not willing to do this, and money continues to be your stopping block, then you might not be ready to pursue a new direction yet.

Education and Experience

You identified the education and experience required and preferred for each of your top three job choices in Chapter 4, "Evaluating Your Training and Educational Needs." Are you willing to complete the education and training that are lacking? Again, if your answer comes back around to doubting whether you have enough money or time to do these things, then you might want to pursue a career choice that's more in line with the education and experience you currently possess. Sometimes we fool ourselves into thinking that we want something, but in reality we're not willing to invest the time, energy, or money necessary to achieve it.

Expectations of Others

Are you living your life according to what others expect of you, or are you living the life you choose? If you pursue certain directions to please others and forgo your own desires, you're bound to end up angry and frustrated. You'll burn out in this situation. On the other hand, if you follow your dreams, you have so much energy to give to others that you'll be amazed. You'll ooze with happiness and enthusiasm.

Are you willing to deal with letdown, disapproval, or lack of support when you pursue a direction you choose that might not be favorable to others? Ask yourself whether it's more important for you to follow your instincts and do what makes you happy or to do what others advocate.

Values

In Chapter 1 (Exercise 1.4, "Career and Life Planning") you fantasized what your ideal scenario would be in all areas of your life. You visualized the kind of lifestyle that's desirable to you. This exercise put you in tune with your values—the things in life that really matter to you.

For each of your top career choices, check to see whether pursuing each direction will conflict with any of your values—the ideal scenarios you visualized for everything from spending time with your children and the amount of leisure time you desire, to your diet, exercise, and spiritual well-being. If you put little value on getting dressed up in professional clothes for work and your career choice requires that (or it's strongly preferred), then you might have a conflict. On the other hand, you might be able to overcome this conflict by working for yourself instead of for someone else.

The idea is to put on your critical thinking cap and see if you have any values that conflict with your top career choices. And with each conflict you find, ask yourself whether it is something that can be overcome or worked around or whether it is best to close the door on this particular career choice because it clearly conflicts with your values.

The Internal Obstacles to Change

Often the hardest part of a change process is getting started. Things stand in the way. Although we might not be able to reverse situations that are external to us—such as violence, aging parents, divorce, a dysfunctional family, or disease—we can change the internal obstacles inspired by others and by ourselves that keep us from being and doing our best.

When I speak of "internal" obstacles, I'm referring to obstacles of a psychological nature. Let's discuss the three most popular internal obstacles that keep us in our comfort zone: fear of change, negative self-beliefs, and procrastination. Then we'll look at a variety of ways to overcome them.

Fear of Change

The fear of change is more or less a generalized anxiety that keeps us from moving forward toward our dreams. When we stay immobile, our anxiety can turn into mild or severe depression. It's almost as if our dreams are a magnet, and the closer we move toward identifying the steps needed to realize them, the more our anxiety and discomfort build.

The important thing to understand is that these anxious feelings are normal, and they pass when you begin to take action and get involved in the process of "becoming" your dream. The fear will dissipate, much as it does when you give a speech. At first you have anticipation anxiety, and the butterflies are running amok in your stomach. But as soon as you open your mouth and start talking, you feel a sense of relief. And as you really get into the speech and forget about yourself, the nervousness vanishes; the butterflies fly into formation, and you've got control.

If you confine yourself to a safe and familiar existence, you place overwhelming limitations on your chance for happiness. By breaking out of old routines and busting through obstacles as if there are no limitations, you have many opportunities to achieve your goals. This is all part of the process of stepping out of your comfort zone. In order to take advantage of opportunities, you must take a risk. As soon as you see progress, your fear will diminish.

Negative Self-Beliefs

Are you allowing situations and people from your past to hold you back? We all have emotional baggage from our upbringings. Our minds are like tape recorders that pick up on and remember everything we hear. As children, the significant people in our lives strongly influenced the image we created of ourselves. Our tape recorders worked overtime when we were exposed to comments such as "You're no good" and "You'll never amount to anything."

Hearing this abuse in our younger years takes its toll on our self-image if we grow to believe these belittling accusations. It stifles our performance and makes us angry. When we're angry, we have a tendency to blame everything and everyone but ourselves—parents, teachers, bosses, the economy, the government—instead of working on what's going on inside. It's always easier and more convenient to assume that the blame lies elsewhere or with others than to hold ourselves accountable for our hurt feelings.

As adults, the anger and negative beliefs can continue to disrupt our lives. If the significant people we've acquired these beliefs from are no longer around to belittle us, our minds take over and do the talking for them. This negative self-talk or chatter keeps us paralyzed. How can you make a move when you're telling yourself, "My family might abandon me" or "Everyone will hate me for doing this" or "I might go broke" or "I'll probably fail"? The good news is that we can use positive self-talk to combat negative self-talk, and I'll talk about that shortly.

Procrastination

Procrastination offers a great place to hide when you want to put something off until tomorrow. It leaves you feeling fatigued and behind. We tell ourselves that we're simply "gathering energy" for our new direction, but in reality, taking action toward our goals increases our energy level, whereas procrastination drains our time and energy and leaves us with feelings of self-doubt. Usually fear is at the root of procrastination when it comes to making big life changes—fear of the unknown, fear of failure, fear of success, or fear of what others might think.

Connie, Age 43

All her life, Connie's father made it clear that girls should grow up and find husbands to take care of them. When Connie wanted to go to college after high school, her father wasn't at all supportive. "I was determined to make my own way, with or without my dad's support," Connie says. "Because he practically shoved the idea of 'finding a husband' down my throat, that was the last thing I wanted to do. I wanted to be able to support myself first."

Connie bounced around from job to job, sometimes holding as many as three jobs at once. "I had no idea what I wanted to do," Connie says, "but in the back of my mind, the one thing I knew for certain was that I wanted to attend college and get my bachelor's degree." Connie allowed a lack of money and time to stand in her way, until she wound up feeling so depressed she sought counseling. She says, "I was tired of putting off my dream of going to school. It was eating away at me, but I had no one to really talk to about it. I finally found a great counselor, who I exchanged services with. I had started cleaning houses part time, and Mary Jo hired me to clean her house each week in exchange for a counseling session."

The counseling was just what Connie needed to work through her depression and take small steps toward going back to school. "I've always been self-sufficient and was embarrassed that I procrastinated and couldn't get going on my own," she says. "That's just not like me. But as far as I'm concerned, those counseling sessions were a major turning point that changed my attitude and changed my life."

Today Connie is a practicing attorney. She made it on her own without any emotional or financial assistance from her parents. Her biggest accomplishment yet? "I recently got married, and my husband and I adopted a son. Having a loving and supportive family of my own means everything to me!"

When you know you really want something and you keep putting it off, you risk losing your golden opportunity altogether. By following through with your dreams and desires, you might not always be successful, but you'll have fewer regrets.

Overcoming Obstacles

Whether you're struggling with fear, procrastination, or negative self-talk, there are a number of ways to boost your confidence. In the sections that follow, you'll find effective strategies to help you get moving in a positive direction.

Jump-Starting Yourself

The following are some ways to kick the procrastination habit so you can live a full life with as few regrets as possible:

◆ Think of the motto "Don't dread, do!" One of the best ways out of a prison of procrastination is to get moving. I use "Sandy's Law of Perpetual Motion." When I'm in a funk, I don't stay idle. I make a conscious decision to try something—to take even the smallest step toward achieving my goals. It's difficult to be active and depressed at the same time.

◆ Concentrate on the successful completion of your current goal. Visualize taking the necessary steps to achieve it, and picture a successful outcome. If you continually focus on positive results, your procrastination fears will vanish.

◆ Take gradual steps. Make a list of five tasks that will bring you closer to making a decision about the new direction you want to take. If you already know what direction to take, then what are five things you can do to get going on your new path?

◆ Seek out and talk to successful role models and mentors. You can learn from the successes and setbacks of others. The more informed you are, the less afraid you'll be, and the less likely you'll put things off.

◆ View challenges as a normal part of the change process. They never stop coming, so gear up to meet them again and again. See them as positive stepping stones rather than as an excuse to stop moving forward. Whatever is holding you back, find a way to get around it, get through it, or get over it.

◆ Don't buy into learned helplessness—the feeling that you have no control and must take whatever life dishes out. You can begin a new life today. You have a voice, and you have the power to create a happy life. It takes almost as much time and effort to lead a mediocre life as it does a good one.

◆ Take on a can-do attitude, and remind yourself of the benefits that will result from getting off your laurels and forging ahead. Think about how good you'll feel afterward. It's amazing how a change of attitude can make a world of difference. If it doesn't, take a good look at the direction you're pursuing and ask yourself whether it's worth the effort. If it isn't, then stop fooling yourself and find something that is.

◆ Find something you can get so immersed in that you forget yourself. If you're so concerned about how you look or whether you'll succeed or get approval from others, you'll concentrate on making mistakes and never get past square one. If you love what you're doing, these things won't matter.

Tapping Into Creativity

A wonderful way to expand your comfort zone and experience tremendous personal growth is to tap into your creativity. Express yourself by creating something that's a reflection of you. Act on your impulse to write, draw, sculpt, dance, compose, or invent. Expressing our creativity makes us profoundly aware of our connection with the universe. These moments bring about peak experiences that take us to the next level.

Creativity brings us a sense of purpose, excitement, and joy. In fact, if we're not expressing ourselves—if we feel locked up or stuck—we feel unrealized and unworthy. Expressing yourself creatively will help you to unleash your raw talents and potential. It will motivate you and put you in the flow of life. Getting involved in a creative endeavor that you enjoy can help you to forget yourself, forget time, and become very clear about what you want and how you'll achieve it.

Here are a couple journaling exercises you can do to get your creative juices flowing:

1.   Think back to the things in life that have really sparked your enthusiasm and made you feel better than usual. If nothing stands out in your mind, use your journal to jot down the best thing that happens to you everyday—the best moment of the day. After tracking this for 2 weeks, see if a pattern emerges. Do you feel best when you're with your children, with friends, or by yourself? Are you talking about a particular subject such as travel, diet, or world affairs? When you target the times you feel happiest, think about how you can creatively express it. If your best times have to do with music, what can you do to develop your creative gifts in that arena? Take guitar lessons? Write songs? If it's travel, make plans to take a cruise or rough it in the outdoors and go camping. Do whatever will inspire your creative expression.

2.   Cultivate curiosity—the sense of awe and wonder. Look for surprises every day and try to surprise someone else. Keep a record of these surprises in your journal. After 2 weeks, look for a pattern of interest emerging from your notes. When you zero in on something that sparks your interest, follow it. This is a way that you can get your creative energy flowing. Concentrate on your interest fully, and don't allow unpleasant thoughts to surface. To keep your newfound interest going, wake up each morning with a small goal that's related to it. Invest your energy and effort into achieving it. Spend time doing the things you enjoy, and you'll find yourself living a full life, taking all kinds of first steps and expanding your comfort zone like never before.

Combating Negative Self-Talk

Unfortunately, our inner voice is usually critical and fault finding. Instead of being nurturing, we beat ourselves up mentally and emotionally—winding up with a lifetime of negative conditioning. It's probably not an overstatement to say that the majority of our stress and emotional suffering comes from how we perceive a situation. Usually, the thoughts that cause us stress are negative, unrealistic, and distorted.

We touched on negative self-talk when we discussed ways to eliminate procrastination. Negative self-talk can have a powerful effect on how you view daily life. Think about it for a moment. We continually talk to ourselves, and the content of our self-talk is usually negative. Our bodies don't realize the difference between what we imagine and what we actually experience. Because we don't normally question our thoughts, after a fashion we not only start to believe them, but our emotions usually match them.

Pay attention to your automatic thoughts. Learn to recognize negative self-talk or irrational beliefs. Notice how your thoughts affect your moods, behaviors, and physical condition. Being aware that negative feelings can result from negative thoughts will help you break out of negative moods. Hence, you can avoid anxiety, depression, anger, or guilt.

The image we have of ourselves regulates our behavior. Therefore, if we think negative thoughts—"I'm a failure"—we feel confined and act accordingly. If, on the other hand, we think positive thoughts—"I'm a success"—we feel free to be and expand on who we are. Here are some strategies you can use to eliminate negative self-talk:

- Make a conscious effort to replace your recurring negative thoughts with positive thoughts or affirmations, and you set yourself up for success instead of failure. Instead of thinking, "I don't deserve to win," think, "I am a winner." Instead of thinking, "Who am I kidding? I'll make a fool of myself," think, "I'm putting my all into <*choose a goal*> and the world will be a better place as a result." Instead of thinking, "I'm not smart enough," think, "When I set my mind to achieve something, I find creative ways to overcome any obstacles in my way." Thought precedes behavior, and the brain doesn't know the difference between thought and reality. These positive affirmations are convincing your brain that these positive occurrences are already happening, and they're preparing you to take those first few steps toward achieving your dreams.

- Choose three goals and say them out loud 100 times for 30 days. For instance: "My goal is to have a family and successfully balance my life," "My goal is to feel totally comfortable with public speaking," "My goal is to pay off my mortgage and take a trip each month." Repetition equals reinforcement. Saying your goals out loud has an amazing effect on your attitude and self-belief. The more you say it, the more likely you are to *do it*. Try it and see.

- Look in the mirror and say out loud, "I'm scared." Then smile and say, "So what else is new?" Every new step we take in life is scary, and sometimes admitting it makes us feel more human and less threatened. When we're less threatened, our inner critics can relax and allow the opportunity for our "inner boosters" to kick in and engage us in a positive pep talk.

- Put a rubber band on your wrist and snap it with your opposite hand each time you catch yourself engaging in negative self-talk. If you make a conscious effort to catch yourself each time, the habit will diminish so that you can pave the way for more positive thoughts and affirmations.

Negative self-talk is the fear of change in disguise. We all fear change, which is normal and healthy. It motivates us and propels us forward. The good news is that about 98% of what we worry about never transpires. Are you going to let these internal energy-zappers stand in the way of your dreams?

Journaling Your Thoughts and Feelings

Keep a journal and write down your thoughts and feelings—anger, fears, happy moments, inspirations. This is a healthy way to get things off your chest on a daily or weekly basis. In my case, journaling served as a cathartic release after my mom's death that paved the way for personal growth.

Sandy, Age 41

I was devastated one day after I called my dad to tell him I was dropping by for a visit. "Your mom isn't up for company right now, sweetie," he said. "She's not feeling good. We think it's something she ate." Two nights later, my dad found my mom nearly unconscious. He rushed her to the emergency room, where they put her on a respirator. For 4 days she remained unconscious, until she died of blood poisoning that resulted from recurring pneumonia.

I thought I'd never survive the loss. Through journaling I made peace and gained a newfound purpose in my life. My mom was my best friend. When I lost her so suddenly—never having a chance to say any last words to her while she was conscious—I felt angry, cheated, and homesick for her. It seemed that everywhere I went, I noticed card displays for moms—especially on Mother's Day. I felt such mixed emotions that I began talking to my mom in my journal. It started with a poem I wrote and read at her funeral. Every day I told her how much I missed her. I let her know what she meant. I told her everything that was going on in my life. I told her about my anger, my fears, and my grief over her passing. I really felt her presence throughout this process. It was as if she were there bigger than life—the angel on my shoulder—showing me the way.

After 4 months of writing to Mom, I decided to finally act on two things that mattered in my life: going back to school to obtain my PhD in psychology and having a baby. Today, about 4 years later, I recently gave birth to a beautiful baby girl. I'm a writer, speaker, consultant, and career transition coach. I love what I do because I have variety, and it allows me to work from home and experience all the miracle milestones of my developing baby. My mom's sudden death sparked me to take action in all areas of my life. Why did it take a tragedy for me to get my act together and make the changes I'd been longing to make for some time?

We discussed ways to eliminate negative self-talk. Use your journal to write about your recurring negative thoughts as you become aware of them. At the same time, jot down a positive replacement thought. Before long, you'll create new mental habits by consciously substituting your negative thoughts with positive thoughts, with the ultimate goal of making your positive thoughts automatic.

Associating with Positive People

If you want to be a positive, upbeat, forward-thinking person, it's important that you eliminate the people in your life who drag you down and deplete your energy. Seek out the people who are on your side and want to support your efforts to find happiness. Lillian Glass has written two excellent books that give insight on how to do just that: *Toxic People: Ten Ways of Dealing with People Who Make Your Life Miserable* (published by Simon & Schuster), and *Attracting Terrific People: How to Find, and Keep, the People Who Bring Your Life Joy* (published by St. Martin's Press). Almost everyone can benefit from the advice and strategies she offers.

Challenging Your Opposite Personality

What if you're a loner by nature but have the desire to expand your comfort zone to pursue a career that challenges your networking capabilities? Maybe you're tired of programming computers and want to sell them. On the other hand, what if you're an extrovert by nature and want to pursue a solitary career as a fiction writer?

By default, we tend to operate in our comfort zones, pursuing directions that come naturally to us. However, each of us has a "displaced" opposite personality just waiting to bust through. Can you think of people who left comfortable occupations to pursue work that challenged their opposite hidden selves? I know a woman who left her job as a successful insurance salesperson to become a writer. I know a woman who left her 10-year nursing career to become an accountant.

Psychologist Carl Jung refers to our opposite hidden self as our "shadow." Every one of our strong points has a repressed, or shadow, side that most of us refuse to acknowledge, such as emphasizing competitiveness over cooperation. Jung believed that mature people don't label one way of being as "bad" and the other as "good." Rather, they delve into and express their shadow selves.

As long as we disown the shadow, we're never whole or satisfied. It causes us to struggle against ourselves, and we're constantly trying to live up to an image that's a distortion of our true being. There's nothing like the feeling you get when you break through fear barriers and allow your hidden desires, talents, and selves to surface and shine through.

Improving Your Communication Skills

A recent survey in *USA Today* ranked the critical success factors for women who have made it to the management level, and the number-one critical success factor is communication skills. Another survey of faculty members of engineering schools revealed that 15% of an engineer's future success is dependent on her communication skills.

If you want to expand your comfort zone and opportunities in the workplace dramatically, improve your communication skills. The ability to communicate well is ranked the number-one key to success in business, politics, and other professions. In times past, the most qualified person got the job; today, among people with equal qualifications, the best communicator gets the job.

One of the top executive search firms in the country surveyed executives making over $250,000 per year and found that the number-one factor attributed to making it to the "big time" was communication skills—even more important than basic job performance, which ranked number four. Intelligence and integrity ranked two and three, respectively.

People spend years in school and training learning the skills of their profession, yet they spend little or no time fostering the skills to communicate. Consider this quote from the days of Pericles: "The thinking human being, not able to express himself, stands at the same level as those who cannot think." As our world continues to change and become more complex, the ability to communicate those changes and complexities in concise terms becomes increasingly critical to our career and life paths.

Identifying Your Critical Success Factors

You can use the following series of activities to create your ideal life:

1. Define your mission.
2. Set your goals.
3. Make your plans.
4. Determine your daily activities.
5. Measure your results.
6. Review.
7. Correct your course.

For any goal or mission, there are *critical success factors*, which are the activities you must do well to be successful. You need to identify them and become very good at them.

Every action has results. The more you can line up all your actions so that they result in what you want, the faster you accomplish your goal. Too often, we want to see the result before we invest the time and effort needed. We must be willing to pay the price in order to get the reward.

You have wonderful resources at your command: mind, body, talent, and skills. You can invest them to accomplish great things, or you can waste them. Take control of them and direct them to accomplish what you want.

Make it a top priority to examine your daily activities. Which ones are moving you toward your goals? Which ones are moving you away from your goals? Prune your life of money-wasting, time-wasting, energy-wasting activities and replace them with activities that lead toward your goals. Make sure your goals build toward your mission and that your mission motivates and excites you.

Building Increased Self-Belief and Confidence

The best way to build your self-belief and confidence so that you're ready to expand your comfort zone is through visualization techniques, also known as *guided imagery*. The idea is to focus on an idea or a picture regularly, giving it positive energy until you achieve what you've been visualizing. Much like positive thoughts and affirmations we say out loud, guided imagery focuses on envisioning successful outcomes. Have you noticed that star athletes often close their eyes and become very still before they begin? They're fully concentrating on stepping through the process of making the perfect putt or doing the perfect gymnastic routine to produce a successful outcome.

This form of psychological training is powerful. Images, even more than thoughts or affirmations, motivate people to perform at peak efficiency, so they're critical to success. Albert Einstein used imagery when he visualized a boy riding a beam of light; this image sparked the breakthrough for his Theory of Relativity. The following are two visualization techniques you can use to promote successful outcomes and increase your self-belief and confidence: fire walking and visualizing the ideal model.

Fire Walking

Fire walking is an ancient ceremonial custom that you can use to conquer your fear of taking the first step toward your goals. The idea is that if you can visualize yourself walking through fire, you can convince yourself that you can do anything. In a quiet place where you can relax and concentrate, picture yourself slowly tiptoeing through a bed of hot coals. Once you've achieved this hot feat, tell yourself the next time you hesitate to step out of your comfort zone, "If I can do fire walking, I can overcome this obstacle with no problem. It will be a piece of cake."

Visualizing the Ideal Model

Think of someone who has the personal qualities and characteristics you'd like to possess—your ideal model, someone you'd like to emulate. Picture the goal that you'd like to accomplish with self-confidence. Imagine your ideal model accomplishing this goal, having all the qualities critical to a successful outcome. What is she wearing? What expression is on her face? Study her closely. What does she do or say to help her achieve the goal? What is her tone of voice? How does she move her body?

After you visualize the scene, move inside this ideal model and become her. Picture yourself in her body, looking out through her eyes. Feel the self-confidence radiate throughout your whole being. You know what you need to know, and you have all that you need to have to achieve this goal. Feel the confidence pouring out of you, into the room and into the universe.

Next, form an anchor by doing a simple action such as crossing your fingers or touching your cheek, realizing that you're pairing your feelings of self-confidence with this physical cue. Whenever you'd like to return to these intense feelings of self-confidence, you can access them by using your anchor. Hold the anchor as long as you choose, noticing that you can actually elevate the intensity of your sense of confidence. Then release it, knowing that you can re-experience these positive feelings of poise and confidence simply by forming the anchor.

Tune into yourself through creative visualization. Learn to trust your intuitive images. Act on them, and you will find a lifelong resource that will boost your self-belief and confidence. These images will support and guide you on your exciting journey to self-fulfillment.

Happiness Is One Step out of Your Comfort Zone Away

Whatever you choose to do with your life, when you experience the first taste of success in stepping out of your comfort zone to achieve your goal, you'll feel happy. Remember that success is not static. It's a continuing process of discovering more and more of your potential, one tiny step at a time. It's a growing and evolving experience that breeds momentum and enthusiasm to keep you going.

Author Doris Lee McCoy lists 12 "megatraits" that are consistently found in the lives of successful people:

1. They enjoy their work.
2. They have high self-esteem and a positive attitude.
3. They use negative experiences to discover their strengths.
4. They are decisive, disciplined goal setters.
5. They have integrity and help others succeed.
6. They are persistent.
7. They take risks.
8. They have developed good communication and problem-solving skills.
9. They surround themselves with competent, responsible, supportive people.
10. They are healthy, have high energy, and schedule time to renew.
11. They believe in God, a higher power, or sometimes just plain luck.
12. They have a sense of purpose and a desire to contribute to society.

Take these traits seriously. Read them over daily as positive affirmations in the first person: "I have high self-esteem and a positive attitude," "I take risks," "I use negative experiences to discover my strengths." Strive to possess these traits and remember that happiness is just one step out of your comfort zone away, and you'll open up new directions that you never thought possible.

CHAPTER 6

GETTING YOUR SUPPORT SYSTEMS IN PLACE

*"Seek out positive-thinking people to energize you
and help you believe that you and what you're
doing are worthwhile and important."*

SANDY ANDERSON, PHD

Making a big change can cause chronic loneliness or intense feelings of disconnectedness. This feeling of isolation can take you on an emotional roller coaster that zaps your motivation, leaving you feeling preoccupied with problems and overwhelmed by trivial issues. Such a scenario leads to increased stress, and the vicious circle repeats, until you finally take control and do something to break the pattern.

It's especially critical in times of transition that we reach out to others for support. In Chapter 1, "Where Are You Now?" you targeted the areas of your life—emotional, personal, and financial—that are lacking. In this chapter we'll discuss the options for handling these needs. This chapter also lists national organizations and Web sites that you can contact for support (e.g., local groups, resources) to help you deal with particular life changes, including pregnancy and child rearing, divorce, death of a spouse, retirement, empty nest, or failing health.

Karin, Age 65

Karin, the youngest of three daughters, always considered herself shy. After her divorce, she decided to do something about it: She enrolled in an assertiveness training workshop at a local community college. "That afternoon workshop changed my life," Karin says. "The instructor taught us how to 'script' so we could learn to speak up and present our case." Scripting involves writing down your main points (first, second, and third) and rehearsing them over and over before confronting a person with an issue by phone or face-to-face. This allows you to stick to your points if the person you're approaching steers the conversation in a direction they're more comfortable with (away from the confrontational issue at hand).

"Scripting worked like a charm for me," Karin says. "I was raising my two kids alone and really needed a pay increase in my position as an editor for a book publisher. When I met with my boss for my annual review, I came prepared with a sheet in front of me, describing all the extra projects I had worked on over the past year that no one knew about. My boss was so impressed that she asked for a copy of the write-up to include in my review package. Instead of getting the typical pittance of an increase, mine was substantial, and my efforts led to a nice promotion—all because I spoke up for myself."

Scripting also comes in handy for Karin when she needs to complain about poor service or merchandise she has purchased. "I just stick to my main points," Karin says, "and my confidence shines through so everything is handled with no problem. In the past I would have stayed quiet, but felt cheated. I learned that the squeaky wheel *does* get the grease—as long as you 'squeak' in a nice, positive way. As a result, the quality of my life and the lives of my children increases every time I squeak, or rather, 'speak,' up."

Managing Personal Needs and Commitments

Look back in your journal at the areas in need of support that you identified in Chapter 1. Now look at the list below, and in your journal, make note of the ways you can achieve the balance you desire. Make sure that first and foremost, you take care of yourself. Attend to your emotional and physical needs. Our health and body image affect how we feel about ourselves. The road to optimal health begins with the basics. Create a personal program by using the following questions as a starting point for a healthy lifestyle:

- ◆ Are you drinking at least eight 8-ounce glasses of water each day?
- ◆ Are you exercising a minimum of 30 minutes per day, three days per week?
- ◆ Are you eating plenty of fresh, healthy foods?

- ◆ Do you have one or two positive-thinking people you can relate to and confide in on a regular basis (e.g., friend, family member, therapist, mentor)?
- ◆ Do you belong to any social or professional groups that support your goals and values and that meet on a regular basis?
- ◆ Do you have role models in your life that you want to emulate?
- ◆ Are there workshops at community colleges or recreation centers in your area that you can attend, to spark your creativity or challenge your personal growth?

If you're interested in joining a personal or professional organization, take a look at the *Encyclopedia of Associations* at the reference desk of your local library. You'll find information on national organizations, focusing on just about every topic and profession you can think of. Most have toll-free numbers you can call to find the local chapter or group in your area. If you can't find a group in your area of interest, consider starting one. If you need support in a particular area, chances are other people do, too.

Personal Relationships

During a time of transition, it's important to ask family members and friends for their support. Let them know what you're doing, and tell them how they can best help you. It's too easy to swallow up into ourselves during challenging times. That's why it's especially critical to make an ongoing effort to keep the lines of communication open with those we love and care about.

Child Care

If you need child care in order to pursue your new direction, you may have several options. More and more firms provide child care referral services to their employees. Others offer child care reimbursement or actually sponsor day care

---

Isolation Busters

It's amazing how much your outlook can take a turn for the positive when you connect with others who are supportive of your goals. Here are some tips to help ward off isolation and keep you in the stream of things:

- ◆ Join a professional networking group.
- ◆ Create a mastermind group that meets regularly.
- ◆ Volunteer in your field of interest.
- ◆ Get some exercise. Join a local gym or take your dog for a daily walk.
- ◆ Make contacts online through the Internet.
- ◆ Attend a class or a seminar in your field of interest.
- ◆ Do some of your job search activities at a local coffeehouse.

centers. Be sure to check this out if you go to work for a company. Decide whether you need child care on a part- or full-time basis. What does your budget afford?

Paid Child Care Options

In considering paid child care options, you should investigate both in-home and out-of-home arrangements.

In-home Child Care

With an in-home child care arrangement, a caregiver comes to the parents' home. The cost of full-time in-home care can range anywhere from $125 to $450 per week, depending on where you live and the level of the caregiver's training. Generally, in-home care consists of one of the following:

- *Baby-sitters* provide in-home supervisory care for children, and no special training is expected of them.
- *Nannies* are employed by a family, to live in or out of the home and provide child care on a full- or part-time basis. Nannies may or may not have formal training.
- *Au pairs* usually live in a family's home and help with child care and light housework. Au pairs tend to come from Europe or various parts of the United States.
- *Sharing care* with another family is an excellent option to consider if you can't afford (or don't need) to hire an in-home care provider full time. Val, a work-at-home travel agent who requires part-time child care, shares her nanny with her business partner, who also works out of her home. "My partner and I alternate with the same nanny—the nanny provides child care for me three days per week and for my partner another three days per week," says Val. "Our nanny is happy with the arrangement because she needs full-time employment. She loves both of our kids, so it works out great."

The following are some of the positive aspects of in-home care:

- You save time not having to drive to and from care centers outside your home.
- You and your children have more flexibility because outside centers are open only certain hours. If your children are asleep, you don't have to awaken them to drive to group care. Also, they can follow their own eating and sleeping routines, rather than have to conform to a schedule in group care.
- Your schedule doesn't have to be altered when your child is sick.
- Your children aren't exposed to the germs of other kids.
- Your children get individual attention.
- Your caregiver can accommodate children of different ages, unlike in most group settings.
- Your caregiver may perform other household duties.

Creative Strategies for Working Without Paid Child Care

If money is tight, you can try some of the following creative strategies during your job search hours without hiring paid child care:

◆ *Arrange play dates:* If your children get along well with other kids in the neighborhood, setting up regular play dates is an excellent strategy that will allow you extra time.

◆ *Reward your children's independence:* Another option is to reward your children for taking care of themselves while you concentrate on pursuing your new direction. This can be something simple like offering a favorite treat or an extra story at bedtime. If they're of the age when money captures their interest, pay them a nominal amount. They'll learn how to take care of themselves and respect your personal time.

◆ *Tire them out:* Carol, an architectural illustrator, uses a strategy with her 2-year-old son that's a bit physical and time-consuming, but effective in allowing her to focus on exploring her new direction. "I devote attention to my son in the mornings, and I find that it gets him good and tired so he'll take a better nap," she explains. "Then I can concentrate on my goals rather than try to work and keep him occupied at the same time. I tried that for a while—it didn't make him happy, and I couldn't get anything done."

◆ *Try the barter system:* Chris, a magazine publisher and mother of 2-year-old Jessica, exchanges child care with another mom in her neighborhood. "I have many friends with kids the same age as mine, so we exchange child care services all the time," she says. And if you don't have neighbors or friends with kids the same age as yours that live close? You might try bartering your work services in exchange for child care. If you have a line of work or special talent that someone in your neighborhood needs, you might be able to do an exchange. Perhaps you can cook or run errands while you're out for someone who is retired and wouldn't mind watching your child on a part-time basis.

◆ *Try a baby-sitting co-op:* Baby-sitting co-ops consist of a group of families who exchange child care services. Basically, you receive as many child care hours as you provide in trade. It's best if the group is large enough to meet everyone's sitting needs. A membership of at least 15 families is best, but fewer can work if the group tends to have opposite work schedules.

◆ *Work in short spurts of time:* "I have time to myself during my daughter's nap time," says Meg, who is researching her options for going back to school. "I always have a 'to do' list made up ahead of time so I can go like a jet when she's down."

◆ *Elicit support from family members:* Do you have family members, such as a spouse, older children, or extended family members, who will regularly pitch in and help with child care? If so, ask for their support in helping you achieve your goals.

Out-of-home Child Care

If you decide to use out-of-home child care, there are many options to consider, depending on your children's ages and dispositions. The cost of out-of-home care varies widely, and can range anywhere from $75 to $400 per week for full-time care.

Day Care Centers and Preschools   In day care centers and preschools, children tend to be grouped according to age. The centers can be privately owned or operated by nonprofit organizations such as churches, schools, or community groups. Good day care centers or preschools offer age-appropriate educational activities.

The following are some of the positive aspects of day care centers and preschools:

◆   They offer a wide range of activities for your child.
◆   The staff is generally trained in child development.
◆   Your child can interact with other kids.
◆   You don't have to worry about turnover of caregivers.
◆   Unlike caregivers, centers don't call in sick.
◆   Most centers are regulated and must meet certain standards.
◆   You can work peacefully, without children at home.
◆   You don't have to deal with the responsibilities of being an employer.

Family Day Care   Generally, family day care providers are moms who want to earn extra income by watching other people's kids while they care for their own. They may also be moms whose children have already left the nest. Typically they care for a small group of children, ranging from four to six kids, including their own. They usually hire an assistant to help out when watching six or more children. Family day care is best suited for infants, toddlers, and preschoolers.

The following are some of the positive aspects of family day care:

◆   It's usually economical.
◆   Your child can interact with other kids.
◆   Providers may be flexible with their hours.
◆   The atmosphere is more intimate than that of a day care center.
◆   You can work peacefully, without children at home.
◆   You don't have to deal with the responsibilities of being an employer.

Subsidized Child Care

Subsidized child care provides free or low-cost care to eligible low-income families. Subsidized child care centers such as State Preschools and Head Start receive funding from government sources to serve eligible families. A sliding-scale fee is used, with rates based on the family's income. A variety of private and public child care providers participate in subsidized child care programs (including family day care and licensed exempt providers). Check with your local YMCA or YWCA for more information.

Evaluating and Choosing a Day Care Center

Here's a checklist of important components to help you evaluate and choose a day care center for your infant or toddler:

- [ ] The building is safe, well maintained, and clean.
- [ ] The building is well ventilated and lit.
- [ ] Fire alarms, smoke detectors, fire extinguishers, and emergency exits are present and well marked.
- [ ] The facility uses window guards, caps on electrical outlets, and gates on stairs.
- [ ] The center has an optimal staff-to-child ratio (one adult to every three or four infants/toddlers).
- [ ] Caregivers respond promptly to signs of distress.
- [ ] Caregivers talk directly to the children.
- [ ] Staff members work well together.
- [ ] The facility is stocked with age-appropriate equipment and toys.
- [ ] Parents are welcome in the center at any time.
- [ ] Scheduled parent/caregiver meetings take place regularly.

School-Age Programs

If your kids are school age and older, look into the variety of after-school activities available. Check out the local YMCA and YWCA, where kids can do their homework as well as participate in activities such as swimming lessons, dance classes, Scouts, and all types of sports. Also look into local churches, community centers, parks and recreational facilities, and private facilities that offer instruction in your child's interest areas (e.g., music, dance, karate).

Summer Camps

During the summer you might be able to send your child to daycamp, where he or she can be around other kids and be exposed to a variety of recreational activities. If your child is older, sleep-away camp is a possibility for a portion of the summer. You can find information on what's available in your community through private schools, community centers, and large day care center chains.

Resource and Referral Agencies

More than 500 government-funded resource and referral agencies across the country can provide the names of licensed day care centers and family day care providers in your community. They also have listings of available school-age programs and summer camps. Check your local yellow pages for the nearest agency, or call one of these resources:

- ◆ Child Care Aware (800-424-2246)
- ◆ The Child Development Associate Credentialing Commission (800-424-4310)
- ◆ The National Association of Child Care Resources and Referral Agencies (800-462-1660)
- ◆ The National Association for Family Day Care (800-359-3817)
- ◆ The CareGuide child care and elder care directory (www.careguide.net)

Elder Care

Finding elder care that's best suited for your needs requires research. Important selection factors to consider include the quality of care, availability of needed services, and personnel training and expertise.

Before starting a search, it's important to determine which types of services you need. You might want to consult with your physician, a hospital discharge planner, or a social services organization such as an Area Office on Aging for assistance in evaluating your needs. When you've completed this assessment, you'll be able to identify the type of home care provider most appropriate to assist you.

Fortunately, most communities have a variety of providers to choose from. Contact your state's departments of health, aging, and social services to obtain a list of licensed agencies. In addition, most state home care and hospice associations maintain directories of existing elder/home care organizations and can assist you in identifying an appropriate provider.

Elder care providers are listed in the yellow pages under "home care," "hospice," or "nurses." If your community has information and referral services available through an Area Agency on Aging or a local chapter of the United Way, check with them. Local churches may also have information about local home care providers.

You can call The Eldercare Locator at 800-677-1116, to find information and resources nationwide, including home-delivered meals, transportation, adult day care, legal assistance, social and recreational activities, senior-center programs and nursing ombudsmen. You can also get local numbers for In-Home Support Services, which is a combined federal, state, and county government program that provides financial aid to qualifying seniors for assistance in helping them stay in their homes. Reference the CareGuide child care and elder care directory (www.careguide.net) for a variety of elder care resources. Also, more and more firms offer elder care referral services to their employees, so check this out if you go to work for a company.

Selecting an Elder Care Provider

When you acquire the names of several elder care providers, you should learn more about their services and reputations. The National Association for Home

Care (202-547-7424) recommends that you use the following checklist of questions to ask providers and other individuals who may know about the provider's track record. Their insight will help you determine which provider is best for you or your loved one:

◆ How long has the provider been serving the community?

◆ Does the provider supply literature explaining its services, eligibility requirements, fees, and funding sources? Many providers furnish patients with a detailed "Patient Bill of Rights" that outlines the rights and responsibilities of the providers, patients, and caregivers. An annual report and other educational materials can also provide helpful information about the provider.

◆ How does the provider select and train its employees? Does it protect its workers with written personnel policies, benefits packages, and malpractice insurance?

◆ Are nurses or therapists required to evaluate the patient's home care needs? If so, what does this entail? Do they consult the patient's physicians and family members?

◆ Does the provider include the patient and his or her family members in developing the plan of care? Are family members involved in making care plan changes?

◆ Is the patient's course of treatment documented, detailing the specific tasks to be carried out by each professional caregiver? Do the patient and his or her family receive a copy of this plan, and do the caregivers update it as changes occur? Does the provider take time to educate family members on the care being administered to the patient?

◆ Does the provider assign supervisors to oversee the quality of care patients are receiving in their homes? If so, how often do these individuals make visits? Who can the patient and his or her family members call with questions or complaints? How does the agency follow up on and resolve problems?

◆ What are the financial procedures of the provider? Does the provider furnish written statements explaining all the costs and payment plan options associated with home care?

◆ What procedures does the provider have in place to handle emergencies? Are its caregivers available 24 hours per day, 7 days per week?

◆ How does the provider ensure patient confidentiality?

◆ Ask the home care provider to supply you with a list of references, such as doctors, discharge planners, patients or their family members, and community leaders who are familiar with the provider's quality of service. Then contact each reference and ask

— Do you frequently refer clients to this provider?

— Do you have a contractual relationship with this provider? If so, do you require the provider to meet special standards for quality care?

— What sort of feedback have you gotten from patients receiving care
from this provider, either on an informal basis or through a formal
satisfaction survey?
— Do you know of any clients this provider has treated whose cases
are similar to my loved one's? If so, can you put me in touch with
these individuals?

Household Support

"I had to let go of what had been stereotyped as *my* job duties in order to find
what I needed to be the best woman I could be, the happiest wife and mother,
and a good business professional as well," says Brenda, an aspiring work-at-
home accountant. "I knew that housecleaning was going to take some very important time away from launching my business—time that would allow me to
make the money it costs to hire someone to come in and clean."

If housework is one of the responsibilities that consumes your time, consider hiring a housecleaner. If your budget doesn't allow for this, barter for services with someone—that person can clean your house in exchange for your
talents in another area. Elicit help from your husband and/or kids if you're not
living alone.

To tactfully divide and conquer the household load with your partner, try
these strategies:

- *Split chores according to abilities and interests:* The best way to split chores
  is according to each partner's abilities and interests. What do each of
  you prefer to do? Jot down the tasks that each of you favors that the
  other doesn't. Although men may prefer doing home repairs and yard
  work, and women may gravitate toward cooking and tidying up, the
  split of chores doesn't have to follow traditional gender roles.
- *Try a team power cleaning:* Chris, a magazine publisher, says that she
  and her husband split the housecleaning chores equally. They use an
  effective strategy whereby they team up to do a "power cleaning" on a
  weekend day. "We'll take a Saturday when neither of us works, and we
  both just pitch in and do it," she says. "It goes much faster that way."

To involve your kids in household tasks, try these strategies:

- *Get an early start:* Children love to imitate their parents. You can buy
  inexpensive toy cleaning tools at garage and yard sales so your kids
  can do just that. By watching you, your children can learn how to use
  a broom and dustpan, push a vacuum, and iron clothes on their own
  toy sets.
- *Give them chores to do:* As your children develop, it's important for them
  to learn that everyone pitches in and does his or her assigned share
  around the house. If you instill the team approach early on, children

are more likely to do their share without being asked repeatedly. In fact, children will want to help.

♦ *Make it fun:* Find ways to make chores fun for your kids, and they'll be more excited about giving you a hand. Some parents assign regular chores to their kids but keep a chore jar with tasks written down on small pieces of paper. Your children can pick their surprise tasks from the jar blindfolded. This gives them a chance to add variety to their usual routine.

♦ *Don't expect perfection:* Perhaps the worst thing you can do is take away your children's sense of accomplishment by redoing their work. A slightly imperfect chore completed is better than no chore at all.

♦ *Give them reminders:* Kids have an easier time remembering their chores if they have reminders. One creative way to remind them is by making up a chart with words or pictures. If your children are old enough, let them use their artistic talents to make up their own charts. Even younger children can attach their own artwork to a chart you've made for them. This gives them the sense that it's their own personalized chart, complete with the tasks they're responsible for. You might have to remind them a bit in the beginning to check the chart daily, but once they're in the habit, it will become second nature.

♦ *Reward them when appropriate:* There are many ways to reward children when they're doing a good job managing their chores. You might treat them to a favorite video or dessert or an afternoon at the movies. Probably the best way to reward them is to regularly express appreciation and recognition for their contributions.

♦ *Make it a family affair:* As much as possible, make household chores a family affair. You can initiate this by scheduling a monthly meeting when you sit down as a family and ask your children what they'd like to do. You might be surprised at what kids will volunteer for instead of being told what to do.

Financial Planning

Most people spend more time planning their vacations than they do their financial affairs. It's not surprising then that 4% of people age 25 today will be financially independent at age 65 and that money is one of the major causes of divorce. The last thing you need to have holding you back during a turning point in your life is money. If you're currently unemployed, make sure to read the last section of this chapter, which offers tips and resources to help you during your time of transition.

Here we'll discuss some strategies to help you take control of your financial affairs. You already took the first step in Chapter 1, where you itemized your income and expenses as well as your goals for the areas you wish to change. This basic information will be your starting point.

Diane, Age 27

Diane and her husband, Paul, had been running a business from home. About 3 years before we spoke, they had gotten involved in a network marketing company that distributes dental hygiene products. They built such a strong downline of distributors that within 2 years Paul was able to leave his construction job to join Diane in the business.

One day, everything changed: The company they distributed for declared bankruptcy and went out of business. Diane and Paul lost their only source of income. To make matters worse, the financial pressure had taken its toll on Diane and Paul's relationship. Paul left, leaving no forwarding phone number or address. "Everything happened so fast," Diane says. "We saw the writing on the wall with this company, but we ignored the strong possibility that they would go under. Instead of creating a backup plan or safety net, Paul and I lived in denial."

Diane scrambled to save her house and maintain their standard of living by generating a financial plan for the interim and getting a temporary job. "It's amazing what you can do when you put your mind to it," she says. "Paul left us high and dry with zero income, zero savings, and big credit card debt. I talked with a credit counselor at the United Way, and we worked together to create a detailed budget and plan to get the kids and me back on our feet. Fortunately, we had some equity in our home, so I did a no-income-, no-asset-verification refinance and was able to pull some money out. With the interest rates being much lower on the new loan, our house payment barely increased. We had an excellent payment history, so there was no problem getting the new loan. I was able to pay off part of our credit card debt. I set the remaining money aside to make six mortgage payments—enough to tide us over until I could find a job."

Diane got a job through a temporary agency as a bookkeeper (something she had learned to do well in her network marketing business). She also applied for financial aid so that she was able to return to school to start earning a business degree with an emphasis in accounting. "It hasn't been easy," Diane says, "but I learned that I can make it on my own with the kids."

Diane's neighbor, whose kids had recently left home to go to college, had extra time on her hands. She agreed to watch Diane's kids while she worked. In return, Diane did her husband's books for a handyman business he ran out of their home. Diane says, "I love working from home and being near my kids. But this time I'm taking the risk on my own efforts, rather than some company or husband that might fold up at any time."

A sound financial plan should accomplish the following:

- ◆ Provide for a financially secure retirement
- ◆ Ensure the financial health of all family members in the event of premature death, disability, or other unforeseen catastrophes (e.g., property loss, job loss, liabilities)
- ◆ Provide for known future financial commitments, such as caring for and educating your kids or caring for your parents

There are three basic ways you can develop a solid financial plan: pay yourself first, invest wisely, and seek help from a financial advisor.

Paying Yourself First

If we would consider our need for capital at retirement to be as important as our need for "things" now, we would better prepare our financial future. Putting aside a portion of every dollar we earn for retirement is as important as the home we own and the car we drive. To decide how much to set aside, consider how much money you'll want to live on, how many years you have until retirement, what financial resources are available, and how the funds will be invested. Develop a systematic investment plan and stick with it so you can achieve your goals.

Investing Wisely

You can't avoid risk, but you can determine what kinds of risk and how much you're willing to take. To determine this, consider the following:

- ◆ What rate of return do you expect? Over the past 25 years, blue-chip stocks have had an average rate of return of 10.8%, which is 4.9% above inflation and 3.6% above money market accounts. Small U.S. stocks and international stocks have performed slightly better.
- ◆ What is your time horizon? If you invest money that will be needed in less than 3 to 5 years, it's advisable to keep the money in short-term fixed-interest-rate accounts. If you're saving for your children's college education or to buy a second home, you have a defined time horizon. If you're investing for retirement, consider your time horizon to be the rest of your life. This long-term investment horizon allows you to ride out the ups and downs of volatile markets.
- ◆ Are you willing to diversify your investments? No matter how much confidence you have in one company, basing your financial future on the success or failure of one or a few financial instruments is risky business. Ask the people who owned IBM stock and saw it drop to under $38 per share!

Seeking Help from a Financial Advisor

The best way to find a financial advisor you trust is through people you know, such as your accountant, attorney, or a knowledgeable friend. Look for a "fee only" advisor who doesn't work on commission. These advisors usually give an introductory meeting at no charge. Here are some questions you can ask at the meeting to see if you'd like to work with the person:

◆ What education or credentials do you have in the financial planning field?
◆ How long have you been in practice in the financial planning field?
◆ What did you do before you became a financial planner?
◆ Can I see a sample financial plan and/or investment report?
◆ What are your areas of expertise?
◆ Will you be working directly with me, or will one of your associates be handling my account?
◆ Will you provide generic or specific investment advice?
◆ How are you compensated? Is there a charge for the financial plan or for periodic reviews and/or revisions?
◆ How will you help me meet my goals?
◆ How often will you meet with me?
◆ Can I have a copy of your Security Exchange Commission (SEC) disclosure document and a sample letter of engagement? (Commission-only planners aren't required to provide these documents.)

Unemployment Survival Tips

If you're unemployed, it's important that you take care of yourself. Maintaining your morale and building a good support system among family members, friends, and acquaintances help ward off some of the negative effects of unemployment. In addition, consider the following suggestions:

◆ Carefully review your financial situation. With less money coming in, it will take more planning and strict budgeting to meet all your needs. Explore ways to reduce costs for basic expenses such as utilities and food. What frivolous items can be sacrificed temporarily, such as magazine subscriptions, cable television, and leisure activities? If possible, discuss your finances with members of your immediate family and work together as a team to manage the situation.
◆ Allow for job-hunting expenses in your budget. If you're looking for a new position in your current line of work, then your job-hunting expenses are tax deductible. These include related résumé typing, printing, postage, telephone expense, travel costs, and employment agency fees. Check the current tax laws to see if your moving expenses are tax deductible if your new position (in your current line of work) requires that you relocate.
◆ Contact your creditors before they contact you. Try to make alternative payment arrangements. If you can't pay everything, pay what you

can so your overdue balance is as low as possible. This lets your credi-tors know that you're trying. Talk to a credit counselor if you need more help. Call 800-411-UWAY for a United Way counselor in your area.

◆ If you're laid off, check into your company's policy on severance pay. Most companies offer 1 week's to 1 month's severance for every year of service. If you can afford it, extend your health insurance. Find out if your company offers outplacement services to help you transition to another job.

◆ Apply immediately for financial benefits, such as unemployment. Your employer is required to pay unemployment insurance while you're work-ing. Since the money has already been paid, check with your state em-ployment department to see if you're entitled to collect benefits in the interim. Your benefit eligibility is as unique as your situation. Don't assume that you do or don't qualify without speaking with the source of the benefit directly. Be prepared for possible delays, and don't let these discourage you.

◆ Make housing costs a priority in your budget. Although help is often available in meeting other basic needs, money for housing is scarce. Consider creative alternatives, such as shared housing, accepting board-ers/roommates, refinancing, or renting your home to meet your hous-ing expenses. Be aware of costs associated with moving.

◆ Consider borrowing against your life insurance policy or retirement account, or accept a loan from a friend or relative.

◆ Take on part-time, freelance, or temporary work to generate additional income during your transition.

◆ Be prepared to fight for your rights. Although free legal information on various areas of the law is often available, free legal representation is scarce. Information is power! (Access www.legal-link.com or www.800wedolaw.com for more insight on legal issues.)

Where to Go for Help with a Specific Life Change

We all experience different life changes that bring us to the decision to pursue a new direction, which is the common thread we share and the reason you're read-ing this book. However, each life change poses different challenges, and it's al-ways easier to make a transition when you can get advice from the experts in the field and relate to others who are going through similar circumstances. For this reason, this chapter concludes with a listing of resources you can access to make your particular life change a smooth one. I've listed numerous national organi-zations you can call for information on local chapters in your area. I've also included many valuable Web sites you can reference.

Wanda, Age 72

Wanda retired from a legal secretarial position at the age of 63. Toward the end of her 30-year career, she started dreading the idea of retiring. "I had heard so many stories about people dying shortly after they retire," Wanda says. "I didn't want to be another statistic. I was so used to leading a routine existence with complete structure in my day. What would I do with all my free time?"

Wanda was recently widowed, and her kids and grandkids all lived on the east coast. Wanda was happy in her small condo on the west coast, and didn't relish the idea of moving. "I hate the freezing weather back there. Makes my arthritis act up," she says. After hearing Wanda's fears about retirement, I encouraged her to join a local seniors' support group that focuses on staying active and healthy. "I couldn't believe how much this group had accomplished since retirement," Wanda says. "They were a bunch of movers and shakers. Many were entrepreneurs who had started part-time businesses. I didn't know how I'd keep up."

After a few meetings, the group encouraged Wanda to pursue a dream she had turned her back on because she had been so busy in her career and raising a family. She had always wanted to paint. The next thing she knew, Wanda was attending a class on watercolor painting at a local community college. "I've found out that painting is my true passion," she says. "My art instructor tells me that I've got a real talent for it." At the age of 68, Wanda learned that her talent for watercolor painting was so strong that her paintings are marketable pieces. In fact, two reputable galleries were so impressed with her work that they've taken her paintings as a part of their collection of offerings. Wanda says, "If it weren't for my supportive group of 'cheerleaders,' I never would have taken the initiative to explore this creative desire on my own. God bless them all."

These days, the Internet gives us infinite ways of staying connected and getting information that can help us, right in the privacy of our homes. If you aren't online with a home computer, I strongly suggest that this be one of the first steps you take toward your new direction. The Internet has a wealth of ideas, information, and support that will help you. For instance, www.ivillage.com and www.women.com are women's networks that offer advice on a wide variety of topics such as parenting, health, career, relationships, food, pets, fitness, finances, and travel.

The Internet is something you'll want to know how to use no matter what you do. If you can't go online at home, call your local library or community college to see if you can use their resources to go online. We'll talk about how to do research on the Internet in Chapter 8, "Exploring Your Options."

Support for Pregnant Women and Mothers

The following are sources for help and support if you're pregnant or raising children:

Healthy Mothers, Healthy Babies (202-638-5577)

Perinatal Care Network (800-675-2229)

www.mayohealth.org/mayo/common/htm/pregpg/htm

www.childbirth.org

www.drkoop.com/centers/pregnancy

www.familyweb.com/faqs

www.nursingmother.com

www.families.com

www.parentsplace.com

family.starwave.com

Support for Single Parents

The following are sources for help and support if you're a single parent:

singleparentresources.com

www.singlerose.com

Support for Divorced and Separated Women

The following are sources for help and support if you're divorced (or are about to be):

www.divorcecare.com (800-489-7778)

www.divorcehelp.com

www.divorcesource.com

www.divorcesupport.com

Support for Empty Nesters

The following is a source for help and support if your kids have recently left home:

healing.miningco.com/library/weekly/aa012299.htm#links

Support for Women Returning to School

The following are sources for help and support if you're returning to school:

www.back2college.com (714-447-0734)

webmaster@back2college.com

Support for Retired Women

The National Center for Women and Retirement Research (800-426-7386) puts out the Pre-Retirement Education Planning (PREP) program, designed to encourage women to plan for their future. The PREP program consists of four workbooks covering topics such as taking control of your finances, social and emotional concerns, health issues, and employment and retirement concerns.

Elderhostel provides travel and educational opportunities to people over the age of 60, and it has more than 1,900 cultural institutions in the United States, Canada, and 47 other countries. For more information and a catalog, contact

Elderhostel
PO Box 1751
Wakefield, MA 01889

The Social Security Administration (800-772-1213 or www.ssa.gov) provides benefits to women over 62. Social Security is money being generated by payroll taxes to pay all benefits for retirees. You receive benefits based on your work record, provided that you've worked long enough under Social Security—usually 10 years—to be entitled to benefits. Apply early—at least a couple months before you'd like to begin receiving your benefits. You'll need

- ◆ Your Social Security card
- ◆ Your birth certificate
- ◆ If signing on a spouse's record, your marriage license
- ◆ Your most recent W-2 form or your entire tax return if you're self-employed

Support for Grieving Women

The Widowed Persons Service of the American Association of Retired Persons offers a variety of free brochures, including "Staying at Home: A Guide to Long-Term Care and Housing" (No. D14986), "On Being Alone: Guide for Widowed Persons" (No. D150), "So Many of My Friends Have Moved Away or Died" (No. D13831), and "Knowing the Facts About the Use of Medications During Bereavement" (No. D13503). To order any of these brochures, include the name and stock number and write to

AARP Fulfillment (EE01135)
601 E Street NW
Washington, DC 20077-1214

You can find additional support and resources on surviving the loss of a loved one at the following Web sites:

www.bguide.com/webguide/love/plus/980204.fabfinds.html

www.fortnet.org/widownet/index.html

Support for Women Whose Health Is Failing

The following are sources for help and support if your health is failing:

Boston Women's Health Book Collective/Women's Health (617-625-0271)

National Women's Health Network (202-347-1140)

National Women's Health Resource Center (202-293-6045)

National Asian Women's Health Organization (510-208-3171)

National Black Women's Health Project (800-275-2947)

National Latina Health Organization (510-534-1362)

American Heart Association (800-242-8721)

Cancer Information Service (800-422-6237

National Osteoporosis Foundation (202-223-2226)

www.yahoo.com/health/women_s_health

www.drkoop.com

Support for Emotional Crises

If you need help with an emotional crisis, call the United Way at 800-411-UWAY and ask for the United Way Info Line toll-free number in your area. Or check out the United Way's Web page at www.unitedway.org.

Support for Alcohol and Drug Abuse

The following are sources for support if you need help with alcohol or drug abuse:

Center for Substance Abuse and Treatment (800-662-4357)

www.health.org

Support for Domestic Violence

The following are sources for support if you need help with abuse or domestic violence:

YWCA (888-305-SAFE)

www.phenomenalwomen.com/help

Support for Sexual Assault and Harassment

The following are sources for support if you need help with sexual assault or harassment:

www.nh.ultranet.com/~sass1/sasslinks.html

www.womenscenter.uconn.edu/harass.htm

Appreciating the Helping Hand

In times of change, we need to build and call on our support systems rather than stay completely isolated, trying to figure out our situations. A healthy amount of alone time is important, and it gives us the opportunity to regroup and redirect our energies more positively. However, support systems can accelerate and accentuate this process immensely. If we ask a question, we'll get an answer. If we ask for a referral, we'll get one. If we talk to someone who has taken the journey we wish to pursue, we'll avoid problems that we otherwise wouldn't have conceived of.

If we ask for and pursue things in an assertive fashion, chances are good that we'll get what we want and end up where we want to be. All these things will bring us closer to our goals.

Appreciate the helping hand that enters your life, and in the process, lend a hand to others who are striving to be where you are. This handshaking, mentoring process will catapult you toward your dreams, and it will help others achieve theirs as well.

CHAPTER 7

CREATING WINNING RÉSUMÉS AND COVER LETTERS

"Recognize and appreciate your talents and traits. Instead of taking them for granted, use them to your advantage."

ANONYMOUS

Regardless of whether you're changing careers altogether or have not worked in years or at all, a professional résumé and cover letter reflecting your qualifications and skills are a must. Your résumé and accompanying cover letter are your personalized selling tools that should convey your clear-cut sense of career direction and momentum. As you'll soon see, developing these tools is a lesson in creativity. There is no right way to create them because they are a summary of personal information relevant to the job or position you're seeking, and they should be tailored accordingly.

Employers spend no more than 20 to 30 seconds scanning a résumé in the initial screening process. Needless to say, in order to make an impact among the hundreds of applicants applying, yours must be outstanding. To achieve this goal, make sure your résumé is brief, clear, neat, honest, and distributed with a cover letter.

This chapter highlights strategies for creating winning résumés and cover letters that are geared to your top career choices. For instance, if you're a stay-at-home mom, you can transfer your household management and organizational skills to a variety of work capacities. To assist you in this process, sample résumés and cover letters are provided.

Creating Killer Résumés

Having résumés developed for your top three job choices prepares you to go out in the field to explore your options, which we'll cover in the next chapter. While in the midst of doing research on your top three job choices, you'll have résumés in hand when you make an important contact at a job fair, or hear from a potential employer as a result of an informational interview. In Chapter 9, "Finding the Work You Love," we'll discuss job search strategies where first-rate résumés are an absolute must. The following sections offer some helpful guidelines to assist you in the résumé-writing process.

Résumé Contents

You should include the following sections in your résumé (some are optional, as noted in parentheses). You should try to arrange them in order of importance to the employer:

- ◆ A heading that includes your name, address, telephone number, and e-mail address.
- ◆ An objective that describes the position you're seeking (optional).
- ◆ Key words listed at the top of your résumé or sprinkled throughout the text that represent skills, abilities, and experience, using nouns taken from position descriptions or technical jargon used in the field (optional). These key words may increase your probability of making it through a computer screening.
- ◆ A qualifications summary (optional) that lists special skills or substantial experience. If you include this section, you should show how and where you obtained the skills or experience in your experience section.
- ◆ An education section, which should be listed first if it's your greatest strength.
- ◆ An experience and achievements section, which should stress accomplishments and results rather than responsibilities (e.g., rather than "Responsible for Red Cross Disaster Supply Department," you should say "Managed Disaster-Recovery Supply Department; instituted new procedures that reduced annual expenditures by 15%").

In general, your résumé should not include personal data, salary history, and references. It's best to have references available on a separate sheet (that matches your résumé in paper stock and overall look) for an interview.

Key Résumé Presentation Guidelines

The following are some general presentation and content guidelines to keep in mind while developing your résumé:

◆ Unless you're applying for a top-level position, keep your résumé to one page.

◆ Use standard $8^1/_2 \times 11$-inch white or ivory 20-pound bond paper (for top-level positions you might want to use more expensive, heavier-weight, or special-grain paper).

◆ Use a 10- or 12-point typeface with a professional-looking font such as Arial, Helvetica, Universe, or Optima.

◆ Use a high-quality office typewriter, a word processor with letter-quality type, or a word processing program on a computer with a letter-quality printer.

◆ Left-justify or center headings. Keep your margins wide and headings clear, and make selective use of bullets to call attention to important points (e.g., skills, qualifications, achievements).

◆ Prepare a résumé that will scan well. Most major employers today scan résumés into an automated applicant tracking system, which can mean quicker retrieval for current or future interviews—if your résumé meets the strict criteria the technology can handle. Avoid using italics and underlining of words, and use boldface sparingly. Also, don't fold your résumé when you send it.

◆ Avoid using paragraphs longer than six lines.

◆ Don't use *I* on your résumé.

◆ Don't include salary or personal information, such as height, weight, or age.

◆ Don't put "References Available Upon Request" on your résumé. (It's understood.)

◆ Be honest and accurate in the information you convey. You want to make yourself look as good as possible, but if you lie, you might be found out and not get the job anyway.

◆ Sell your skills and accomplishments, slanting them toward the position you wish to obtain. De-emphasize accomplishments that are irrelevant to the position you wish to obtain.

◆ Itemize the sections of your résumé in the order of importance to the potential employer you're submitting it to.

◆ Stress results. This is no time to be modest—be positive about what you've achieved and how you contributed to your past employers (e.g., reduced costs, improved a product, implemented a new program). Where applicable, use dollar amounts and statistics (e.g., "increased annual sales by 20%").

◆ Be brief and direct, using short and concise phrases to make a point, as opposed to using long-winded sentences that meander. Table 7.1 lists some action verbs that will bring life to your résumé. Choose those that will make yours sparkle.

◆ Proofread your résumé, checking grammar, punctuation, and spelling. Check for awkward or illogical sentences and those that can be omitted.

Table 7.1

Action Verbs to Use in a Résumé

Accelerated	Accomplished	Achieved	Adapted
Administered	Advised	Analyzed	Appointed
Arranged	Assisted	Attained	Authored
Balanced	Budgeted	Built	Calculated
Cataloged	Chaired	Collaborated	Compiled
Completed	Composed	Computed	Conducted
Constructed	Consulted	Controlled	Convinced
Coordinated	Counseled	Created	Decided
Delegated	Delivered	Demonstrated	Designed
Developed	Devised	Directed	Edited
Educated	Employed	Encouraged	Equipped
Established	Evaluated	Examined	Executed
Expanded	Expedited	Extracted	Facilitated
Formulated	Founded	Generated	Guided
Handled	Headed	Helped	Identified
Illustrated	Implemented	Improved	Increased
Initiated	Innovated	Instructed	Integrated
Interpreted	Launched	Led	Maintained
Managed	Marketed	Mediated	Monitored
Negotiated	Operated	Organized	Performed
Persuaded	Planned	Prepared	Presented
Prioritized	Processed	Produced	Programmed
Promoted	Proposed	Provided	Published
Recruited	Reduced	Regulated	Reorganized
Represented	Researched	Resolved	Restored
Restructured	Retrieved	Reviewed	Revised
Scheduled	Served	Shaped	Sold
Solved	Streamlined	Summarized	Supervised
Taught	Trained	Upgraded	Utilized
Worked	Wrote		

Writing Accomplishment Statements

When stressing what you've achieved in various jobs you've performed, think about the problem or situation that arose, the action you initiated, and what resulted from this action. Summarize the result, and if possible, use percentages or quantify how the result benefited the organization. For example, say the following are your problem, action, and result:

Problem: Clients weren't receiving information needed to make decisions, which caused errors, delays, and inefficient use of staff and client time.

Action: Determined information needs of clientele, selected format and style of writing to communicate information. Organized, edited, printed, and distributed a newsletter to convey the information.

Result: The newsletter improved information flow between the department and clients, decreasing the number of staff errors and increasing client satisfaction.

From this problem, action, and result, you might come up with the following accomplishment statement:

Researched, wrote, edited, and distributed monthly newsletter, which significantly improved information flow between the department and clients, and decreased costly department errors by 60%.

Types of Résumés

There are three basic types of résumés: chronological, functional, and chrono-functional (or *combination,* which combines the first two types).

The chronological résumé is the most widely used and accepted résumé. It's the best format to use if you have no large employment gaps in your work history and your previous jobs relate to the job you're currently pursuing. It's actually a reverse chronological résumé because your current or most recent position and schooling are generally listed first, with previous positions following in reverse chronological order. The names, dates, and places of employment are listed, with education and work experience grouped separately. This format is best for women moving up the career ladder.

The functional format is less common than the chronological format. It focuses on skills and talents you've developed rather than positions you've held. You might choose the functional format if you have no work experience, have significant gaps in your employment record, have a pattern of short-term jobs, or have held several positions in which you've exercised the same skills. This format is appropriate for first-time job seekers, including recent graduates and at-home moms and homemakers making the transition to the job market.

The chrono-functional résumé is a good choice for job seekers with a solid employment background and special skills they want to emphasize. In this format, job history and education are listed chronologically, with highlights on qualifications that are particularly marketable. This format is suitable for recent graduates with some job experience, career changers, and at-home moms and homemakers returning to the job market.

Highlighting Your Relevant Background

Each résumé format emphasizes different aspects of your background, depending on where your strengths lie in relation to the position you're seeking. Here are some of the points you should convey in your résumé, regardless of the format used. You might want to highlight those that relate to your job objective so that you can easily find them when you're putting together your résumé:

◆ Specific job skills that relate to your objective.

◆ Your education. What classes have you taken? Have you taken any special workshops or seminars? Have you earned any degrees, licenses, or certificates?

◆ Special achievements or recognition (e.g., Salesperson of the Year). This could be almost anything, such as publishing an article, receiving an award or a scholarship, graduating with honors, raising a family, coaching a softball team, organizing group vacations, or planning a wedding. Choose accomplishments and achievements that relate to the position you're seeking. Planning a wedding, for instance, would be appropriate on a résumé submitted for a planning-type job, but might not be appropriate for other jobs.

◆ Volunteer work. Have you volunteered for any organizations, or raised funds for a special cause or charity?

◆ Committees and organizations you're active in. These could be social or professional. Are you active in your children's school? Are you a member of the PTA? Are you a board member of a homeowners' association or a professional organization such as Toastmasters?

◆ Classes, internships, or research or special projects (especially those that relate to your job objective).

◆ Computer knowledge. Are you familiar with any word processing or spreadsheet software? Have you created a family budget on the computer? Are you familiar with the Internet? What kinds of research have you done on the World Wide Web? Have you created a Web page?

◆ Language skills. Are you fluent in a foreign language? Can you write or read as well as speak it?

◆ Unique talents. Do you have artistic or musical abilities? Are you a writer or an inventor? What creative endeavors spark your enthusiasm and bring you to life?

◆ Extracurricular activities that relate to your job objective, such as camping (outdoor work), dancing (fitness instructor), travel (travel agent), antique collecting (antiques salesperson), cooking (chef), or walking (tour guide).

Prioritize your background information derived from the previous points in the order of importance to a potential employer you're targeting. This will help determine what résumé type you choose and the order in which you'll place the information on your résumé, with the most important items such as work experience, special skills, and education generally being first.

General Résumé Pointers

Here are some additional pointers to keep in mind while tailoring your résumé to your career objective and deciding which format to use:

◆ Tailor your résumé to the specific job you're seeking. If you're pursuing a position as an administrative assistant, your résumé should emphasize your office organization and management skills.

◆ Use a brief and general objective that's focused but keeps your opportunities open. You can always address a particular job, skill, or company in your cover letter. This is especially helpful for entry-level positions. For example, "An entry-level intern position as a counselor" doesn't limit Beverly in the first sample résumé to only working with battered wives. During an interview, her preference can be discussed, but if there are no openings for counselors of battered wives, then Beverly's résumé won't eliminate her from consideration.

◆ Unless you have more than two years of full-time work experience, emphasize your education by placing it first on your résumé.

◆ When placing your education first on your resume, if you've already graduated, begin with "Awarded the degree of...." If you're still working on your degree, begin with "Candidate for the degree of...." If you didn't graduate and aren't currently pursuing your degree, then list the dates you attended college and the courses you studied.

◆ Don't include a grade point average (GPA) under 3.0 on your résumé. However, do include your GPA for the courses you took in your major if it's better than your overall GPA.

◆ Include special classes you took, achievements you've made, awards you've received, and volunteer work you've done (e.g., student government, teaching assistant, school newspaper, tutoring).

◆ Don't include high school information unless you haven't made significant progress in your college achievements, part-time jobs, and volunteer work.

◆ If you've held several jobs, include the two or three that are most relevant to the position you're seeking and place the others under the heading "Other Experience," without individual job descriptions.

◆ List personal information, interests, or hobbies only if they relate to the position you're pursuing, or if they emphasize personal qualities that would be desirable for the position. For example, the fact that you meet weekly with a group of seniors to play cards may be relevant if you're seeking a job at a seniors' organization that prefers someone who has a good rapport with this age group.

◆ Be brief in your writing. Filter out the important points and create a concise résumé. Unless you're applying for a top-level position, keep your résumé to one page.

Résumé Tips for Special Scenarios

As I said at the beginning of this chapter, writing a résumé is a lesson in creativity. Each résumé is unique to the individual and his or her situation. Here are some additional tips on résumé writing for special situations:

◆ *Gaps in employment history:* Use the functional résumé format. Embed the dates of your employment in your job descriptions so they aren't conspicuous.

◆ *Part-time employment history:* Treat part-time experience like full-time experience on a résumé.

◆ *Brief employment history:* Emphasize educational and relevant volunteer experience to compensate for brief employment history.

◆ *Some college but no degree:* List courses you've taken that are relevant to the position you're applying for. List any supportive qualifications or experience, paid and unpaid.

◆ *Temporary employment history:* Treat long-term temporary assignments like full-time permanent positions on a résumé. Short-term assignments that are relevant to the position you're applying for can be listed under "Other Experience."

◆ *Weak or irrelevant educational background:* De-emphasize your limited education and emphasize your relevant work experience.

◆ *History of freelance work:* List three or four of your major clients in the "Experience" section, along with your accomplishments and the results you achieved for each client.

◆ *Moving up the career ladder:* Emphasize the progress you've made in your career, with the primary focus on your current or most recent job (e.g., specific accomplishments and achievements). Do not use a job objective. Your résumé presumably shows a strong career path. An objective could eliminate you from consideration for positions other than the one for which you're applying.

Julia Bauer, founder and owner of Résumé Resources, a résumé and career coaching business in Northern California, encourages recent college graduates and women who are transitioning to new careers and have little or no work experience to brainstorm their accomplishments and achievements on paper.

You can start by creating a list such as the following:

◆ President of the Chess Club
◆ Assisted on a committee for the holiday food drive
◆ Organized a golf tournament to raise funds for a children's charity

After you've created a list of your accomplishments, Julia suggests that you add the details under each, as in these examples:

◆ *President of the Chess Club:* Established the first Chess Club at the school during my freshman year. Original club had 5 members. Through advertising (putting up flyers around the campus and making announcements on the school PA system) and talking to friends, we now have 25 members, and I was named president.

◆ *Food drive committee:* Worked as the team leader of 20 people to collect food, toys, and clothing for underprivileged families and children. Organized groups of people to collect items outside local grocery stores. Left flyers at homes in neighborhoods and organized students to go house-to-house to collect canned goods, toys, and clothing.

◆ *Golf tournament fundraiser:* Organized and oversaw all aspects of a golf tournament fundraiser, including planning and coordinating the event, advertising for sponsors, and searching for high-profile celebrities.

After you've jotted down the details of your achievements and accomplishments, try to find ways to relate them to the position you're seeking. For instance, recruitment activities involved in establishing the Chess Club and fundraiser are perfect for a position in sales, marketing, advertising, or public relations. The presidency position would be useful experience for a management position. The activities involved in organizing the food drive and fundraiser would be helpful in a variety of jobs involving management or leadership, as well as jobs involving event planning, coordinating, or organizing. Potential employers would not only be impressed with your accomplishments, but also with the fact that you did volunteer work.

Where to Begin

If one of your top three job choices is related to something you're already doing work-wise or in which you already have an extensive background, you might want to begin by developing a chronological résumé targeting that job objective. Chronological résumés are the most widely used and accepted, so this is a good place to start. They're also fairly easy to write because you're focusing on your accomplishments in prior work capacities that relate to the position you're seeking.

After you've prepared a résumé for one of your job choices, take notes on what type of résumé you'd use for your remaining job choices, as well as the areas you'd like to emphasize in each résumé. Consider what's most important to potential employers. If your work experience is most desirable, emphasize its strength by putting it first on your résumé. If your education or personal accomplishments are your biggest strengths, put them first.

Winning Résumé Samples

The following pages walk you through the most common scenarios among women seeking jobs. A sample résumé that applies to each case is presented. General tips for gearing your résumé to your career objective are offered. These tips will help you determine which résumé format to use. Additional résumé pointers for special circumstances are provided later in this chapter.

Beverly, Age 24, Psychology Major

Beverly is a psychology major at California State University, Los Angeles. She is seeking a position as a counseling intern, working with battered wives. Her work history is weak; however, she participated in a teaching assistant position and an internship position that supported her job objective, so those things should be emphasized on her résumé; this gives her a competitive edge. Her part-time employment during college reflects her ability to handle multiple responsibilities. Her education is her strongest point, so we should put that first on her résumé and use a chrono-functional format.

Beverly Jones
212 3rd Avenue
Los Angeles, CA 99999
(213) 555-5555
bjones@email.com

Objective
An entry-level intern position as a counselor

Education
California State University, Los Angeles   **1996–Present**
Candidate for the degree of bachelor of arts, to graduate in June 2000, majoring in psychology. Courses have included assertiveness training, human relations, public speaking, and Internet research. Independent study topic is the psychological impact of commercial advertising on battered wives. Won the Carl Rogers Award for Outstanding Student of Humanistic Psychology in 1998.

College Activities and Memberships   **1996–Present**
Teaching assistant for human relations psychology class. Student member of the American Association of University Women (AAUW). Volunteer for the Red Cross. Helped organize a clothes donation drive for the homeless; collected more than 2,000 articles of clothing that were distributed to more than 600 families.

Internship   **Summer 1998**
Women's Resource Center, Los Angeles
Filed, answered phones, researched patient information for various counselors. Observed group counseling sessions. Participated in weekly counselor meetings.

Work Experience
New World Bookstore, Los Angeles
Sales Clerk   **Summer 1997**
Helped customers make selections, registered sales. Was named Salesperson of the Month in August.

The Hollywood Wax Museum, Hollywood
Museum Assistant   **Summer 1996**
Prepared and delivered brief talks on museum exhibits. Guided tours for up to 100 people per day. Participated in organizing creative educational programs for children.

Sabrina, Age 32, Entering the Job Market for the First Time

Sabrina is an at-home mom entering the job market for the first time. A functional résumé is perfect for her because she can emphasize the skills—including her household management skills—that will help her in the entry-level administrative position she wants. Sabrina puts her relevant skills and accomplishments in categories under a "Summary of Qualifications" heading.

Sabrina Smith
168 Green Street
Toronto, OH 43964
(614) 555-5555
ssmith@email.com

Objective
To obtain an entry-level administrative position

Summary of Qualifications

Administration:
Accurate typing at 60 words per minute. Experienced in office administration, including record keeping, filing, and scheduling/planning.

Accounting:
Coordinated finances for a middle-income family of five on a personal computer. Processed accounts payable in a timely manner without compromising the expenditure budget.

Computer Knowledge:
Experienced in using PC software including Excel, Word, WordPerfect, PageMaker, and PhotoShop.

Organization:
Organized a fundraiser to renovate the James Kahn Writing Center. Raised over $5,000.

Organized a rotating carpool with five other mothers. Generated a monthly newsletter to keep the mothers abreast of the carpool schedule, the school lunch menu, and special school activities.

Leadership:
Led a monthly women's group focusing on finding your lost creative soul. Developed artistic exercises that address the hidden spiritual elements in modern women's lives. Motivated members to channel stress, uncertainty, and fear into creativity. Acted as a mentor and friend.

Coached a YWCA soccer team, for girls ages 7–11, from September through November. Provided players with the instruction, motivation, support, and outlook that will enable them to leave each game with satisfaction and pride, no matter what the score.

Notable Accomplishments:
Wrote and published several articles on creativity for various magazines, including *The Writer.*

Education:
Toronto Community College, Toronto, OH; completed a business administration certificate program, 1996
Courses in creative writing, Excel, and bookkeeping

Carol, Age 56, At-home Mom Returning to the Job Market

Carol is an at-home mom who has been out of the job market for 9 years. While in the workforce, her extensive professional experience in the field of nursing created the perfect foundation for a challenging position in the health care industry. In her résumé, she focuses on her experience, using a chronological format.

Carol Baker
123 Post Drive
Holland, MI 49423
(616) 555-5555
cbaker@email.com

Objective
　　To utilize my extensive experience in nursing in a challenging position within the health care industry.

Professional Experience
1988–1990　　　　　　　　　　Holland Memorial Hospital, Holland, MI
Staff nurse, addictions treatment program
- Cared for patients on 40-bed mental health unit, including assessing patients in crisis, interviewing and counseling patients, administering medication, consulting with emergency room staff members, and collaborating with health care providers.
- Assessed and evaluated patients with substance abuse problems.
- Managed the verification and precertification of insurance providers.
- Assessed medical complications.
- Led and co-led educational groups for patients and their families.
- Collaborated with the treatment team to implement inpatient and continuing care plans.

1985–1988　　　　　Psychiatric Addiction Emergency Service, Holland, MI
Staff nurse, psychiatric care unit
- Assessed psychiatric patients to determine severity of illness and level of care needed.
- Collaborated with health care providers and medical team.

1983–1985　　　　　　　　Holland College/Nursing Program, Holland, MI
Instructor, medical assisting techniques
- Instructed students in office medical procedures.
- Organized and planned curriculum, and tested and graded students in written and practical methods.

1981–1983　　　　　　　City of Holland School Department, Holland, MI
Substitute school nurse
- Administered first aid for students in grades K–12.
- Performed eye and ear testing and counseling.

Education
　　BSN, Holland City Hospital School of Nursing, Holland, MI, 1980
　　RN: Registration Number 19527, 1981

Activities
　　Volunteer, Holland Nursing Home, 1993–Present
　　Coach, women's soccer league, 1993–Present

MaryAnn, Age 60, Career Changer

MaryAnn would like to obtain a position as a fashion designer. Her 7 years of experience with women's apparel indirectly relate to her objective, so she needs to prepare a functional résumé, emphasizing her relevant qualifications rather than her job experience. This allows her to tailor her résumé to her field of interest.

MaryAnn Downs
1345 A Street
Sumter, SC 29150
(803) 555-5555
mdowns@email.com

Objective

To apply my seven years of experience with women's apparel as well as my educational background to a career in fashion design.

Summary

- Area of expertise is creativity, from conception and design to marketing and sales.
- Self-starter, good attention to productivity and workmanship.
- Excellent communicator, adept at sizing up situations and developing new ideas or alternative courses of action in order to design, sell, or increase production.

Qualifications

Design

Conceptualized, coordinated, and designed in-store and window displays, including the massive front window of a major fashion center. Operated within a streamlined materials budget appropriated by the manager, yet consistently generated award-winning window themes for a $2.1 million department store.

Buying

Attended fashion shows in New York, Milan, and Paris, and assisted in the buying process. Perused fashion magazines during off time, and provided head buyer with information about upcoming styles.

Employment

Display Coordinator/Associate Buyer, The Chess Queen, Sumter, SC, 1989–1994
Window Dresser, Stella's Castle, Sumter, SC, 1987–1989

Education

AA in fashion design, Sumter's School of Fashion Design, Sumter, SC, 1994

Marge, Age 44, Moving Up the Career Ladder

Marge has a diverse background that makes her a good candidate for a management position in retail sales. Because she doesn't want to be excluded from positions other than the one she applies for, she doesn't want to put an objective on her résumé. This leaves her advancement opportunities open, and employers might consider her qualifications for a variety of positions. Marge uses the chronological résumé format, which focuses on her most current (and relevant) position. She lists her education at the bottom of her résumé because her practical experience outweighs her degree.

Marge Thomas
949 Taylor Street
Providence, RI 02912
(401) 555-5555
mthomas@email.com

Experience

Jones Corporation, Providence, RI   1992–Present

Sales assistant: Act as a liaison between the customer and the sales division. Provide customer service via telephone. Ascertain order accuracy. Track and expedite more than 1,000 orders per month. Cooperate in team endeavors.

Musical Memories, Providence, RI   1988–1992

Sales assistant: Coordinated sales efforts of a staff of 20 for a large musical instrument dealership. Developed and maintained working relationships with manufacturers and customers. Supported top account executives. Maintained open files to ensure greatest customer satisfaction.

City of Providence, RI, Treasurer's Department   1984–1988

Research assistant: Assisted in the collection of delinquent real estate, personal property, and motor vehicle excise taxes. Processed title searches and petitions of foreclosure for the legal section.

Traffic and Parking Department, Providence, RI   1982–1984

Senior claims investigator: Investigated and expedited claim settlements relating to ticket disputes and information requests.

Central Savings and Loan, Providence, RI   1980–1982

Bank teller: Interacted with customers, processed money and check transactions, balanced transactions at the end of each shift. Operated an IBM word processor and CRT and TRW terminals, and developed a working knowledge of money market funds and IRAs. Increased the number of money market accounts by 25% in one month.

Education

Providence College, Providence, RI
AS in business management, 1980

Rhode Island Institute of Banking, Providence, RI
Completed courses in bank organization and employee relations, 1980

Writing Killer Cover Letters

A good cover letter should be your best sales pitch, conveying why you're the perfect person for the job you're applying for. This is where you can distinguish yourself from other job seekers and show that you've researched the company you're interested in working for. Always mail a cover letter with your résumé. It's not professional to send a résumé without one.

Cover Letter Contents

Following are the ingredients of a successful cover letter:

◆ The cover letter shouldn't be more than four concise paragraphs long.

◆ Your address on the cover letter should be the same as the one on your résumé. It should appear in the same spot on your cover letter as it does on your résumé (so if it's centered on your résumé, it should be centered on your cover letter). It's best to avoid abbreviations (e.g., use *Street* rather than *St.*); however, abbreviating the state name is acceptable.

◆ Two lines beneath your address, put the date. The date can be left justified, centered, or aligned to the right. Always write out the date (e.g., June 9, 2000), rather than use an abbreviated format.

◆ Two lines beneath the date, put the name of the addressee, preceded by *Mr.* or *Ms.* List the individual's proper title on the next line, the company name on the next line, and the address of the company on the next two or three lines.

◆ The salutation should be two lines beneath the company address, and should begin with *Dear Mr.* or *Dear Ms.,* followed by the individual's last name and a colon or a comma.

◆ In the first paragraph, state the position you're applying for and what makes you the best candidate for the position. Let the employer know how you learned about the position.

◆ In the second paragraph, tell the employer what you'll contribute to the company, and show how your qualifications will benefit the firm. For example, "In addition to my strong background in caregiving, I also offer significant business experience, having worked as an administrative assistant and a real estate agent. My bachelor's degree in psychology will also prove particularly useful in the position of managed care manager."

◆ In the third paragraph, describe your interest in the firm, subtly emphasizing your familiarity with the industry and respect for the firm's accomplishments. This shows that you've done your research. For example, "I admire the recent rapid growth and superior reputation of Technosystems, Inc. After researching different technology firms, I've concluded that Technosystems, Inc., is in a strong competitive position, offering cutting-edge products and excellent customer service."

◆ In the fourth and final paragraph, request an interview. Include your phone number and when you can be reached, or mention that you'll follow up with a phone call within the next few days to arrange an interview at a mutually convenient time. In general, it's best not to include your salary requirements. If you feel that not stating your salary requirements might jeopardize your chances of getting an interview because the employer specifically requested this information, then state a salary range you're seeking, such as, "I seek a starting salary between $25,000 and $30,000."

◆ The closing should begin two lines beneath the final paragraph, aligned with your return address on the righthand side of the page. Keep the closing simple. "Sincerely," works best. Space down four lines, and type in your full name, including your middle initial. Sign your name in black ink above your typed name.

◆ Type an enclosure line (i.e., "Enc. résumé") two lines below your typed name, on the left side of the page, to let the employer know that a résumé is enclosed. This reflects your good attention to detail.

Key Cover Letter Presentation Guidelines

Here are some general presentation and content guidelines to keep in mind while writing a cover letter:

◆ Keep your cover letter shorter than one page.

◆ Make your cover letter an attention-grabbing selling tool. I can't emphasize this enough. You don't want to go overboard or sound sappy, but this is your chance to make a good first impression. If you don't impress the employer, she or he might not even look at your résumé.

◆ Use standard $8^1/_2 \times 11$-inch white or ivory 20-pound bond paper (for top-level positions you might want to use more expensive, heavier weight, or special-grain paper).

◆ Use 10- or 12-point typeface with a professional-looking font such as Arial, Helvetica, Universe, or Optima.

◆ Use a high-quality office typewriter, a word processor with letter-quality type, or a word processing program on a computer with a letter-quality printer.

◆ Use proper English, and avoid abbreviations and slang. Use short sentences and common words.

◆ Use action verbs to make your letters interesting (e.g., *developed*, *guided*, and *produced* sound much more active and specific than *was* or *did*).

◆ Personalize each letter. Don't send form letters or generic copies.

◆ Proofread your cover letter, checking grammar, punctuation, and spelling. Check for awkward or illogical sentences and those that can be omitted.

◆ Avoid using correction fluid or making messy corrections that detract from the professionalism of your cover letter.

Winning Cover Letter Samples

Three types of cover letters are commonly used in the process of seeking a job: a warm mailing, a response to a classified ad, and a cold mailing.

A Warm Mailing Cover Letter

A warm mailing is the friendliest approach to job hunting and by far the most effective because you've already made a contact within the company that gives you the edge over other applicants. In the opening of a cover letter to a warm lead, describe your connection and objective. State the name of someone significant who referred you, such as a company representative at a job fair, or a familiar colleague or friend of the potential employer.

If you already spoke directly with the person you're contacting, jog his or her memory in the opening paragraph with the date and content of your conversation. For example, "I'm following up in response to our phone conversation on June 8, when you requested a copy of my résumé to review for the database analyst position."

4385 Birch Drive
Knoke, IA 50553
(515) 555-5555
dmiller@email.com

September 14, 1999

Mr. John Doe
Equipment Purchasing Manager
St. Joseph's Medical Center
123 Oak Knoll Road
Knoke, IA 50553

Dear Mr. Doe,

It was enjoyable meeting your representative, Dr. George Cole, at the Purchasing Management Association Conference on August 19. I was interested to learn that you are looking for a buyer with computer capability.

I feel that my background would prove valuable in the reorganization and expansion that you're planning for your medical center. My expertise lies in two areas. The first area is the way a health care facility delivers patient care, from scheduling to billing. The second and most relevant area is the way health care and office supplies and equipment are actually researched, put out to bid, purchased, and delivered to the correct department.

I am aware that the mission of St. Joseph's is to offer top-quality health care, incorporating proven leading-edge techniques and state-of-the-art equipment. I am eager to support this mission with my extensive background and experience.

I'd appreciate the opportunity to meet with you to review my qualifications for this position. Should you require additional information, you can reach me at (515) 555-5555 between 9 a.m. and 5 p.m.

Sincerely,

Debbie M. Riley

Enc. résumé

Responding to a Classified Ad Cover Letter

Newspaper and online ads are the most popular ways to hunt for jobs, but not the most effective. Companies often place ads because of regulations, even when they've already chosen internal candidates. If a company is really looking for someone through an ad placement, you're still competing with hundreds of applicants. That's why it's critical that your cover letter be sparkling.

When you respond to an advertised position, specify the position you're seeking and the name and date of the publication in which you saw the ad. This clarifies your objective because companies often run several ads at once.

---

678 Daisy Lane
Boston, MA 02115
(617) 555-5555
mparker@e-mail.com

September 14, 1999

Ms. Maggie Smith
Todd Jones and Associates
8989 State Street
Boston, MA 02115

Dear Ms. Smith:

My interest in the business development manager position you advertised in the September 13 *Boston Herald* has prompted me to forward my résumé for your consideration. I received my BA from Boston University in 1997 and am currently a principal and manager at a growth-stage Internet company.

My most recent experience with Marketing Systems, Inc., an online career-planning Web site, has allowed me to participate in all facets of an expanding business, including product development, marketing, sales, and promotion. I have worked closely with a Web development firm to design the content and features of the site, which includes a powerful database, passwords for advertisers, an onsite search engine, and elaborate graphical interface and content.

My writing, collaboration, and presentation skills are excellent, and I am committed to creativity and excellence in new media business development. I am interested in working in the fast-paced, team-oriented environment that Todd Jones and Associates offers, and to making a significant contribution to a growing Internet company.

If you would like additional information, you can reach me at (617) 555-5555 between 9 a.m. and 5 p.m.

Sincerely,

Michele T. Parker

Enc. résumé

Cold Mailing Cover Letter

Cold mailings might be the toughest way to get your foot in the door of a company. The employers don't know you, don't know anyone who knows you, and didn't ask you to contact them. The biggest advantage of cold mailings is that they show your initiative and genuine interest in a company. Some companies keep résumés on file and pull them when they begin hiring. However, many wind up tossing résumés in the circular file.

When doing a cold mailing, you should call the company and ask for the head of the department in which you're interested. Generally, people within each department, not the Human Resources Department, make hiring decisions. Contacting an individual may create a feeling of responsibility that might save your résumé from being tossed.

---

444 B Street
Woodside, NY 11377
(718) 204-2113
abarnes@email.com

September 7, 1999

Ms. Jane Phillips
Union Bank
1244 5th Street
Woodside, NY 11377

Dear Ms. Phillips,

I majored in mathematics at Woodside University, where I also worked as a research assistant, and I am confident that I would make a successful addition to your Economics Research Department.

In addition to my strong background in mathematics, I offer significant business experience: I worked in a data processing firm, a bookstore, and a restaurant. My courses in statistics and computer programming would prove particularly useful in an entry-level position.

I am attracted to Union Bank because of its rapid growth and the reputation of its Economic Research Department. My research shows that Union Bank will be in a strong position to benefit from upcoming changes in the industry, such as the phasing out of Regulation F.

I would appreciate the opportunity to interview with you at your earliest convenience. Should you require additional information, you can reach me at (718) 555-5555 between 9 a.m. and 5 p.m.

Sincerely,

Nancy M. Bennett

Enc. résumé

Standing Out from the Crowd

In order to stand out from all the other job hunters, it's important that you make your résumé and cover letter crisp and concise. Be specific in each of your résumé entries, and be clear about your job objective so that a potential employer will know what you're looking for. She or he won't be willing to sift through a bunch of unorganized data to find out. It's likely that the manager doing the hiring to fill the vacant positions is already working extra hours and won't have time to read lengthy cover letters and résumés. Employers are simply looking for experience that realistically fits the job being sought; it's best to save all the exciting details for the interview.

Now that you have the necessary information to create winning résumés and cover letters, you're ready to go out in the field and explore your top career choices. When someone asks about your background along the way, you'll be prepared—with your dynamite selling tools in hand.

CHAPTER 8

EXPLORING YOUR OPTIONS

"If what you want lies buried, dig until you find it."

ANY DOG

N ow that you've prepared résumés for your top three job choices, it's time to do field research so you can get a hands-on feel for each job. The idea is to explore as many directions as possible—talking to people, asking questions, making connections, asking for referrals, working on a trial basis in the field—so that you can make the best job choice possible for *you*.

Before committing time and money to a specific educational program or job, it's best to do some research and experimentation first. You can pick and choose the research strategies you're most comfortable with. In this chapter we'll explore six key methods: library and career center research, Internet research, informational interviewing, job fairs, job shadowing, and hands-on experience.

In the last portion of the chapter, we'll walk through a step-by-step decision-making process. Once you've explored your options, you'll be in a knowledgeable position to decide which of your top three job choices you'd like to pursue further. Field research can be lots of fun. You'll be amazed at the gold nuggets you turn up in terms of connections and opportunities, just by putting yourself out there.

Library and Career Center Research

To gain more in-depth knowledge about the specifics of your top three job choices, you can do an information search. Start by visiting a local library or career center that has good career resources, such as the following:

- National occupational classification and other occupational binders (e.g., *Occupational Outlook Handbook,* published by JIST Works)
- Books and videos on various occupations
- Career directories
- Alumni directories
- Association directories
- Magazines and newspapers
- Salary guides
- Computers with Internet access

In Exercise 8.1, make note of the important aspects of your top career choices. Use the points in the left column as a guide for your research. If you need help, ask the library or career center staff for assistance.

Internet Research

The Internet offers great ways to network with others who work in a field you're interested in pursuing. It's also a wonderful job-hunting resource. You can go directly to a Web site if you have the address. You can do searches on specific companies to learn more about them and decide whether you'd be interested in working for them. You can join mailing lists (e.g., listservs, newsgroups) that are focused on a certain occupation (e.g., writers, accountants) or work style (e.g., telecommuters). You can also do research by exploring subject directories or using search engines. The following sections give a brief overview of these methods to help you get started.

Internet Terms

The Internet has its own vocabulary. Here are a few of the most commonly used words, acronyms, and phrases that will help you feel more comfortable in cyberspace:

address An e-mail address, which can be a series of letters and/or numbers. Also called a Web site address or a URL.

chat An Internet feature that allows two or more people to communicate with each other in real-time. It's something like a telephone conversation, except with keyboards.

cyberspace A term that refers to the space that seems to exist within computers and computer networks.

e-mail Short for electronic mail.

Exercise 8.1

Occupational Exploration

Topic	Notes
Occupation to research	
Knowledge required	
Skills required to perform the job (e.g., computer, problem-solving)	
Duties and responsibilities	
Working conditions (e.g., hours, environment, physical demands, level of stress)	
Salary range	
Opportunities for advancement	
Related occupations	

FAQ Frequently Asked Questions, which are grouped together along with their answers and posted at Web sites to inform newcomers about specific topics.

FTP File Transfer Protocol, which is a system for transferring computer files (e.g., documents, programs, graphics) over the Internet.

home page The first or main page of a site on the World Wide Web, often leading to other pages. *Home page* and *storefront* are often used interchangeably.

hotlist A feature of most browsing software that lets you save the addresses of your favorite World Wide Web sites. Also called Favorites (in Internet Explorer) and Bookmarks (in Netscape Navigator).

HTML Hypertext Markup Language, which is a programming language used to make information compatible with the World Wide Web.

hypertext (or hyperlink) A highlighted word or underlined screen area on a Web page that enables you to jump from one page to another when you position a mouse on it and click.

Internet A powerful network of interconnected computer networks that share information and do not have a central authority.

Netiquette Internet etiquette—basically an informal attempt to establish rules for online conversations.

server A computer on the Internet that provides files and information to Internet users.

spamming Sending massive e-mail broadcasts to other Internet users that advertise a product or service, especially those advertising illegal money-making schemes. This includes "junk" e-mail, unsolicited e-mail, e-mail sent out in bulk, and excessive cross-posting in newsgroups.

timed out The equivalent of getting a busy signal or being cut off from the computer you're accessing. You'll often see a message such as "Access to this server has timed out."

URL Uniform resource locator, which is an electronic address on the Web. Any variation to this address (e.g., an extra space, a capital letter, a missing period or slash) will not work.

WWW World Wide Web, which is a collection of interconnected Internet sites that can be traversed through hypertext links. Web sites can provide text, graphics, input fields, audio, video, and access to a wide range of Internet features.

Directly Accessing a Web Site

If you know the Internet address of a site you wish to visit—let's say a company you're interested in knowing more about—you can use a Web browser to access that site. Many companies have their own Web sites, which provide job seekers with information to help them decide whether to pursue a certain position. Company Web sites often list current job openings.

To access a particular site, type the URL in the appropriate window. The URL specifies the Internet address of the electronic document. Every file on the Internet has a unique URL. Web browsers use the URL to retrieve the file from the host computer and the directory in which it resides. This file is then displayed on the user's monitor. Here are some Web sites and their URLs that you can access directly to help you get started:

- ◆ *Careers & Jobs:* www.starthere.com/jobs (This is a great source for links to career services and college job lines. Check out the cities listed under "Cybercampus" and "Riley Guide.")
- ◆ *Career Mosaic:* www.careermosaic.com (This source also provides a useful link to resources that job seekers use to find everything from job postings to résumé-writing advice.)
- ◆ *Boldface Jobs:* www.boldfacejobs.com (Want to check out your competition before conducting a job search? Review the résumés online.)
- ◆ *America's Job Bank:* www.ajb.dni.us/index.html (You can use this government-sponsored site to see what federal agencies are advertising jobs on the World Wide Web.)
- ◆ *Monsterboard:* www.monsterboard.com (Good source for links and direct job searches.)
- ◆ *CareerBuilder:* www.careerbuilder.com (Try the personal search agent at this site. It provides free, useful information via e-mail. You can also subscribe to a free magazine at this site.)
- ◆ *CareerPath:* www.careerpath.com (This interactive site allows you to choose a field, try keywords, and select newspapers, and then it gives you all the ads from those papers that fit your criteria. It's especially helpful if you're moving or are looking into trying a new area of the country—you don't have to subscribe to newspapers and search manually.)

Using E-mail, Listservs, and Newsgroups

E-mail, listservs, and newsgroups allow you to network with people working in a variety of fields of interest. Listservs are automatic mailing systems in which an e-mail message sent to a network address is automatically sent to all other members of the list. These lists work like journals in that submissions are accepted, sometimes edited, and then forwarded to subscribers. In order to subscribe to a list, you need to know the name of the list and its address. (Note that there is a difference between the address to which you send postings for the listserv list and the address you use for subscribing.)

You can join literally thousands of listserv lists. To keep them all under control, there are several collections of listserv lists. One good collection groups lists by topic: www.1soft.com/catalist.html.

A newsgroup is an electronic conference or bulletin board system. Newsgroups are similar to listservs except that the postings don't come into your account as e-mail messages. Rather, you have to go into a newsreader to view and respond to the messages. This allows you to access the messages at your convenience, and limits the number of messages coming into your account. Like listservs, there are thousands of newsgroups, on every subject conceivable, from sports and history to fan clubs and hobbies. A good site to access for groups and topics of interest is www.dejanews.com.

You can also scan the member profiles of commercial services such as America Online, Prodigy, and CompuServe to find e-mail addresses of people who work in a field you might be interested in pursuing. When you have their e-mail address, it's easy to write a brief introductory letter, explain your situation, and ask for a response.

E-mail messages are more likely than a cold call to generate a response because communication via computer is much less threatening to most people. Because the technology is still fairly new, it's exciting to get a computer message from somebody you don't know. If you converse through e-mail with a number of people, it could help open doors when your e-mail pen pals learn of a job opening in their industry.

Exploring Subject Directories

Subject directories such as Yahoo! are similar to card catalogs at the library. They file everything in categories such as careers, jobs, and computers. They consist of links to Internet resources relating to these subjects. Most directories provide a search capability that allows you to query the database on your topic of interest. When you find your topic in a Web directory, you're given a handful of key sites to start with. Directories offer a useful research tool to get the job done quickly. When you're looking for information on a general topic, a directory is the best place to start. Some of the most prominent and useful directories are the following:

- *Argus Clearinghouse:* www.clearinghouse.net
- *BUBL Link:* bubl.ac.uk.link
- *INFOMINE: Scholarly Internet Resource Collections:* lib-www.ucr.edu
- *Librarians' Index to the Internet:* www.lii.org
- *Scout Report Signpost:* www.signpost.org/signpost
- *The WWW Virtual Library:* www.vlib.org/home.htm
- *Yahoo!:* www.yahoo.com

Using Search Engines

Web directories cover only a small fraction of the pages available on the World Wide Web. That's where search engines like those found on AltaVista, HotBot, and Lycos come into play. You enter keywords relating to a topic, and the search engine retrieves information about Internet sites containing those keywords.

Among the most prominent and useful search engines are these:

- *AltaVista:* www.altavista.com
- *Excite:* www.excite.com
- *HotBot:* www.hotbot.com
- *Inference Find:* www.inference.com/infind
- *Infoseek:* infoseek.go.com

- *The Internet Sleuth:* www.isleuth.com
- *Lycos:* www.lycos.com
- *MetaCrawler:* www.go2net.com/search.html
- *MetaFind:* www.metafind.com
- *Northern Light:* www.nlsearch.com
- *ProFusion:* www.profusion.com

A good search engine to start with is Infoseek. It's quick and accurate, and it offers several field searching options, as well as simplified keyword and phrase searching. Infoseek clusters all your results from different sites. This makes it easy to scan for a variety of documents brought in by your search. The technique for formulating a search depends on the search engine you're using, so read the directions on how to conduct searches at each site. You'll find a wide variety of options available among the different search engines.

Informational Interviewing

We hear a lot about informational interviewing in relation to career changes and job searches, but what exactly is it? In a nutshell, it's research—gathering information by asking questions of those who are in our field/occupation of interest. It's a great place to start after you've done some library and career center research, or research on the Internet. We do informational interviewing all the time when we invest money or make big purchases, such as buying computers or cars—we question the "experts" to find the right fit for our needs. And it's no different when choosing a line of work.

Marilyn, Age 30

Remember Marilyn from Chapter 4, "Evaluating Your Training and Educational Needs"? She went through vocational school to learn the medical transcription business so that she could start a business at home and be able to care for her 3-year-old daughter, Tracey. Marilyn ended up starting a business as a result of an informational interview. She cold-called medical transcriptionists listed in the yellow pages to conduct informational interviews. One woman she called had too much work on her hands, and asked Marilyn if she'd be interested in helping her on a part-time basis to familiarize herself with the business.

"What started as volunteer work became a part-time job," Marilyn says. "I was able to learn the medical transcription business under an experienced mentor, and I was paid in the process. What could be better?" Eventually Marilyn went to work at home on her own, taking her knowledge base and a couple clients with her. "The first person I cold-called changed my life," she says. "I'm sold on informational interviews."

OUACHITA TECHNICAL COLLEGE

Informational interviewing is a great way to build a "beehive" of connections. As you meet and talk with a variety of people in potential fields of interest, they'll introduce you to others in the field. Before you know it, you'll have a strong network of contacts. All you have to do is ask for referrals each time you talk to someone.

Informational interviewing is also discreet job hunting. It's a way to uncover at least 50% of the job market because you'll be talking to people who work in your field of interest—people who are likely to know where the job openings are. Be cautious, however, and never use an informational interview to find out whether jobs exist in a company. Instead, relax and let the jobs and referrals come to you. And come to you they will—in abundance—especially if you use this opportunity to sell yourself.

What Is Your Goal?

The first thing to do before conducting informational interviews is to define your precise goal. Here are some reasons that you might use informational interviews as an effective strategy to gain information:

- To explore your interests
- To find a work direction you feel passionate about
- To learn more about alternative work arrangements
- To find a job by being in the right place at the right time, or by word-of-mouth
- To learn more about a school or training program you're considering (e.g., distance learning program) by talking to faculty members or students

Where to Conduct Informational Interviews

People who are successful in their careers like to talk about it. After all, they've been in your position at some point. Informational interviews give you the opportunity to get feedback on specific questions you have in relation to your top career choices. They can be done briefly by phone, e-mail, fax, or regular mail, or in person. Some say that in-person is best. I say whatever is most comfortable for you is best—especially when you're starting out—so that you can build confidence and gradually take things to the next step.

I prefer to do informational interviews by phone. Not only do I save time because I can forgo having to travel and dress up for the occasion, but I can have all my notes and résumés scattered about me so I can concentrate on the conversation rather than making "appearances." Besides, phone interviews are a less threatening way to build rapport, and they often lead to in-person interviews, so it allows for a smooth and gradual transition to the next step.

The Benefits of Informational Interviewing

I've conducted hundreds of informational interviews for a variety of reasons, and they're an excellent vehicle for learning and networking, not to mention a lot of fun. When you show a genuine interest in someone's work, you get a positive response. In fact, if the experience is positive, people don't hesitate to refer you to other people you can talk to, who may also be working in similar lines of work. Just ask. Here are some of the many benefits you'll experience in conducting informational interviews:

◆ They often reveal the hidden job market.

◆ They provide a way to learn about alternative work arrangements (i.e., part-time, temporary, job sharing, telecommuting, entrepreneurship, home business, portfolio careers, internships, volunteer work).

◆ You can learn the ups and downs of a particular profession.

◆ You can build credibility and rapport with people.

◆ People appreciate it—it offers them a chance to talk about themselves and their business.

◆ You can make a friendly contact—someone you can get in touch with again down the road.

◆ One person leads to another (building a network of connections if you always ask for a referral to someone else who might be able to help you).

◆ They build confidence.

◆ They enhance your communication and listening skills, and they teach you how to take control of a discussion.

◆ They prepare you for job interviews by giving you preliminary practice in a low-stress fashion and offer a nonthreatening way to get to know the decision makers in a company.

◆ They provide free research that's current and right at your fingertips.

◆ You might find a mentor who wants to help you find your way.

◆ They could lead to the creation of a "mastermind" group, consisting of people with similar goals and interests (for sharing of information, contacts, and resources; for problem solving, brainstorming, goal-setting, and life/career planning).

◆ They could lead to an actual position you're excited about or an opportunity to shadow someone on the job or do volunteer work that serves as a self-created internship that enables you to get hands-on experience in your field of interest.

◆ It's a proactive, rather than a reactive, way of conducting a search—you're taking control of your future, charting your course, and moving toward your ultimate goal rather than away from dissatisfying experiences.

◆ It's fun!

Who to Contact for Informational Interviews

The best way to get started doing informational interviews is to write down in your journal all the people you know who work in your top career choices. If you can't think of people, ask your friends or family members. The average person has at least 350 people in his or her circle of influence, so you're bound to find someone who qualifies. Think of everyone as a huge bank of referrals.

People you know are the easiest and least threatening to approach because they're "warm" leads. These include friends, family members, coworkers, fellow students, instructors, bosses, and people you come into contact with on a regular basis (e.g., at establishments you frequent while eating, shopping, having coffee, getting your hair cut).

After you get your feet wet and build confidence with warm leads, you might want to tap into other directions to find potential interviewees:

◆ *The Internet:* Use e-mail, listservs, and newsgroups.
◆ *Cold calls:* You can call companies you find in the yellow pages or in ads in newspapers or newsletters surrounding your occupation or area of interest.
◆ *Creative:* Brainstorm your own ways (e.g., contact authors of articles or books, attend seminars or networking events surrounding your field of interest).

If your career choice is uncommon or you have difficulty gathering names of people who fall within your parameters, take out your local yellow pages and search by business type (or a related business, if your interest is new or unusual).

Another way to find people working in different capacities is by attending a meeting put on by a professional organization—preferably one that's aimed at your field of interest. Call the organization's membership services and leave a message. When you get a return call, ask for a referral to members who work in your career(s) of interest. The representative will most likely give you names and numbers and, if the group meets regularly, invite you to attend one of the upcoming meetings. This will give you a chance to talk to people face-to-face.

Before you attend a professional meeting, create a 1-minute commercial about yourself and practice saying it ahead of time. Role play your 1-minute commercial with someone you know. You might say something like this:

"Hello, I'm _____. (They'll introduce themselves, and then you'll most likely have the opportunity to say your 1-minute commercial.) Most recently I have been (<u>in what industry or at what school, etc.</u>). My interests are strongest in _____ and _____, so now I'm looking for information about _____ and would like to meet people who _____. Do you know anyone I can contact who might be able to help me?"

If you have access to the Internet, consider joining newsgroups and mailing lists that are geared toward your job choice. You can e-mail your questions to the group and wait for responses. You can also participate in online discussions. The beauty of this type of research is that you only have to ask the question once, and it's posed to a targeted audience. Plus, these groups are free to join. Just be on the lookout for people trying to make a quick buck off you. Some people want to prey on people who are in transition and try to sell you the business opportunity of a lifetime.

How to Conduct Informational Interviews

"Call people and ask what you need to do," advises Jenny, a secretarial services provider. "That's how I got started. I called everyone in the phone book." When you cold call people from the phone book, be yourself. Generally, if you're friendly, you'll get a warm response. Always remember to smile. Have a script in front of you so you exude confidence. Also, have your questions handy in case the person has time to talk when you call. I have found this to be the case about 25% of the time. You might start the phone call with something like this:

> "Hi, my name is _____, and I'm interested in working in the field of _____. I saw your ad in the yellow pages (or I was referred to you by _____) and wonder if I could possibly ask you a few questions about your work at a time that's convenient for you."

If people are quick, gruff, or disinterested, don't push. Just move on to the next person. You want to talk to people who are as enthusiastic as you are. You're looking for the 20% of people who feel passionate about what they do and are eager to share.

After you establish a rapport with a person, set up a time for an informational interview or proceed with your questions if the time is right. Keep the interview brief (10 to 15 minutes) unless your interviewee has enough time for a longer interview. When you're done, let the person know how much you appreciate his or her valuable time and willingness to share. Confirm the person's address, and immediately send a handwritten thank-you note. This kind gesture will be remembered, and you will have established a warm contact with someone you might want to touch base with down the road. Some people will tell you to call again if you have questions, or to keep them posted on your progress. Do keep in touch. You might get a referral someday, or even a job.

Starting Off on the Right Foot

To help you get started on the right foot in conducting informational interviews, keep the following pointers in mind:

- Establish your goals in doing informational interviews.
- Create a 1-minute commercial about yourself.
- Generate a telephone script that feels comfortable for you when contacting people.

- Build a contact list of people you know.
- Contact your list of people to see if they know people who can help you meet your goals.
- Be persistent in making contacts, and don't give up.
- Be enthusiastic and polite. No one likes to talk to a "wet noodle."
- Jot down the phone numbers and addresses for recommended points of contact. Use index cards and keep a file of all the contacts you make for each of your top three job choices.
- Use scripts for initial phone contacts and the 1-minute commercial for in-person or phone contacts.
- Set an informational interview appointment with your point of contact (be prepared with your questions in hand to do on-the-spot interviews).
- Confirm your appointment the day before if you make it a long time in advance.
- Keep your interviews brief (15 to 20 minutes). If your interviewee wants to take longer and you're interested in what the person has to say, go with it.
- Always ask for a referral to someone else who might be able to help you further.
- Have your résumé on hand in case you're asked for one. It also makes it easier to talk about yourself on the phone if you have your résumé in front of you.
- Always send a hand-written thank-you note within 24 hours of the interview so you're fresh in the person's mind. Few people do this, and it makes a lasting impression. (You can even send an e-mail message and a hand-written note—this "double whammy" is quite effective.)

Informational Interview Questions

Here's a list of typical informational interview questions you can modify or add to. They focus on gaining knowledge about a particular job position. Keep in mind that you can use informational interviews to acquire information on just about anything, from work styles such as home business or temporary work to various school programs of interest:

- In your position, what do you do on a typical day?
- What are the responsibilities of your position?
- Does your position have variety?
- Does your position allow you to use your creativity?
- Do you have to work overtime, and if so, how much?
- Do you bring work home with you?
- Do you have to meet deadlines in your position? If so, are they realistic and is your workload pretty consistent over time?
- Does your position require travel, and if so, how much and how often?
- Is your position flexible in allowing you to set your own hours or to do work at home?

- Can this position be part time as well as full time?
- Would you be able to work on your own as a consultant in this position?
- What are the educational and/or experience requirements for a position like yours?
- What is the best way to obtain a position to start a career in this field?
- What are the salary ranges for various levels in this field?
- What aspects of a career in this field do you consider particularly good or bad?
- How much burnout/turnover do you see in this field?
- Is there a demand for people in this field? Do you view this field as a growing one?
- What is the future of this industry? Is it seasonal or driven by the economy?
- What do you wish you had known about this job before you accepted it?
- What kinds of benefits are provided by this or similar firms?
- Does your company encourage and provide support (e.g., financial) for continuing education and training?
- What professional organizations in this field can I join or visit?
- What trade journals or magazines do you recommend?
- What advice would you give to someone just starting out?
- Can you recommend others who are working in a similar position to yours that I can talk to?

Job Fairs

Job fairs bring together scores of employers that have job openings. It's an opportunity for you to make contacts galore, and gather accurate, wide-ranging employment information in a friendly, practically risk-free environment. Some job fairs target a particular field such as computer-related careers. More often, employers of all types—from both public and private sectors—are represented at job fairs. City, county, state, and federal employers cover an array of careers, including law enforcement, environment, personnel, recreation, and transportation. Private employers represent such fields as retail, medical, financial, insurance, telecommunications, and temporary services.

At a job fair, each employer is assigned a table or booth and has representatives to answer questions and distribute literature. Information is usually available on levels of training and education required for each job, necessary skills and abilities, salaries, and application and interview procedures.

Job fairs can be a great way to network, make contacts, and get answers to questions about a particular career path. You might meet someone you'd like to conduct an informational interview with or shadow on the job. You might turn up a great opportunity for an internship, volunteer work, or even a paying position in one of your fields of interest. You might find another direction that interests you—something you hadn't turned up in all your research thus far.

Janet, Age 43

Janet was burned out in her graphic design career. She'd been working in the field for 8 years and was ready for a career change. "I went to a job fair at a local college," Janet says, "and was intrigued by a company that was looking for people with artistic backgrounds and experience in multimedia programming." Janet had a strong art background and a degree in interior design, but had barely even turned on a computer, let alone programmed one. She says, "All my prior graphic artwork had been done by hand, and then I became a manager for several years, where I always delegated computer tasks to others. I was always afraid of computers and went out of my way to avoid them."

Janet enrolled in a multimedia certificate program at the local community college, where she excelled beyond her expectations. "I was amazed at how quickly I picked things up on the computer, considering the fact that I never used them before," Janet says. "Of course, I never worked harder in my life, and I had to scrimp to get by financially, but I enjoyed every minute of it. My boyfriend wasn't crazy about the long hours I put in, but I had the time and wanted to go for it. I was on a mission to complete the program and go out and give something back to society." And give back she did. During the course of her program, Janet created numerous Web sites on the Internet for various departments and faculty members at the college she attended. Her performance was so outstanding that she was given an award, written up in the local newspaper, and presented with more offers for work than she knew what to do with. Her story was the talk of the town. Janet says, "If I can do it, so can you!"

When you attend a job fair, don't show up unprepared. Here are some tips to help you make the most of the opportunity:

◆ *Investigate:* Speak with as many employers as possible. You don't have to worry about walking into someone's office and interrupting something important. This is your opportunity to conduct mini informational interviews. Make a note of the key questions you want answered. Choose from the sample list of informational interview questions in this chapter or create your own list. Take your time and make the most of the event. The employers are there to answer your questions.

◆ *Take notes:* You'll be talking to several employers, so don't rely too much on your memory. Bring a notebook or something on which to take notes. Bring a carrying bag or briefcase to hold any literature you pick up.

◆ *Be prepared:* Review all the information provided by the job fair producer and the attending companies. Company literature, job descriptions, and advertising by the company is usually available. If you're able to read it prior to meeting them, you'll be prepared and ready to make conversation and ask intelligent questions.

◆ *Sell yourself:* Be ready to sell your talents and skills, and the key features that make you unique.

◆ *Be assertive:* Show the employers that you're excited about getting started. Ask what you can do for the company as a worker, and then use that information to sell yourself. If you're genuinely interested, let them know! Say something like, "I'm quite excited about the possibilities your company offers, and I think I have the talent to help you achieve your goals. What do I need to do to arrange a second interview?" Smile a lot! A positive attitude is a winning attitude.

◆ *Present a positive image:* Present yourself in a professional, memorable manner. As the saying goes, you don't get a second chance to make a good first impression. Only a small percentage of hundreds of interviewees will stand out at the end of the event. Dress well, practice your best handshake, use an award-winning smile, and make eye contact!

◆ *Bring your résumé:* Bring your résumé, along with letters of reference from past jobs. You might bring samples of your work to have on hand when an employer expresses interest.

◆ *Collect business cards:* Business cards are easy to file, and they contain valuable information—a connection with someone you might want to contact again for an informational interview or an opportunity to shadow someone on the job.

◆ *Follow up:* Get the names of your contacts when you get applications, and then follow up with phone calls and/or letters.

◆ *Send a thank-you note:* If you find an employer particularly helpful, consider sending a thank-you note—it will help you be remembered and will establish you as a sincere person. Remind the employer of your qualifications, and reiterate your interest in pursuing a second interview. Few people follow through this way, so you'll stand out from the crowd.

◆ *Don't forget to network:* There are hundreds of other careerists onsite. Many of them have interviewed at other companies that might have an ideal position for you. Some might be leaving the ideal job for you. Share resources, leads, and ideas.

Job fairs are usually advertised in the local papers. Call your local chamber of commerce for information on upcoming events.

Job Shadowing

Job shadowing involves following someone around on the job to learn more about the true ins and outs of a particular position. It's an opportunity to see whether a job you're interested in is a good fit for your interests and capabilities, with no strings attached. During successful job shadowing, companies often share information on industry trends, samples of work, company safety and training manuals, evaluation processes, and sample hiring procedures, including application requirements, interviewing skills, and screening tests.

To find someone to shadow on the job, use the same strategies you use to find people who are willing to do informational interviews. Write or phone to make arrangements to meet with your contact for a half day or an entire day. Do your research on the company beforehand. Read the company's materials (e.g., marketing brochures, handouts), and gain as much knowledge as you can about the company's history and mission.

During your shadowing experience, ask questions similar to those you'd ask during an informational interview. Observe what the person does on a typical day, and take good notes about the expectations and requirements of the job, the work environment, the interactions with other people, and what you liked and didn't like about the position. You might even offer to help.

Your job shadowing experience will prove fruitful even if the job doesn't appeal to you as you had hoped. You might decide to end your information gathering as a result of what you learn from seeing the real thing. On the other hand, you might be so excited by what you see that you want to take the next step. This might involve an internship, volunteer work, or an entry-level position—possibly working for the same company with which you had the job shadowing experience.

Within a day or so of your job shadowing experience, write and mail a personalized thank-you note to your contact. Stress what you found helpful. Your contact will probably not be concerned with whether you decide to work in the field or not, only that your time together helped you clarify the career path you want to pursue.

Hands-on Experience

One of the best ways to find out whether your top three job choices are a good fit is to go out there and try them. Instead of searching for an entry-level position in the field, you can test the waters and get short-term hands-on experience through cooperative education, internships, and volunteer work. In addition to the job content knowledge you'll realize, you'll also gain the following:

◆ Referrals for future jobs through a network that you build
◆ Knowledge of the strengths and weaknesses of your work-related skills
◆ Development of communication, leadership, analytical, organizational, problem-solving, and creative skills
◆ Demonstration of your initiative and establishment of a track record for potential employers

As you get involved in some of these hands-on experiences, take time to reflect on your experiences. Write your thoughts in your journal to keep a permanent record:

- What is the work you're doing?
- How are you doing the work, and when?
- What interpersonal relationships help or impede your progress?
- What are you having fun doing?
- What do you find boring?
- Are your surroundings and interactions what you had visualized?
- Do you see other job opportunities that interest or suit you better?

Cooperative Education

Cooperative positions are full time, usually for 4 to 8 months, or even a year, and they provide you with the opportunity to have paid employment in positions that complement your academic program. The advantage for you is that you get a formal structure through which you can try out different jobs to see what you like and are good at.

With regular performance evaluations by your supervisors, you can acquire an employer's perspective on how well you measure up to the quality of other people working in that position. You'll also have an in with the various companies you work for, which will give you a competitive advantage if you decide that you want to pursue a particular job or work for a particular company.

Internships

An internship gives you the opportunity to have a structured experience combining work and learning in a field you're considering for your career. The work is usually unpaid, although you might find a position with a stipend or an hourly rate typical for that kind of job. The work can be part or full time. You should select an internship that will help you meet an immediate or a relevant objective. For instance, if you're looking for a career in human resources, an internship that offers the skills to screen and interview potential employees would be optimal.

There are many ways to locate internships, whether they're paid or volunteer, or whether they're for academic credit or not:

- Consult a college or county career center—ask professors and advisors for referrals.
- Talk to friends, colleagues, and former coworkers for ideas and possible contacts.
- Refer to internship books at your local library or bookstore.
- Surf the Internet to check on job sites or to conduct a keyword search on internships.
- Contact the personnel departments of companies that you have an interest in working for.

Volunteer Work

Volunteering allows you to check out many types of work. Some fields where volunteering is common are animal care, environmental preservation, health education, marketing, computer programming, and management (by working on a volunteer board of directors). Anyone can volunteer in practically any organization.

If you're not concerned with obtaining paid employment to learn about the work world and expand your employable skills, volunteering is beneficial. If you're interested in counseling, for instance, consider volunteering at a mental health clinic. Counseling is a burnout profession, and after volunteering, you might opt to get out before you get in. On the other hand, you might see that a job as a counselor is perfect for you.

Ask yourself what you'd like to give to the community, and what you'd like to get back in return. Civic and social organizations, whether local, national, or international in scope, provide opportunities for individuals to give something back to society. List three to five organizations or community needs that you're interested in helping. Interview the person in charge to determine whether your goals and theirs are compatible, and whether working together will meet both your needs.

When you've made a decision on where you'd like to volunteer, agree on the number of hours, the times you'll be available, your specific duties and responsibilities, any training you require, your out-of-pocket expenses, and so on. Having a written, signed contract can alleviate any misunderstandings that might jeopardize your reputation in the future.

Making the Decision

After you've had an opportunity to explore your options, you'll be in a better position to decide which of your top three job choices to pursue. Or maybe you've exhausted the top three, reached a dead end, and are ready to investigate the next three job choices on your list. Remember in Chapter 2, "Where Do You Want to Be?" where you prioritized your top career choices in your journal as a result of the jobs you turned up in Exercise 1.5, "Identifying Your Passion"? Now that you're a pro at research, if need be, you can investigate the next three job choices on your list much more quickly.

Somewhere along your research path for each job choice—talking to people, making connections, exploring your options—the answer will come to you. Sometimes the picture is so clear that you have no doubt about which way to go. Sometimes, with just a little thought, the decision comes easily. If you're having trouble making the decision because none of your choices really stand out as being the one for you, try the following exercises:

◆   Are areas of your personal life standing in the way of making your decision? Are there personal or financial things you need to take care of in order to feel right about pursuing any direction at this point? Look back on your list of needs in Chapter 6, "Getting Your Support Systems in Place," where you identified areas in need of support and Chapter 1, "Where Are You Now?" where you targeted areas in which you feel off-balance emotionally, personally, and financially. What can you do to correct things so that you feel free to move on?

◆ Imagine how things will turn out—in the immediate future and some years down the line—if you pursue each of your top three job choices. Which path are you most drawn to? Most major decisions produce a mixture of outcomes.

◆ Continue brainstorming and looking for alternatives while doing your research for each job choice. Keep your eyes and mind open. Don't worry about having too many choices. The one for you will come along, and you'll know when it's right and you're ready to make a commitment.

◆ List the pros and cons of each alternative. If you're still stumped after this process, listen to your intuition. At some level, you usually know which choice feels right for you.

◆ Consider your job choices in terms of your values, as you defined them in Chapter 1. If you want to live simply, then it doesn't make sense to seek a high-powered, energy-consuming job for which the only reward is money. If having a family and a career are important, then find a job, position, and/or work style that accommodate your needs. Allow your career choice to reflect your priorities.

If you're still unable to choose a career after exhausting all your career choices, you might want to take more time to gain confidence and clarify your values so that you're ready and willing to cross over from process to action. All the support and research in the world won't be sufficient to make the decision for you. If you decide to take a time-out and not take action at this point, you can always pick up where you left off at a later date. The important thing is that you will have arrived at a decision—to not make a decision yet. And that's okay. Time can be our best ally.

After you've made the decision on which career choice to pursue, the next step involves developing a good set of strategies that will take you there. This includes creating a detailed plan that has milestones with dates rather than general statements such as "I'll start job hunting next week." In Chapter 9, "Finding the Work You Love," we'll establish a game plan that will allow you to overcome obstacles and stay on track so that soon your dream will become a reality.

PART III

GOING FOR IT

CHAPTER 9

FINDING THE WORK YOU LOVE

"Opportunities multiply as they are seized."

SUN TZU

Y ou've zeroed in on one of your top job choices, so now it's time to put forth the effort to find the work you love. This takes a detailed plan that spells out your goals and how you'll manage your time, yourself, and your personal obligations. That's your sole mission in this chapter—to create a plan with milestones and time frames. We'll begin with a discussion of effective job search strategies that you can incorporate into your plan. The two keys to success in any job search are perseverance and the ability to handle rejection.

Job Search Strategies

There are a variety of ways to find the work you love. In this section we'll explore the most and least effective ways to find jobs. You might be surprised to learn that some of the most popular job-search methods, such as responding to newspaper ads and contacting employment agencies (especially for entry-level positions), are the least successful. After you review the following strategies, you can decide on one or two approaches that you'd like to begin with.

Two types of job searches can be conducted using the strategies that follow: reactive and proactive. A reactive search involves reacting to job postings, want ads, and recruiting activities. A proactive search is goal directed, involving networking and contacting people and organizations related to your field of interest.

The reason most job searches are prolonged or come to a standstill is that the job seeker doesn't know what type of job she wants. Staying reactive will limit you to posted opportunities (e.g., want ads, search firms, career fairs). On the other hand, staying focused and proactive will allow your goal-directed efforts to enhance the networking process and eventually pay off. I strongly urge you to take a proactive approach to job searching.

If you maintain a take-charge attitude toward your job search, you'll wind up exactly where you want to be rather than reacting passively (e.g., aimlessly flooding the market with your résumé, not following up on résumés you send to cold contacts). Put yourself in the driver's seat, continually ask for referrals to other people who can help you, and ask potential employers you contact for an interview. Assertiveness will win hands down over passiveness in paving the way to finding your dream job.

Newspaper Classified Ads

Few people find jobs by sending résumés to companies that advertise openings for positions in the newspaper. In fact, fewer than 3% of all job openings are advertised in classified ads. So many applicants apply for these positions that the competition is fierce. Even if you're well qualified for the position, your chances of being contacted for an interview are slim. Consider the fact that IBM receives about one million résumés per year. Needless to say, it's easy to get lost in the crowd. For this reason, the classifieds aren't the best method to focus on in your job search.

Barrie, Age 49

Barrie gave up a solid, unchallenging career to return to school, assume new debts, and start off on a search for her elusive calling. The longer it took, the harder it became for her to cope. "I was afraid of poverty," Barrie says, "of losing my self-confidence and self-worth." Changes in direction came through little clues, especially her dreams. She took many detours that, looking back, were like mini-workshops or training camps that gave her the experience she desired.

"A major breakthrough was when I broke my ankle the day after a tremendous dream about mountain gods! It helped me leave a dead-end job I hated and join a job club," Barrie says. "Because I was having such a hard time figuring out what to do, I thought teaming up with others would help me get focused. Ironically, I ended up becoming a coach and trainer for the members, and ended up staying in the club well beyond the average time. I created motivational courses, taught, and gave workshops to inspire the group. In the process, I learned new skills that I know will be a part of my next step, which will most likely involve starting a business of my own."

However, the newspaper classified ads offer a great pool of research that you'll want to take advantage of. Read through the ads in the local and national newspapers, as well as magazines. You might find a good lead but concentrate your efforts on gaining a broader picture of the current labor market. What fields are hot? Who is advertising, and for what kind of jobs?

If you come across a company of interest, research it further to see if it's a firm you might want to work for. Start a list of companies you eventually want to contact directly for a position. Make up a file folder for each company, where you can store their marketing materials and literature and any other bits of research you acquire on the firm.

Blind Ads

Generally, blind newspaper ads don't identify the employer. They specify that résumés be sent to a post office box. Blind ads are often legitimate; however, they are sometimes used for deceitful purposes (e.g., scams, agencies asking for payment in return for a job or access to the "hidden job market"). If an ad seems suspicious, cold, distant, or superior, trust your gut instincts. It's probably not a good place for you to consider working.

Job-Wanted Ads

Placing a job-wanted ad in the general newspaper is not likely to be effective. On the other hand, placing a job-wanted ad in a newsletter or magazine that targets the profession you're interested in might prove fruitful. Employers tend to read job-wanted ads in sources that target their trade rather than ads that are run in the general newspaper.

Job Banks

Job banks can be a good source for leads. Check out the job banks maintained by any group you belong to (e.g., alumni association). Employers are likely to be more receptive to you because you're part of the association. You can also search state job banks that contain thousands of job openings for anyone seeking a job.

Job Clubs

Job clubs can be an effective part of your job search. They're composed of groups of 15 to 20 people looking for jobs that get together regularly to swap leads, and offer support and motivation. An intense form of networking, job clubs are usually free of charge or require a minimal fee. The rule is that all members stay in the group until the last person gets a job. In order to get the support of the group, you must be willing to commit for the duration. Many churches, community groups, and libraries sponsor job clubs. Check with your state employment office as well.

Job Fairs

We covered job fairs in Chapter 8, "Exploring Your Options." Job fairs are also a great resource for finding jobs. You'll see job fairs advertised in the newspapers now and then. Even if they don't post any openings that interest you, there might be employers attending in your area of specialty that you'd like to make contact with. Contact your local chamber of commerce to request information on up-coming events. Many people get job interviews as a result of attending job fairs. The idea is to keep your eyes and options open.

Employment Agencies

Employers who want to find qualified job applicants often hire employment agencies. The agency's main responsibility is to satisfy the needs of the employer rather than focus on finding a suitable job for you. Generally, employment agencies are somewhat effective job search strategies for experienced professionals; however, only a small percentage of professional, managerial, and executive positions are listed with these agencies.

Employment agencies often place entry-level candidates in clerical positions. So unless you're interested in a clerical position, it's best to steer clear. It's not uncommon for employment agencies to send applicants out on job interviews for work they can't or don't want to do, and for a salary that's way below what they rightfully expect to make.

If you decide to use an employment agency in your job search, ask for referrals to reputable agencies from your friends and associates. Again, beware of scams. Any agencies that advertise 900 numbers you can call or that guarantee you a job or ask for payment before you've been placed are likely to be bogus.

Check the agencies you're interested in with the Better Business Bureau (BBB) at 703-276-0100 or www.bbb.com. Find out whether the agency is licensed, how long it's been in business, whether valid complaints have been lodged against the agency, and whether the firm was responsive to the complaints. If you're asked to sign a contract, you might want to hire an attorney to look at it first. Be sure to avoid any agencies that ask you to pay rather than be paid by the company that hires you.

Executive Search Firms

Executive search firms—also known as *headhunters*—are similar to employment agencies in that they don't work for you; they represent the companies that hire them to fill job openings. They seek out and screen candidates for high-paying executive and managerial positions. Unlike employment agencies, however, they generally approach qualified candidates rather than wait for candidates to approach them.

The most efficient way to use executive search firms in your job search is to send your résumé to agencies that specialize in your line of work. Executive search firms are not licensed. Check out the reputation of any firm you're interested in using with the Association of Executive Search Consultants (AESC) at 212-949-9556.

Temporary Agencies

As discussed in Chapter 3, "Choosing a Suitable Work Arrangement," taking on job assignments through temporary agencies gives you the opportunity to check out a job position or company to see if you're interested in pursuing it further. Temping also offers a great way to supplement your income during your job search and adds experience to your résumé.

When you're on a temp assignment, you can ask about job openings. You're already "inside," so it's not unprofessional to ask the person in the Human Resources Department or the head of the department who brought you aboard if any positions in your area of interest are open.

You'll find temporary agencies listed in the yellow pages. Start by sending your résumé and cover letter. Follow up with a phone call within a week or so to schedule an interview.

Internships and Cooperative Education Programs

Like temporary job assignments, internships and cooperative education programs offering work experience in your field of interest are two more ways that you can inquire about job openings since you already have your foot in the door with a company. If the firm doesn't have any positions available, ask whether it has heard of any opportunities elsewhere in the industry or if it can give you names of people to contact.

Job Counseling Services

Another useful job search option is job counseling services offered by your city or town. Check your phone book for listings in your area. Another good resource to consult is *The JobBank Guide to Employment Services* (published by Adams Media Corporation). It lists career counseling services as well as executive search firms, employment agencies, and temporary agencies located throughout the United States.

Nonprofit Agencies

Nonprofit community agencies frequently offer counseling, career development, and job placement services to specific groups such as women and minorities. Check your phone book for listings in your area.

College Career Centers

If you've attended college or are a recent graduate, or even if you've long since graduated, your school's career center is a great place to start your job search. You'll find up-to-date job banks and a wealth of information about every aspect of job hunting.

Also, you can contact the head of the department your degree is in and ask for a list of job leads. Because many academicians also work as private consultants, they have excellent contacts and are aware of what's currently happening in the field.

Community colleges offer both career guidance and local job listings. In the process of doing research at one of these places, you might learn that you're one skill or one course short of your dream job, so you're in the perfect place to satisfy that requirement.

State Employment Services

Your state employment service can also provide job placement assistance and career counseling. You pay for this service with your taxes, so don't be reluctant to ask for help. Check your local phone book for the office nearest you.

Computerized Online Networks

You might consider devoting some of your job search to registering with computerized online networks of job listings. Electronic databases compile information on job seekers to be searched and scanned by hiring companies. They usually charge between $30 and $50 to list your résumé for a year.

The Self-Placement Network, Inc., in New York sends résumés to 7 major online networks used by 16 million people in 145 countries. It also searches weekly for job leads among 110,000 listings in electronic job banks and classified ads put online by 55 major newspapers. Check with the local college, vocational schools, and professional associations in your field of interest to see if they're a part of an online job bank.

Spreading the Word in Cyberspace

On a more informal basis, you can network in cyberspace via listservs and newsgroups targeting your field of interest to see if anyone knows about a good job opening. We discussed this research strategy in Chapter 8, and it can be an effective job search tool. Rebecca Smith's eRésumés & Resources, at www.eresumes.com, offers a wealth of advice on how to post your résumé on the Internet via e-mail and electronic forms (also known as *e-forms*). The best thing about this job search method is that you don't have to leave home to do it.

Direct Contact

Better known as the "cold call," contacting a company cold with a cover letter and a résumé is one of the most effective job search methods. Therefore, we'll cover the how-to's of this strategy in the sections that follow.

Doing Your Homework

Throughout your job-hunting journey, you've been keeping a list of companies that interest you. Now it's time to do your homework by researching industry trends and acquiring information on the firms you're interested in working for so you can talk knowledgeably with the appropriate people. You can gain a lot of information about the industry through the Internet, industry trade journals, professional trade associations, and informational interviews.

To gain information on individual employers, check the references at your local library or bookstore. Ask the reference librarian for help in locating directories that list basic information about companies in your field of interest. Many fields such as law and advertising have industry-specific directories.

Here are a few publications that provide valuable information on hundreds of companies:

◆   Local chamber of commerce publications
◆   Dun & Bradstreet's Million Dollar Database
◆   *The Encyclopedia of Business Information*
◆   *Fortune's* latest 500

You can also ask for the *JobBank* books, a series of employment directories listing most of the companies with 50 or more employees in larger cities in the United States. These books provide the latest information on each company, including key contacts, common positions the company hires for, background required, and benefits offered. Many of these resources are available on CD-ROM, and you can easily print the information you need.

Check the *Guide to Periodical Literature* for any recent articles on companies and industries of interest. You can also learn about companies by calling them directly. Ask for the Human Resources Department or Public Relations, and tell them you'd like to learn more about the background of the company. Request marketing brochures, handout materials, or annual reports. This will show your genuine initiative.

Focusing on Smaller Companies

Rather than focus on the Fortune 500-type companies, you should concentrate on midsize firms (with 100 to 1,000 employees) and small companies (with fewer than 100 employees). These firms are where the majority of new jobs are being created every year, and they offer significant room for career growth. Small companies aren't as visible to the public as large ones, so competition for new openings is much less fierce.

Making the Initial Call

When you contact companies directly, it's best to have a telephone script that gives a clear and concise summary of yourself in about 30 seconds. You need to convey the kind of work you do (or want to do), your strongest skills and accomplishments, and the kind of position you're seeking. For instance

"Hi, I'm Mary Brown, and I'm a freelance writer and desktop publisher. I've been doing business writing for the past 3 years, and I have extensive experience in the development of desktop procedures and company newsletters. I read the article in last Saturday's newspaper about your company's recent expansion, and I am impressed with your innovative approach and fast growth. I recently sent you my résumé, and am wondering if you can use someone with my communications background to round out your team?"

Practice, practice, practice role playing your script with a friend or family member. Then call your list of firms and ask for the name and title of the person who manages the department that hires people in your field. You can then use one of two methods, depending on which is more comfortable for you:

◆ Confidently ask to speak to her or him. Deliver your script. Generate interest and ask for a meeting. If you get no for an answer, ask for the name of someone else who might be hiring or might know someone who is hiring in the field.

◆ Contact the department head with a cover letter and résumé, followed by a phone call a week later. Deliver your script. Generate interest and ask for a meeting. If you get no for an answer, ask for the name of someone else who might be hiring or might know someone who is hiring in the field.

Getting Past the Gatekeeper

One of the most challenging things about cold calling companies is getting past the gatekeepers—assistants and receptionists who screen all calls, making sure that only the important ones get to the top. When you ask to speak to the department head, you commonly hear responses like "she's busy," or "she's in a meeting." Here are some tips to help you bypass the gatekeeper and get to the head of the department you wish to reach:

◆ Ask when it's best to call back. Keep trying at that time every day for 5 days.

◆ Ask for your contact by first name, with confidence and authority, and you might get through immediately.

◆ Call while the gatekeeper is likely to be out of the office—early in the morning, at lunchtime, or afterhours. Employers often answer their own phones during offhours.

◆ Call the office of the vice president and ask who's in charge of your field of interest. Ask for the name of the person who gives you the point of contact to call. We'll say that Mary Kane from the vice president's office suggests that you contact John Myers, who is the head of the finance department. You then call back and ask for John Myers. If you reach John's assistant, tell her or him that Mary Kane from the vice president's office suggested that you contact John. Works like a charm!

◆ When asked what you're calling about, tell the gatekeeper that you've been corresponding with John Myers and he's expecting your call. (Don't say this unless you've sent a résumé and cover letter first.)

◆ Ask the gatekeeper for help. Explain that you've been trying to reach John Myers for some time and you wondered if she or he has any suggestions on how you can speak to him.

Cold calling can be challenging and frustrating because you hear a lot of no's. Keep revisiting those no's by phone or mail—you might eventually get a positive response. No matter how frustrated you get, keep smiling and dialing. Be friendly and polite to everyone you talk to. You never know who will open up the opportunity you've been searching for. Remember that each no brings you one step closer to the yes you've been waiting for.

Networking

Networking is the most effective job search strategy. As many as 86% of all jobs are found through networking. It's a powerful approach that can uncover opportunities galore. The beauty of networking is that it's an extension of informational interviewing. If you get comfortable making contacts for informational interviews, then networking for a job position will be a breeze. All you're doing is letting people know that you're looking for a job.

Much like making direct contact with companies, when you network with people in the field, make sure you've done your homework first. Get a good understanding of what's going on in your field of interest by reading trade journals and attending professional trade association meetings. Gain as much knowledge and background on the industry as you can while conducting informational interviews.

As when conducting informational interviews, when networking, the people you know are the easiest and least threatening to approach because they're warm leads. These include friends, family members, coworkers, fellow students, instructors, bosses, people you come into contact with on a regular basis (e.g., at establishments you frequent while eating, shopping, having coffee, getting a haircut).

After you get your feet wet and build confidence with warm leads, you might want to try the following:

◆ *The Internet:* Use e-mail, listservs, and newsgroups.
◆ *Cold calls:* Read the yellow pages, ads in the newspaper surrounding your occupation or area of interest.
◆ *Creative:* Brainstorm your own ways (e.g., contact authors of articles or books, attend seminars or networking events surrounding your field of interest).

If your career choice is uncommon or you have difficulty gathering names of people who fall within your parameters, take out your local yellow pages and search by business type (or a related business, if your interest is new or unusual).

Another way to find people working in different capacities is by attending a meeting put on by a professional organization. Call the organization's membership services line and leave a message. When you get a return call, ask for a referral to members who work in your career(s) of interest. The representative will most likely give you names and numbers and, if the group meets regularly, invite you to attend one of the upcoming meetings. This will give you a chance to talk to people face-to-face.

Create a 1-minute commercial about yourself and say it to every new contact you make. Practice role playing your 1-minute commercial with someone you know. You might say something like this:

"Hello, I'm _____. _____ suggested that I contact you. Most recently I've been <u>(in what industry or at what school, etc.)</u>. I'm very interested in pursuing a career as _____. I'm wondering if we could meet at your convenience to discuss the _____ industry."

If you get a negative response, ask for a referral: "Do you know anyone I can contact who might be looking for someone with my qualifications?"

If you have access to the Internet, you can join newsgroups and mailing lists that are geared toward your field. You can introduce yourself to each group and give your 1-minute commercial. Your goal is to try to get at least one referral or job lead from each contact. You'll find that this system works so well that you'll have more leads than you know what to do with. Just make sure that you keep following up with your leads (much as you should do when contacting companies directly) and send a thank-you note to any networking contacts that are particularly helpful. You'll be the first person that comes to mind if something new and exciting opens up.

Charting Your Course

After you've chosen your job search strategies, it's time to put them into action. The best way to do this is to set goals with time frames and establish ways that you'll help yourself stay on track. Finding the work you love *is* work, but it can be a lot of fun when you get into it. The more focused and determined you are, the more quickly you'll achieve your goals.

Setting Goals

Don't begin your job search haphazardly. Chart your precise course so you know exactly where you're headed and how you'll get there. How soon do you want or need a job? How many hours per week are you willing and able to devote to your job search? Job hunting can easily take more than 40 hours per week; consider all that goes into it—phone calls, research, interviews, thank-you notes, follow-up calls, and evaluating your progress and performance. Always assume that a job search will take months, not days or weeks, and plan accordingly.

To help reach your goals, create a job search contract. Ask someone close to you, who will be supportive—a friend, family member, or fellow job seeker—to sign it and hold you accountable to your goals. You can accomplish this by checking in with your friend each week, for instance, and discussing your progress. If your search is stalled and you need a jump-start, you can ask for feedback on possible solutions to get back on track.

Exercise 9.1 is a form you can use or modify to suit your needs. Notice that the contract focuses on results (e.g., number of follow-up calls made) rather than time spent (e.g., number of hours per day).

Exercise 9.1

Job Search Contract

1. I will begin my job search on _____.
   Date

2. Each week I will:

   ◆ Make _____ job search phone calls.

   ◆ Send _____ cover letters and résumés and/or job applications.

   ◆ Make _____ new network/job contacts.

   ◆ Ask for _____ job interview appointments.

   ◆ Aim to go on _____ job interviews.

   ◆ Assertively follow up on all job leads and networking contacts.

3. _____ will hold me accountable to the job search process.
   Name of individual

I will enthusiastically pursue the goals of this contract, managing my time effectively, so that I will successfully complete my job search and find a high-quality job that excites me by _____.
Projected date

Signature:_____

Date:_____

Managing Your Time

Another thing you need in order to conduct an effective job search is a job search schedule. Pick up one of those spiral-bound weekly appointment books at an office supply store. These books are great to use for logging your job search activities in a daily schedule that you can track weekly. They're usually broken

Twelve Steps to Time Mastery

1. Establish where your time goes by keeping a daily log of your activities.

2. Find out why your time goes where it does, and make the distinction between productive and nonproductive use of your time.

3. Minimize your time commitments by not taking on more than you can comfortably handle.

4. Prioritize your activities by sorting out what needs to be done from what can wait until later.

5. Cut down on time-wasting activities such as watching TV or being involved in long personal phone calls.

6. Be ruthless about getting rid of distractions by establishing boundaries, rules, and schedules.

7. Create systems to help locate information in a hurry. Searching for and handling information occupies up to 20% of your time, so efficiency in this area can make a big difference.

8. Establish daily, weekly, and monthly job search goals.

9. Break the procrastination habit by not putting off difficult or unpleasant tasks.

10. Use other people's time to your advantage. It's not time- or cost-effective for you to try to do everything yourself. Recognize personal and professional tasks that can and should be delegated (e.g., housecleaning, using online résumé posting services that target your industry), and you'll end up increasing your effectiveness.

11. Be creative with the use of your time. Traditional ways of doing things are often the least effective. In terms of your job search, this would ideally involve finding creative ways to stand out from other job seekers. You might, for instance, give a talk to a professional group in your career area of interest. This would put the spotlight on you and your abilities, and would likely turn up more leads to job opportunities than simply attending the meeting as a guest.

12. Add hours to your time budget by working smarter, not harder. This includes using technology to your advantage.

down by the quarter or half-hour, so you can specify what you'll be doing during any short block of time during the day.

Be sure to block out personal time, such as a lunch hour, breaks, or appointments. Treat your job search campaign like you're going to work every day. If you think you don't have the time to devote to job search activities, take a look at how your time is being spent in the journal exercise (Exercise 1.1, "Time Commitments") you performed in Chapter 1, "Where Are You Now?" See where you can make the time, even if it's only a couple hours a day to begin with.

Staying on Track

You should establish some boundaries and rules of conduct for yourself, your family, and your friends while you're in job search mode. Put everything in writing in your journal, and discuss it with the people you care about. Elicit their support by asking for their cooperation. This will help you stay accountable and on track. It will also let you and others know what to expect. Here's a sampling of personal rules and boundaries you might consider:

- Set up a home office—preferably one that's private.
- Dress up, go to the "office" each day, and work at getting a job.
- Establish regular office hours.
- Work during your peak energy periods.
- Take periodic stretching breaks.
- Use rituals to ease in and out of your workday (e.g., read the newspaper and drink coffee in the morning, before starting your job search activities, and create a to-do list at the end of the day to transition out of your job search role).
- Create a daily job search activity to-do list of items that you can check off as you complete them. (You can use your weekly calendar for this purpose.)
- Keep a file of all job contacts you'd like to pursue further. After each meeting or networking event, take some time to enter your business cards into a database so you can access a number easily—by type of business, for instance—if you forget someone's name. Then you can store the cards in a card file box or save space and throw them away.
- Follow up religiously with all contacts.
- Don't do any housework during office hours.
- Don't do any personal computer activities during office hours that aren't job search related (e.g., personal e-mail, Web surfing, games, online chats). To establish a boundary with this, use separate screen names or e-mail addresses for business and personal use. Log on to the computer using your business address during your job search working hours. Then you won't be constantly enticed to check your personal e-mail and you won't be available to friends who are looking to catch you online to chat.
- Don't watch TV during office hours.
- Don't take or make personal phone calls during office hours.

What happens when your children don't understand that you're home but not available because you're actively conducting your job search? It's imperative that you teach your kids to respect your job search time and space. The best way to do this is to set limits and guidelines.

Setting Limits and Guidelines with Children

Depending on the ages and personalities of your kids, what kind of rules of order can you realistically and fairly expect them to follow? You want to be able to achieve your daily job search goals but at the same time allow for a family-friendly environment. Here are some guidelines you might establish with your children:

- No TV or stereo allowed during job search hours.
- Unless something is urgent, don't interrupt.
- Don't touch office equipment without asking.
- Don't answer the phone during job search hours.
- Dress and feed yourself in the mornings.
- Pack your lunch each day.
- Do your daily chores without prompting or complaining.
- Do your homework without prompting or complaining.
- Keep noise levels down during work hours.
- Control noisy pets.

Helping Your Children Understand

There are many effective ways to help your children understand and respect your job search commitments. Depending on your child's age and personality, try the following strategies:

- *Foster empathy:* If your children constantly interrupt, explain to them that you need focused time to work. Involve them by asking for help with a solution to your problem.
- *Have mutual respect:* Be clear with your children about your needs and encourage them to do the same. It's critical that you have mutual respect and that you take each other seriously, but understand that it takes time because kids tend to forget rules when they're excited. Even if your kids interrupt, don't make the mistake of taking out your job search frustrations on them.
- *Bring it to their level:* Communicate at your child's level. "The toddler stage is the hardest," says Wendy, a newspaper editor who decided to leave the newspaper she was working for to start a home-based freelance writing business. "That's when you've got to start setting limits. It takes time, though. You need to tell them, 'Look, I'm busy, I can't read to you right now. You have to respect that Mommy has to do this. If you want these nice toys, you have to leave Mommy alone so she can make the money to buy these nice toys.'"
- *Offer explanations:* Don't just lay down the law; explain the rationale behind any rules or guidelines you implement. You might have to do a lot of explaining at first, but give your children the gift of time.
- *Post your job search schedule:* Always let your children know your job search schedule. Put it on paper, read it to your kids, and post it in a prominent place. If your children interrupt during your work hours, remind them of your schedule. Tell them you'll be with them as soon as you take your next break or finish for the day.
- *When desperate, bribe:* Mary, an aspiring insurance agent and mother of two young boys, admits that sometimes when she's on the phone and

her son interrupts or gets noisy, she resorts to bribery. "If you don't say a peep while Mommy's on the phone, I'll play a game with you on my break," says Mary.

Maintaining Motivation

A job search campaign can be grueling work—no doubt about it. Cold calls and rejection certainly are not easy. Understand that your motivation to keep at it will probably run in cycles. Fortunately, there are many things you can do to give your morale a regular boost:

- ◆ Accept that your job search might last a long time. If it ends sooner than expected, you get a pleasant surprise, but if it takes some time, you are mentally prepared.
- ◆ Eliminate distractions by establishing rules and boundaries.
- ◆ Set clearly defined, achievable career goals. Don't take on more or less than you're able and willing to do.
- ◆ Visualize and write down your reasons for working, besides making money (i.e., clarify your personal goals and dreams).
- ◆ Stay away from negative people who don't support your efforts.
- ◆ Don't personalize rejections. Realize that rejection is a part of life and welcome it, knowing that you're one step closer to success. Find someone to share your job hunting war stories with, and quickly move on.
- ◆ If you're tired, take a nap or get some fresh air and exercise.
- ◆ When you get discouraged and don't feel like job hunting, don't. Take a break and do something you enjoy. Allow yourself to rejuvenate.
- ◆ Vary your activities when you're bored with job hunting.
- ◆ Don't deal with personal problems while performing your job hunting tasks. Set aside specific times for taking care of personal issues that are upsetting you.
- ◆ Take care of your health and morale. Reward yourself regularly for meeting your job search goals. Go to an occasional afternoon matinée or have a dinner out.
- ◆ Remember that perseverance is the key to success!

Tracking Your Progress

To ensure that you stay on track with your goals, keep a log of your weekly job search performance in a notebook that holds your job search contract. You might use a form like the one in Exercise 9.2.

Adjusting Your Course

Compare your weekly performance with your goals on your job search contract to see whether you need to adjust your course. If you're falling off track, look at how you're spending your time. Are your goals too ambitious? If so, tone them

Exercise 9.2

Weekly Job Search Performance Form

The week of _____
                            Date

This week I:

- ◆ Made _____ job search phone calls.

- ◆ Wrote _____ job search/cover letters.

- ◆ Sent _____ cover letters and résumés to potential employers.

- ◆ Completed _____ job applications.

- ◆ Completed research on _____ companies.

- ◆ Attended _____ professional association meetings, conferences, or other networking opportunities.

- ◆ Followed up on _____contacts, _____ referrals, and _____ leads.

- ◆ Received _____ invitations to a job interview.

- ◆ Went on _____ job interviews.

Next week I will:

- ◆ Make _____ job search phone calls.

- ◆ Write _____ job search/cover letters.

- ◆ Send _____ cover letters and résumés to potential employers.

- ◆ Complete _____ job applications.

- ◆ Complete research on _____ companies.

- ◆ Attend _____ professional association meetings, conferences, or other networking opportunities.

- ◆ Follow up on _____contacts, _____ referrals, and _____ leads.

- ◆ Aim to go on _____ job interviews.

- ◆ Actively follow up on all job leads and network contacts.

Here is a summary of my progress this week in relation to my job search contract:

_____

_____

_____

down a bit. Does your motivation need a boost? Take a look at the tips in the preceding section. Talk to the person who agreed to hold you accountable. If your job search isn't producing results, check the following:

◆ Are you sending out enough personalized letters and résumés to prospective employers?

◆ Are you following up by phone with every résumé submitted?

◆ Are you contacting smaller companies that are less known and sought after?

◆ Are you qualified for the positions you're seeking?

◆ Are there courses or seminars that will make you a more competitive candidate for the job you're seeking?

◆ Are you networking as much as possible to keep new contacts coming?

If what you're doing isn't working, try new approaches. If your letters and résumés aren't getting results, try new formats. If you're way off the mark, ask yourself, "Do I really want the job I'm aiming for?" Do a gut check, and explore why you're not following through with your goals. Write down your feelings in your journal. Freely express whatever comes to mind, even if it's anger and frustration. Let it out so that you can relieve stress and move on. No one said that job hunting is easy!

Amy, Age 36

A single mom with a 4-year-old son, Amy panicked when she was laid off from her position as an administrative assistant, working for a large aerospace firm. "I needed a job quickly," Amy says. "I was willing to do whatever it took to land a position fast." When I talked with Amy, she asked what would be the quickest route to finding a job. I told her cold calling companies directly and networking for contacts in her field of interest. Her response? Reluctance. She said, "I've never made one cold call, and I'm not a social butterfly. I'm terrified of rejection. Besides, I'd be embarrassed and feel like I'm begging."

I asked Amy if she'd ever struck up a conversation with a stranger and ended up sharing a helpful tip on a great restaurant or place to shop. "Yes, with no problem." I asked how it made her feel. "Good about myself because I helped someone." I told Amy that she would be doing others a favor by giving them the opportunity to share, simply by asking if they know someone who has an opening for an experienced administrative assistant. "That's a great way to look at it," she said. "I'd be happy to share whatever connections I have with someone who is actively and responsibly seeking a particular position. In fact, I'd want to hire them myself if I could."

Two weeks later, Amy was gainfully employed as an office manager for a smaller firm, making 30% more money annually. "As soon as I learned to love the word *no*," she says, "I got the job."

Handling Rejection

Active job search methods encourage you to step out of your comfort zone and risk being rejected. But remember what we said about comfort zones in Chapter 5, "Expanding Your Comfort Zone"? With the risk comes opportunity, so don't let rejection get you down. It's your key to success.

The One-Month, No-Nonsense Job Search

You can use the "1-month, no-nonsense job search" approach in any situation where you're faced with a continual stream of no's, and you'll forever view rejection in a different light.

How many contacts would you have to make to find your dream job? 25? 50? Let's just say hypothetically that you'd have to talk voice-to-voice to 100 different people in your field of interest to land a good position. You might do this by cold calling heads of departments at companies you're interested in working for, talking to someone in your field of interest at a networking event, or talking to a friend or colleague who works in the industry.

In other words, 100 no's would lead to a job offer in your field of interest. Let's spread that out over a 1-month period—we'll say 4 weeks. That's 25 new contacts you'd have to make each week, which equates to 5 new contacts per day if you're job searching 5 days per week and rejuvenating on the weekends.

To continue with this scenario, let's say you're searching for a job with a potential salary of $30,000 per year. If it takes 100 new no's to find the position, you're earning $300 per no. If you're getting 5 no's per day, you're earning $1,500—not a bad day's work in anyone's book!

So every time you hear a no throughout your job search, quietly say to yourself, "Yes! Thank you," and pat yourself on the back because you just earned $300. You'll feel better and better, and in less than 1 month, you'll be earning your $30,000, and *no* will be the most exciting word you've ever heard.

CHAPTER 10

THE ART OF JOB INTERVIEWS

Whatever you can do, or think you can, begin it.
Boldness has genius, power, and magic in it."

JOHANN WOLFGANG GOETHE

You're all set. You've got a job search plan all mapped out, and you've established rules and boundaries to manage yourself and your personal responsibilities so you'll stay on track. Now it's time to talk about job interviews and job offers. Isn't that what all this research and planning is leading up to?

In this chapter we'll discuss how presentation and preparation are the keys to successful job interviews and job offers. We'll talk about what to do before the interview and during the actual interview—how to present yourself as the ideal candidate, how to respond to typical questions, and what questions to ask so that you can screen companies to see if you'd like to work for them. We'll also cover negotiation strategies for handling benefits, salary requirements, and job offers.

Preparation and Presentation

Successful interviews are directly related to the amount of time and energy you invest in preparation beforehand. This involves everything from your knowledge of the company, the clothes you wear, and your attitude, to emphasizing how your skills, experience, and qualifications closely match the needs of the company.

The bottom line is that employers want to know whether you're the right person for the job and whether you're enthusiastic about working for their company. If you convince employers that the answer to their concerns is an emphatic yes, then you stand a good chance of getting a job offer. The following sections offer some tips to help you stand out as the winning candidate.

Researching the Company

In Chapter 9, "Finding the Work You Love," you conducted employer research to see if you'd be interested in working for various organizations of interest. It's also important to research companies in preparation for interviews—but not so you come across as a know-it-all.

Shelly, Age 24

Shelly had just gotten her bachelor's degree in business, with an emphasis in marketing. She was excited about all the job opportunities she could explore. She was interested in an entry-level marketing position for a local company. She concentrated on networking with people in the industry. One of her leads resulted in a job interview with a very reputable medium-sized company that was a 5-minute drive from where she lived. She was eager to make a good impression. Prior to the interview, her friends and family told her to go to the library and study the firm and amass an array of facts and figures to impress the interviewer with her knowledge of the company and the industry.

Shelly researched the company thoroughly and read that the company would be launching a new product. During the interview, she asked the recruiter how the new product campaign was going. Shelly learned that although it seems logical to make a good impression by showing off how much you know, you might be setting yourself up for a fall.

"I was completely thrown off when the interviewer told me that the new product campaign was pulled from the shelves shortly after its introduction," Shelly says. "To top it off, the interviewer happened to be the supervisor for the product introduction, and I could tell he was annoyed at me for asking about the failed effort. The mistake I made was in coming across as a know-it-all. The information I read wasn't up-to-date. You have to be careful not to say things that might be inaccurate or rub the interviewer the wrong way. That blunder blew my chances for that position and maybe even with that company, but it taught me to listen attentively and to answer the questions in a way that will make my qualifications fit the job description. I don't need to show off my knowledge of the company. If I've done my homework, the knowledge will naturally surface throughout the conversation."

The more you know about the company and the position you're applying for, the more confident you'll be during the interview. Learn as much as you can about your prospective employer. What does the company make or what services does it offer? What are the industry trends, technological breakthroughs, and the company's rank in relation to its competitors? Here is some of the information you'll be looking for:

- History and potential growth for the employer and the industry
- Restructuring, downsizing, re-engineering activities
- Products and services
- Location(s)
- Annual sales for past year(s) compared to industry trends
- The employer's major competitors
- Ownership of the organization (and the impact of family ownership on possible advancement potential)
- For nonprofit organization—its purpose, funding, clientele, and functions/activities
- Management style and corporate culture
- Number of employees
- Organizational structure, working climate/atmosphere, and workload
- The amount of subordinates' participation in decision-making activities
- Training and development programs
- Typical career path
- Promotion policy
- Use of technology, and amount and type of equipment
- Company benefits offered to employees
- Salary range for the position you're interviewing for (Check with professional associations or trade groups, and the library. Ask friends in the field or anyone working at the company you're interviewing with. Also, call the local office of the U.S. Bureau of Labor Statistics.)

There are a variety of resources you can access for information on a company:

- Packets prepared for a company's stockholders
- Annual reports (which include a company's financial, marketing, and product reports)
- A prospectus (which includes the names of the CEO and major players)
- A 10K report (which contains a company's historical and financial information)
- A recruitment package or any other information for job seekers
- A company newsletter or brochure
- Trade magazines
- Trade associations
- Libraries (e.g., business directories, recent articles written about the company)
- The chamber of commerce
- Career centers
- Someone who works at the company
- The company's Web site

Learning as much as possible about a company before the interview will not only make you feel confident, but it will help you know exactly what the company needs and wants, and you'll be prepared to demonstrate how you're the best candidate to meet those needs. Because most interviewees skip this very crucial step, the interviewer will appreciate your ability to converse knowledgeably about the company. The time you take to do your homework will easily pay for itself in interview success.

Collecting References and Letters of Recommendation

Prior to your interview, you need to collect three to five references, with at least two of these being professional references (e.g., previous employers, business associates). You can also get valuable references from teachers, professors, volunteer committee heads, and friends who are well respected in the business arena. Don't list family members as references. Also, don't list references on your résumé. It's best to have references available on a separate sheet (that matches your résumé) for an interview.

Before you give out names, call and ask for permission to cite your chosen people as references. Create a list of people who agree to give you a positive reference; the list should include each reference's job title, company name, and work address and phone number. At the end of your job search, you should send each reference a thank-you note and let them know about the great position you landed. This will keep your connections up-to-date and the doors open. You might want to contact these references again in the future if you decide to change companies.

Besides references, it's helpful to have two or three letters of recommendation on hand at job interviews. These should be from professional connections (e.g., former bosses, well-respected colleagues in the business arena). Ask that letters of recommendation be sent directly to you rather than to potential employers. You can make multiple copies and have them available at job interviews. Follow up with a thank-you note to anyone who writes a letter of recommendation for you.

Role Playing

Get a stack of about 20 index cards and write a typical interview question on each card. (See the list of typical interview questions and how to respond, later in this chapter.) Develop solid answers to these typical questions. Shuffle the cards, and practice responding to them until the words flow easily.

Answer the questions in front of a mirror, paying attention to your posture and body language. Are you relaxed and composed, or stiff and uptight? Smile periodically. It will let the interviewer know that you're calm and confident. Record your responses on a tape recorder. When you play it back, think about ways that you could improve your responses. Are you able to formulate answers quickly? If not, keep practicing.

Perhaps the most effective interview preparation strategy is to find a friend or family member who's willing to play interviewer with you. Role play a mock interview and ask for reactions to your body language, your way of expressing yourself, and your aura of self-confidence. Ask for feedback on your speech. Do you articulate well or do you mumble? Is your voice enthusiastic or monotone? Try to make adjustments that improve your presentation.

If you have little nervous habits such as twirling your hair, talking too fast, or tapping your pencil, it will help to have someone point these out in advance so you can keep the behavior at bay during the real interview. The goal is to practice enough so that you can confidently walk into your interview and present a calm and polished impression to your potential employer.

Presenting Yourself as a Professional

How do you want to present yourself during the interview? Evaluate your look— your hair and the clothes you wear. What might be fitting for an advertising agency could be inappropriate for an engineering firm. When you have a sense of the kind of company you're interested in, attend meetings or workshops of the professional associations for the industry to see how members dress. You can also call the personnel office of the company you'll be interviewing with and ask anonymously about the dress code. If you know someone in the field, ask for advice.

Put together a professional-looking dress or suit with low-heeled shoes. In more conservative industries such as law or banking, a suit is a safer bet. In more creative industries such as graphic design or publishing, a more informal look reflecting your individuality might be more appropriate. Make sure your clothes are clean, well-fitting, and pressed, that your hairstyle is neat and business-like, and that your shoes are clean and attractive. Believe it or not, people are often judged by their shoes. Also, don't wear excessive jewelry, makeup, or perfume.

Timing It Right

Don't arrive late for your interview as many job seekers do. Give yourself plenty of time to travel to your destination and pull yourself together before the interview. This means allowing time to deal with traffic, slow lights, getting lost, and finding a place to park. Arrive at the interview site at least 20 minutes early so you can go to the restroom. It's a good idea to tend to loose strands of hair and look for undone buttons or zippers and runs in your nylons.

If you've never been to the interview location before, visit the place ahead of time so you know exactly how to get there, find the building, and locate parking. This means investing extra time, but it will make your travel to the interview site much less anxiety provoking because the dry run will help you know what to expect.

Acing the Interview

The interviewer you meet with might be a department head, a project director, or a number of people familiar with various aspects of the job. A group of staff members, for instance, might act together as an interviewing committee.

Sheila, Age 58

Sheila decided to interview for a position as a stock analyst with a new brokerage firm. She felt she had reached a dead end and was rather burnt out in her current job as a stockbroker, but realized that her qualifications and background were perfect for the stock analyst position. During her second interview with the same firm, she felt calm. The interview appeared to be going well, and Sheila thought she was making a good impression. She answered the questions in a relaxed and rambling style. When the interview was over, she shook hands with the recruiter and exited with a smile.

"I didn't get the job," Sheila says. "They must have thought I was the nicest person in the world, but after the interview was over, I realized that I didn't indicate in any way that I wanted the job. I think I came across as unexcited about the position. I could kick myself, but next time I'm going to give strong clues that this is the job for me—'I can and want to do this job.'"

In a small business, the owner might interview you briefly and casually. Large corporations, on the other hand, often employ professional interviewers or recruiters.

An interview can be conducted in a structured format, where the recruiter asks a prescribed set of questions, seeking brief answers. Or it can be unstructured, where the recruiter asks more open-ended questions to encourage you to give longer responses and reveal as much as possible about your qualifications and aspirations.

Regardless of the interview format, with practice and preparation beforehand, you can walk into any interview and get the job. Here are some additional pointers to ensure that you interact naturally with the employer and convey the image you want to project:

- Get a good night's sleep before the interview.
- Be punctual. Arrive at least 20 minutes early to collect your thoughts, observe the working environment, and double-check your appearance in the restroom.
- Memorize the interviewer's name and use it once or twice throughout the interview. Make sure to get a business card from the interviewer.
- Don't smoke or chew gum during the interview.
- Bring a watch, a pen and pad of paper for taking notes, extra copies of your résumé, and a briefcase or portfolio of your previous work (e.g., sketches, designs, writings). Carry these items in your left hand so that you won't have to juggle them to shake hands.
- Avoid carrying a purse.
- Be friendly. Smile before being greeted and acknowledge introductions with a firm handshake.

◆ Maintain good eye contact and smile when appropriate. This conveys confidence and calmness to the interviewer.

◆ Sit comfortably and alertly, without slouching. Lean slightly forward, toward the interviewer. Don't put anything in your lap that you'll be tempted to play with. Keep your briefcase, note pad, and portfolio at the side of your chair, within easy reach.

◆ Don't fidget. Avoid displaying nervous habits. If the interviewer is trying to be funny, don't be too nervous to laugh.

◆ Be enthusiastic and animated in your responses. Remember that low tones convey confidence and competence; high tones convey insecurity.

◆ Pay attention to the interviewer's nonverbal cues. Watch for signals indicating that your responses are too short or too long. If the interviewer becomes silent after your responses, your answers might be too brief (or perhaps the interviewer is testing you to see how comfortable your are with silence, or maybe she or he just ran out of questions). If the interviewer looks away while you're talking, wrap up your answer as quickly as possible.

◆ Know your past achievements and relate them to the company's needs. Talk about opportunities and successes, not limitations and failures. Never downplay your achievements. Always project a positive, upbeat attitude.

◆ Don't criticize your former employers or coworkers, under any circumstances.

◆ Don't bring up salary requirements during the interview. This is one of the main reasons prospective jobs are lost. Discussing monetary needs before the potential employer has a chance to understand whether your qualifications match the needs of the position conveys that you're placing your own interests over those of the interviewer or the company.

◆ Focus on what you can do for the employer. It's not true that employers only hire candidates with experience in their industries. Applicants from other industries who are intellectually curious, ask questions, see options, and volunteer applications for solving problems can be just as desirable.

◆ Avoid interrupting the interviewer midsentence or tuning out of the conversation.

◆ Answer questions truthfully.

◆ Avoid using trite expressions.

◆ Answer all questions clearly and concisely. Be direct in your responses. Don't ramble on, giving long-winded answers, or go off on unrelated tangents.

◆ Think quietly before you speak. A pause to organize your thoughts before talking is quite acceptable.

◆ Give descriptive examples or proof whenever you can throughout your interview. Try to paint a visual picture that the interviewer will remember. The true stories you tell about yourself will differentiate you from the other applicants.

- If you feel you want the job, let the interviewer know that you're interested in the position. Don't seem overly anxious, but give strong messages that this is the job for you, such as "I can do this job."
- Be an active listener. Concentrate on what the interviewer is saying rather than on formulating what you'll say next. If you've practiced ahead of time and if you relax, your answers will flow naturally. If you're in doubt about what the interviewer wants you to discuss, ask for clarification.
- Remember that more than 90% of what we communicate is conveyed nonverbally. This is especially true of first interviews with companies. The actual words spoken account for only about 6% of the first impression. If you radiate a positive and confident presence in your posture, manner, and expressions, you'll have won the interviewer over.
- Ask intelligent questions about the company and the job, based on your research.
- Thank the interviewer as you're leaving and again in a follow-up note by mail.

Responding to Typical Interview Questions

The following is a list of typical interview questions or probing statements that you can expect and prepare for, along with winning strategies to help you formulate your responses. Remember to practice your responses beforehand, until they're clear, concise, and free flowing:

- *Tell me about yourself.* Spend about 1 or 2 minutes answering this question. Talk about the reasons you feel your skills and background are a good fit for the job and how you see your future with the company. This is your golden opportunity to talk about yourself, so don't ramble aimlessly, but use it advantageously to start the interview on the right foot.
- *Why are you switching careers?* It's best not to give a trite answer here, such as "I wanted to try something new." Instead, explain how your skills, personality, and goals are more suited to the new career or that you want to add something to your experience that will help you achieve a longer-term goal.
- *Your résumé indicates that you've been in and out of the workforce quite often. What were you involved with in those periods?* The interviewer is probably posing this question out of concern that you'll leave after being trained for the job or that your skills are not up to speed. After answering the question, offer assurance that you plan to stay with this job and that you're qualified to handle the job. Know your abilities as they relate to the requirements of the job so that you can clarify this for the interviewer.
- *Why did you leave your last job?* (or *Why are you leaving your present job?*) Don't offer personal or emotional problems as an answer. Don't criticize your former (or current) boss, coworkers, or company. Many people leave their jobs because they don't like their employers. If your

boss or the conditions of your present (or most recent) position were unpleasant, few employers will want to hear it. Instead, focus on the business reasons for leaving. If your boss was controlling or your co-workers were disagreeable, a move can provide the opportunity for growth in a variety of ways. You might say that you've reached a point where there's little potential for growth or you've learned your job well and want to challenge your abilities in a growing (or larger or more innovative) company. Express appreciation for what you learned in your most recent (or current) position and what you'd like to learn with the new company. Turn it into a positive statement. If you're looking for a job because of factors beyond your control, such as layoffs or office closure, be honest but brief. Tell the interviewer, for instance, that the organization you're working for is being reduced in size and you're interested in using your skills and experience to benefit their company. If you were fired because of a conflict with a boss, however, you might be better off telling the interviewer rather than having that person find out through industry gossip.

- ◆ *Why do you want to work for our company?* If you've done your research on the company prior to the interview, you'll have no problem answering this question. Point out some positive aspects of the company's mission, policies, procedures, products, or services that you can discuss with enthusiasm. The interviewer wants to know that you care about the company.
- ◆ *How long do you expect to work for us?* Most companies won't keep their employees if they can't use their skills. You might simply tell the interviewer that you expect to work there as long as it's good for both of you.
- ◆ *Where do you want to be 5 years from now?* Give an answer that's consistent with the company's goals. Make long-term goals a part of your answer, but focus on the short term. You might, for instance, tell the interviewer that you'd like to be a CEO in 5 years, but you realize you have other things to learn first and the next logical step is to be a division manager. Then explain why you'll be ready for the position of CEO in 5 years.
- ◆ *What's your greatest accomplishment?* Don't talk about responsibilities; talk about results you've achieved. Review your notes from Chapter 7, "Creating Winning Résumés and Cover Letters," where you put accomplishment statements together for your résumé. Rather than say that you balanced the books and did the financial statements, talk about ways that you cut overhead costs by a certain percentage or improved system performance or employee morale. Describe the big picture and how it benefited the company (or others), not just the activities you performed.
- ◆ *What are your strengths?* Present about three strengths and relate them to the position you're seeking. Show the benefits to the company.
- ◆ *What are your weaknesses?* Give one weakness, but turn it into a strength. You might say, for example, that you used to push back deadlines to

turn in higher-quality work. However, you've learned to delegate more and have only slipped once in the past year. One word of caution: A pet peeve of many managers is hearing "I'm a perfectionist" stated as a weakness. Being a perfectionist in some jobs can indeed be a positive thing, but so many people give this answer that it can sound like a coached response rather than a genuine one.

◆ *Tell me about a time you failed.* On this question, take the approach that you fell off your bike, learned what you did wrong, and got back on and rode it better. Show how you learned from your mistakes, always turning a negative into a positive. Don't say that you've never failed. Interviewers will think you're not telling the truth or aren't trying hard enough to come up with an answer.

◆ *Will you get along with your potential boss?* Here you might say that you concentrate on the job and the results, and you are flexible enough to work with almost anyone. If you're asked to describe the worst boss you've worked for, frame your answer as a disagreement over a business issue or a difference in styles, not as a personal dislike. You might also be asked what kinds of people rub you the wrong way. Don't get into personal likes and dislikes. The interviewer wants to see if you get along well with people and focus on getting the job done.

◆ *What would you do if...?* Many interviewers make up scenarios that test your knowledge of the job. Begin your answers with statements like "One of the things I might consider would be...." Don't commit to a process of what you would do because the employer might disagree. Instead, offer several choices and indicate that you'd carefully assess the situation. This shows your willingness to explore all the courses of action and make a knowledgeable choice.

◆ *Would you accept part-time or temporary work?* Employers are more inclined to hire for full-time work from their pool of part-time and temporary workers than to hire someone from the outside. If you'd like to stay with the company, ask whether the part-time or temporary position is likely to result in a permanent position before you say yes.

◆ *What are your salary requirements?* If asked what your salary requirements are, you might say, "I would expect a salary that's comparable to the going rate for someone with my qualifications. I'm excited about this opportunity and your company because I believe that my skills and expertise are a good match for the position. What kind of figure do you have in mind?" If pressed for a figure, be nonspecific and state a range, indicating that you're willing to negotiate. Convey the attitude that the job is more important than the money.

Answering Difficult Interview Questions

You need to prepare to talk about any topic that you're concerned or feel uncomfortable about because chances are good that the issue will come up. This

What Not to Do in an Interview

◆ Don't stretch out on the floor to complete the job application.

◆ Don't challenge the interviewer to arm wrestle.

◆ Don't brush your hair or teeth or apply makeup in the interviewer's office.

◆ Don't chew gum and blow bubbles constantly.

◆ Don't announce that you haven't had lunch and proceed to eat a hamburger and fries in the interviewer's office.

◆ Don't interrupt the interview to phone your therapist for advice on answering specific questions.

might include a poor work record, being fired for serious problems, or having been convicted of a crime.

How has the difficult situation been a learning experience that's made you a better person? Formulate your answer and practice saying it aloud. You might want to include some recent experience as evidence that you've made changes in your life. Be brief and to the point. Don't overexplain. If you come across as confident rather than angry or defensive, the interviewer will be more likely to accept your answer.

Handling Illegal Interview Questions

Interview questions that inquire about your age, race, ethnic background, sexual orientation, religious beliefs, or disabilities are illegal. Any questions that probe into your private life and background are forbidden. Although it's the responsibility of the interviewer to know the law, not all interviewers do. Many employers don't know what's legal and illegal.

Do some reading and know your rights as they pertain to the interview. Women in particular are asked many questions about their family responsibilities, despite Title 7 of the 1964 U.S. Civil Rights Act, which prohibits sex discrimination in hiring. You might be asked about the size of your family, if you plan to have more children, whether you're available to travel, what you'd do if your husband were transferred, or what you'd do if your child got sick and you had to be at work.

If you're asked whether you plan to have kids, for instance, try to identify the employer's underlying concern. You might say, "I don't quite understand your question and how it's relevant to the position. Could you please explain?" The employer might reconsider or clarify the question. If the employer is concerned about your ability to travel or work overtime, offer reassurance that you're extremely responsible in fulfilling all your obligations on the job.

You might decide to answer the question if the issue isn't important, rather than risk offending the employer. If you prefer not to answer the illegal question or aren't interested in working for the company, you might say, "I don't feel obligated to answer that," or "That question is inappropriate." In choosing this option, you'll either enlighten (the employer might not have realized that the question was illegal and will appreciate your pointing it out) or alienate (the employer might not consider you for the position). Try to avoid reacting in a hostile fashion. You can always decline a job offer later. You don't have to work for a discriminatory company, but you can use their job offer as leverage to find something better.

Posing Questions to the Interviewer

Toward the end of your interview, the interviewer will probably ask if you have any questions. Most interviewers judge job applicants by the questions they ask as well as the questions they answer. Ask three or four intelligent questions that will impress the interviewer and provide you with additional information. Pose questions about the company and your future with it, and avoid questions of a personal nature. Also, make sure that your questions don't reflect your inexperience or unfamiliarity with the field or the company. Here are some potential questions you might ask:

- Why is this position available?
- Could you show me a copy of the detailed job description?
- Can you describe a typical day on the job?
- How many people are in the department? To whom would I report?
- What are some of the drawbacks of this position?
- What is the most rewarding aspect of this job?
- How easily do people advance from this position? Where do they go from here?
- Is this a good position to learn about this industry?
- Would I be eligible for any training programs?
- How are employees evaluated and promoted?
- What is a realistic time frame for promotion?
- Why do you enjoy working for this company?
- How would you describe this company's management style and working environment?
- What do you see as the greatest threat to this company?
- What are the greatest opportunities for this company?
- What do you see as the future of this company?
- I feel confident that I would be able to do the job well. Do you have any questions about my suitability?

Following the Interview

After you've completed the interview (whew!), relax and take a few minutes to jot some notes in your journal. Ask yourself these key questions:

- What does the position involve?
- What do I like and dislike about the position and the company?

- ◆ What points did I make that interested the employer?
- ◆ Did I pass up opportunities to show how my abilities can benefit the position and the organization?
- ◆ Did I talk too much? too little?
- ◆ Did I make any mistakes or have trouble answering any of the questions?
- ◆ Did I feel well prepared?
- ◆ What could I do to improve my performance during future interviews?
- ◆ Did I find out enough about the employer and the job to allow me to make a knowledgeable decision?

Consider all these issues. If you felt that your presentation was lacking, find ways to improve it. Follow up immediately with a one-page personalized letter, thanking the interviewer. Express your appreciation for the opportunity to interview and your enthusiasm about the position and the company. Reiterate your strengths as they relate to the requirements of the job and the company. Close the letter with a request to meet again.

Allow about a week for the employer to contact you after receiving the letter. If you haven't heard anything by this time, follow up with a phone call to check on the status. Again, express your enthusiasm and interest in the firm and position. Ask whether any decisions have been made and when you'll be notified.

In the meantime, continue to schedule more interviews. Don't place too much importance on one interview experience, or you'll waste valuable time and energy. The right job for you might be around the next corner.

Negotiating Job Offers

Before accepting a position, take the time necessary to evaluate the offer. Don't jump at the first job offer you get. If you act too quickly, you might feel stuck in an unsuitable position. If you're offered a desirable job with a salary and benefits package that you think are fair, by all means accept it. If based on your research, the offer is far below your expectations, negotiate a better one. Negotiating will be worth your while. Not only can it result in a better starting salary and benefits, but it will also affect later pay raises and future earnings with this and other employers.

Realizing that the company is interested in you, make a counteroffer that's fairly close to what you actually want. Show the person hiring you the data you've collected about salaries for this specific job. This will show that you've done your homework and will increase the likelihood that the employer will offer a better deal.

If asked what your salary requirements are, you might say, "I would expect a salary that's comparable to the going rate for someone with my qualifications. What kind of figure do you have in mind?"

The employer will probably state a salary range. If, for instance, the employer indicates that the position pays between $30,000 and $36,000, ask for a salary toward the top of that range or slightly higher. If the employer offers a specific figure, it's most likely at the midpoint of the range for the position. If,

Debbie, Age 32

Debbie was an accomplished graphic designer, working for a firm in Los Angeles. She was raising her two kids alone as she and her husband had separated the year before. She had always wanted to relocate to a rural area. She figured that now was the time to make a job change and work for a different company. The only problem was that she was shy and rather modest about her accomplishments and dreaded having to do interviews. Her résumé contained an impressive work record and list of achievements and awards.

When I talked to Debbie, she had just completed her first job interview and felt she had blown it. "During the interview," she says, "I completely glossed over my work record and discussed insignificant things that relate to my present job. I should have communicated my relevant accomplishments as they relate to the job I'm seeking. Somehow I thought that my résumé clearly spells out my qualifications, but I don't think the interviewer even looked at it. I certainly learned that I can't expect my work record to speak for itself. If I don't toot my horn, nobody else will, and I won't stand out from the rest."

for instance, the employer indicates that they can't offer more than $33,000, it often means that $33,000 is the midpoint. Try to negotiate the initial offer upward. Most companies will negotiate up some degree if they feel your requirements are reasonable.

If you have other job offers, this puts you in a better negotiating position, as does being employed. Research reflects that employed job seekers are offered higher starting salaries than those who are unemployed. On the other hand, the competition for jobs in some industries is so fierce that they're less open to negotiation. This might include fields such as entertainment, advertising, public relations, and publishing.

If the salary really bothers you, but you realize that the offer is a firm one and you still want the job, consider accepting it, with the agreement that you'll have a salary review in 6 months. And remember that salary is just one part of the total package. People who work only for the money tend to become unhappy when the newness of the position is gone. Assess the entire picture when deciding whether to take a job. Here are some important points to consider:

Company and Management

Your comfort in the field or type of industry (e.g., government, private sector)

The size, growth rate, and market potential of the company

Facilities and working conditions

Your desire to work there for a period of time

The stability of the company's management

The company's interest in employee well-being (e.g., pay, benefits, training, flex schedules)

Job

Your duties and responsibilities

The opportunities initially offered to you

Whether you'll be able to use your abilities

The company's training programs (inside and outside the company)

The broadening of your experience for future jobs

The amount of travel and/or overtime the job requires

The compatibility of the job with your medium-/long-range career goals

Potential for Promotion

How and by whom performance is judged, whether a salary review is included

The number of realistic opportunities for promotion and to what level

Compensation

Starting salary and long-term outlook

Other benefits (e.g., insurance, profit sharing, tuition assistance, rental car, flexible benefits packages or menu plans that allow you to choose from a variety of options)

Community

The geographic area and the environment of the company

Desirable amenities in the area of the company

Cost of living, distance from work, length of time to commute

When deciding whether to take a temporary position, an internship, or a volunteer position, evaluate the benefits in terms of your longer-term goals. Employers often use this type of short-term employment as a method to determine whether they'd like to offer you a permanent position in the future.

Competition for many positions is fierce, so keep your expectations realistic. Don't ask for the moon. The most important thing is to decide whether you'll be happy with the job and accomplish what's important to you. You can always ask to renegotiate after you've proven your value to the company. Strive to make an informed decision based on what's right for you, taking the entire picture into consideration.

Writing the Acceptance/Decline Letter

It's always best to follow up on job offers in writing. If you wish to accept a job offer, state your acceptance in a letter, along with the terms you've agreed upon with the employer (e.g., salary, benefits). Thank the people who made your employment possible. To confirm your starting date, state the day and time you'll see them.

If you wish to decline the job offer, do so politely over the phone and follow up with a letter. Always keep doors open for the future. You might change your mind down the road. Let the employer know that you received a better offer or have decided to pursue another direction, such as a freelance or consulting career, at this time. Close the letter by thanking the employer for his or her time and consideration.

Excelling on the Job

Work life in the United States is becoming more competitive. Jobs are harder to get, and after you're hired, you're often expected to work harder than was the case 20 or 30 years ago. Here are some tips to help you excel on your job:

- *Welcome change:* How well you accommodate change will determine your success. Look for ways to take advantage of it. For instance, stay abreast of technology and software developments in your area of expertise. This will keep you on the leading edge in your industry.
- *Be your own manager:* Think of yourself as self-employed, regardless of where you work. Take the responsibility of managing your career. Continually assess your skills and determine what you need to advance in your current position.
- *Connect with others:* Develop quality relationships with your colleagues and clients. Teamwork is a must these days. Develop a variety of contacts inside and outside the company you work for. Find mentors who will help you and extend yourself to others who are just starting out and would appreciate your wisdom.
- *Do it now:* Nothing impresses as much as immediate follow-up. If you're given an assignment, try to complete it as soon as possible and ask for the next one.
- *Exceed your employer's expectations:* Look for ways to go beyond the mere "satisfactory" in your assignments. Do them faster and do them better this time than the last. Show up ready for new challenges.
- *Know what your boss wants:* You're going to be judged on how well you do what your employer wants, not on your conception of the job. Periodically meet or check with your supervisor to make sure that you give

your assignments the proper emphasis and that nothing of major importance is neglected.

◆ *Get good at what you do:* Seek out areas where your special skills and interests are most fully used. Hopefully, you'll become so good at certain things that if a reduction in force is forthcoming, you'll be that much more indispensable.

◆ *Know your organization's history and objectives:* Learn as much as you can about how your company developed. Read everything you can about how it operates today, particularly the relationship between various divisions and departments. Know your company's competitors.

◆ *Maintain a positive attitude:* People like coworkers who are optimistic and cheerful. Even when the negatives pile up, look for challenges that will help you stay on an even keel and encourage those around you.

◆ *Take a long view:* Don't let temporary setbacks discourage you. Remember that the good and bad will occur in your working life, and the important thing is to take a long view—look at where you're going and your progress toward your goal.

◆ *Invest in yourself:* Attend professional meetings, participate in in-house training opportunities, and take night or weekend classes at a nearby college or university to acquire skills (and maybe even contacts) that will be helpful as your career expands and advances.

◆ *Take time to plan:* Spend at least 5% of your time planning what you're going to do, in what sequence, and with what results. Purchase a daily planner and spend some time with it every day.

Moving On

We've established that preparation beforehand is the key to successful interviews and resulting job offers. Interviewers will be sizing you up for various positions, but this is also your opportunity to screen potential employers to see if you'd like to work for them. If you feel good about a job offer, congratulations—your practice, preparation, and research have paid off. If you aren't selected, don't take it personally—you could have been up against the boss's cousin.

Whether you or the interviewer decides that it's not the right match doesn't matter. What's important is that, as in any relationship, it's better to part ways rather than plunge into a commitment that both parties don't feel strongly about. Treat each interview as a learning experience. Keep a running list of ways you can improve your performance and move on to the next opportunity, remembering that the best is yet to come.

CHAPTER 11

MASTERING CHANGE

"Change is inevitable, growth is a choice."

NORMAN COUSINS

E dmond B. Szekely vividly captures the essence of change in his essay on the fear of transformation (*Gospel of the Essenes*, published by National Book Network):

> *Sometimes I feel that my life is a series of trapeze swings. I'm either hanging on to a trapeze bar or swinging along or, for a few moments in my life, I'm hurtling across space in between trapeze bars. Most of the time, I spend my life hanging on for dear life to my trapeze-bar-of-the-moment. It carries me along at a certain steady rate of swing and I have the feeling that I'm in control of my life. I know most of the right questions and even some of the right answers. But once in a while, as I'm merrily (or not so merrily) swinging along, I look ahead of me into the distance, and what do I see? I see another trapeze bar swinging toward me. It's empty, and I know, in that place in me that knows, that this new trapeze bar has my name on it. It is my next step, my growth, my aliveness coming to get me. In my heart-of-hearts, I know that for me to grow, I must release my grip on the present, well-known bar to move to the new one.*

> *Each time it happens to me, I hope (no, I pray) that I won't have to grab the new one. But in my knowing place, I know that I must totally release my grasp on my old bar, and for some moment in time, I must hurtle across space before I can grab onto the new bar. Each time I am filled with terror. It doesn't matter that in all my previous hurtles across the void of unknowing, I have always made it. Each time I am afraid I will miss, that I will be crushed on unseen rocks in the bottomless chasm between the bars. But I do it anyway. Perhaps this is the essence of what the mystics call the faith experience. No guarantee, no net, no insurance policy, but you do it anyway because somehow, to keep hanging onto that old bar is no longer on the list of alternatives. And so for an eternity that can last*

a microsecond or a thousand lifetimes, I soar across the dark void of "the past is gone, the future is not yet here." It's called transition. I have come to believe that it is the only place that real change occurs. I mean real change, not the pseudo-change that only lasts until the next time my old buttons get punched.

I have noticed that, in our culture, this transition zone is looked upon as "nothing", a no-place between places. Sure the old trapeze-bar was real, and that new one coming towards me, I hope, that's real, too. But the void in between? That's just a scary, confusing, disorienting "nowhere" that must be gotten through as fast and as unconsciously as possible. What a waste! I have a sneaking suspicion that the transition zone is the only real thing, and the bars are illusions we dream up to avoid the void, where the real change, the real growth occurs for us. Whether or not my hunch is true, it remains that the transition zones in our lives are incredibly rich places. They should be honored, even savored. Yes, with all the pain and fear and feelings of being out-of-control that can (but necessarily) accompany transitions, they are still the most alive, most growth-filled, passionate, expansive moments in our lives.

And so, transformation of fear may have nothing to do with making fear go away, but rather with giving ourselves permission to "hang out" in the transition between the trapeze bars. Transforming our need to grab that new bar, any bar, is allowing ourselves to dwell in the only place where change really happens. It can be terrifying. It can be enlightening, in the true sense of the word. Hurtling through the void, we just may learn how to fly.

A support guide for women in transition wouldn't be complete without a discussion on mastering change. In this chapter we focus on strategies to help embrace the void and develop inner resiliency so that change can be a welcome event rather than something to be feared and avoided. We'll also talk about methods for handling stress.

Stepping Into the Void

The void is something most of us fear and tend to avoid, as the opening essay of this chapter so beautifully illustrates. I mentioned in Chapter 1, "Where Are You Now?" that in *LifeLaunch* (published by Hudson Institute Press), Frederic Hudson and Pamela McLean refer to this process as "cocooning"—periods of time when you take stock of your life, talk to yourself, and get in touch with your core values and feelings. William Bridges, author of *Transitions: Making Sense of Life's Changes* (published by Addison-Wesley), refers to the void as the "neutral zone."

According to Bridges, in order to face up to and experience the tremendous personal growth of the neutral zone, a person must first give in to the emptiness and stop struggling to escape it. The gap between our old and new lives (the void between our trapeze bars) allows us to experience self-renewal through a process of reintegration.

The neutral zone allows us to view life from a place of emptiness that we can't see anywhere else. A succession of such views over a lifetime produces wisdom—wisdom that allows us to make well-grounded choices and embrace change with confidence and self-knowledge. In essence, it allows us the opportunity to realize what matters most in life, so that the next trapeze bar we grab is a choice we feel passionate about.

How can we encourage ourselves to step into the neutral zone and gain self-knowledge? Bridges offers these helpful tips:

◆ *Find a regular time and place to be alone:* When making a big change, you might be tempted to surround yourself with people constantly. What you really need at this time are brief periods of alone time when your inner values can make themselves heard. It might mean getting up early every morning and spending a half hour by yourself, sitting in the living room with a cup of coffee.

◆ *Begin a log of neutral-zone experiences:* Try to capture a daily or weekly account of your experience. Ask yourself, "What was my mood?" "What was I thinking about?" "What unusual things happened?" "What decisions do I wish I had made?" "What dreams did I have?" The process of identifying the next chapter of our lives comes from within; it's not external to our situation.

◆ *Write an autobiography:* Often it's only in seeing where you have been that you can tell where you're headed. Things look different from the neutral zone, and one of the things you let go of when ending one chapter of life and starting another is the present and the need to see the past in a particular way. This letting-go process makes it easier to conceive of a new future.

◆ *Take the opportunity to discover what you really want:* Don't think about what you should do or have to do. Think about what you want, what you desire, what you dream for—without limitations. Listen to your inner signals. Explore how you're feeling in the present.

◆ *Think of what would be unlived in your life if it ended today:* What has been unlived in your life—what dreams, convictions, talents, ideas, and qualities in you have been unrealized? How would you have lived your life or expressed yourself in a significant way?

◆ *Go on your own version of a passage journey:* Spend a few days alone in an unfamiliar place that's quiet. Eat simple meals, and don't distract yourself with activities such as reading or watching TV. Take this time to journey into the emptiness and reflect consciously on your current transition process. Allow yourself to *be.* If you're happy, be happy. If you're bored, be bored. Take along a journal to jot down your thoughts—whatever they might be.

Creating Temporary Support Structures

During a time of transition, we stand a much better chance of allowing ourselves to experience the void if we have structures and support systems in place to relieve us of some of our usual responsibilities. In our busy everyday lives, how can we take regular time-outs or 3-day journeys to be alone with our thoughts?

In Chapter 1 you accounted for your time and how you spend it in your daily routine. You checked off the commitments you feel are out of line with what you desire. In Chapter 6, "Getting Your Support Systems in Place," you thought about support systems that could alleviate some of your responsibilities and free up time so that you have the opportunity to embrace the next chapter of life. This is a critical step in the transition process because we often avoid new beginnings because of our busyness. It is this idle busyness—the minutes and hours of the day that we spend doing the things we least desire—that keeps our hands frozen to the old trapeze bar. We hang onto it for dear life and miss the chance to swing onto the new bar and start fresh.

Transitions that you initiate for yourself are easier if you approach them in phases. If you see a big change coming, experiment with the unknown before you let go of the familiar. This will make the change less scary.

Sudden transitions can be followed by a period of shock, bereavement, anger, depression, and confusion. These are normal, unavoidable reactions because change involves loss—the closing of one chapter and the opening of another. Allow yourself to go with and live through these emotions.

Take stock of the changes you've successfully negotiated in the past. Ask yourself, "How did I do it?" and "What did I learn that can be applied now?" Think of the ways that you created temporary support structures that enabled you to swing from one trapeze bar to another.

Developing Emotional Resiliency

When you free up time and allow yourself to embrace the void, emotional resiliency can be your best friend. Your inner resiliency determines how well you manage change, handle stress, and bounce back from adversity. Are you a victim who constantly blames others for your discomfort, or do you take responsibility for your feelings (e.g., "Feeling guilty is a choice I make; no one is 'making me' feel guilty")? Highly resilient people take responsibility for their feelings.

If you don't think your resiliency is where it ought to be, then feel reassured that much as physical health and strength can be improved, research suggests that a person can develop excellent mental health and emotional strength as well.

Al Siebert, PhD, author of *The Survivor Personality* (published by Practical Psychology Press), has studied the traits of survivors who beat the odds in the face of adversity. His work reflects that highly resilient people show many similar qualities, and that emotional resiliency comes from developing these attributes. The following sections describe some of the most prominent traits, along with action plans on how to develop them.

Being Curious, Playing, and Laughing

Resilient people laugh and play like children. They have a good time almost anywhere. They have a childlike curiosity and love to learn how things work. They wonder about things, make mistakes, get hurt, and laugh. They ask lots of

Katrina, Age 20

When Katrina told her family that she wanted to leave their home in San Diego to go to college in Chicago, their reaction was varied. Her parents were supportive and understanding, but Katrina knew her mom went to her room and sobbed, and she saw that her dad had tears in his eyes when she boarded the plane. Their first child was leaving the nest—something many parents don't look forward to—but they knew she had to make her own decisions and mistakes.

"That year in Chicago provided me with opportunities I never would have had if I hadn't ventured out beyond the neighborhood I grew up in," Katrina says. "I learned quickly that San Diego girls are not meant to live in Chicago's bitter weather. At the end of the school year, I moved to the one place I always swore I'd never go, Los Angeles, which made my family unbelievably happy. It never would have happened had I not had my time in Chicago."

Just 2 months ago, Katrina made another monumental decision. She realized she had an opportunity to do something few people can, so she's taking a couple years off from school to pursue a film career. "Let's just say that most of my family is vocal against this turn of events, but I know who I am and how I want to live my life. Vikram Chandra summed it up best when he said, 'For some the unfamiliar holds the promise of love, of perfection.' To me, changing my life is not scary or a mistake; it's completely necessary for me to develop into the person I was meant to be."

questions such as "What if I did this?" or "What's funny about this?" They gain an accurate understanding of the world around them. The ability to play and laugh at what's happening improves your chances of coping well. It enables you to remain calm during times of change, rather than overwhelmed, so that you can absorb useful information rapidly.

Action plan: Ask more questions, be curious, experiment, and laugh more. Learn how to laugh at yourself and challenging situations so you don't have to rely on outside sources.

Learning From Unpleasant Experiences

Resilient people rapidly take in unpleasant experiences and see how they can make a change for the better. They ask what lesson can be learned or they say, "The next time this happens I'll...." They gain strength from their mistakes. On the other hand, less resilient people react to unpleasant experiences by protesting "Look what's happened to me now!" or "If only other people would change, my life would be better!" They have what's called a *victim reaction*. They blame others for their unhappiness and portray upsetting people as villains.

Action plan: People tend to react to an upsetting or a distressing experience with either a victim/blaming reaction or a learning/coping reaction. To develop the learning/coping habit, accept responsibility for your reaction to what other people do or say. For example, instead of feeling that other people are *making you angry*, realize that *you feel angry* when other people act or talk a certain way. If you practice the learning/coping response over and over for weeks and months, you'll develop confidence in yourself. You'll anticipate either handling something well or learning something useful. This will do wonders for your stress level.

Developing Strong Self-esteem

Self-esteem is how we feel about ourselves. It determines how much we learn when something goes wrong. Resilient people have high self-esteem, which can be thought of as a protective thick skin. When people have strong self-esteem, they have such a high opinion of themselves that they're able to shrug off criticism without feeling wounded. At the same time, strong self-esteem allows them to receive compliments gracefully.

Action plan: Generate a list of all the things you like and appreciate about yourself. Practice positive self-talk on a regular basis. (See Chapter 5, "Expanding Your Comfort Zone," for ways to combat negative self-talk.)

Valuing Your Paradoxical Traits

Resilient people are mentally and emotionally flexible. They're comfortable with contradictory personality qualities. They can be serious and playful, self-appreciating and self-critical, angry and forgiving, trusting and cautious, selfish and unselfish. They can, for instance, be pessimistic and optimistic at the same time by thinking in negative ways to reach positive outcomes: "What could go wrong here and how can I avoid it?"

Action plan: Make up a list of your opposing personality traits. The more pairs of opposites you have, the better. Validate your opposing qualities. Tell yourself, "It's good to be both optimistic and pessimistic."

Practicing Empathy for Difficult People

Resilient people view things through the perspectives of others, no matter how difficult people might be. They ask themselves, "What do others think and feel?" "What is it like to be them?" or "What's legitimate about what they feel, say, and do?"

Having empathy for someone you know and like generally comes easily. How do you react to difficult people? Do you give them a negative label? Labeling others is a sign that you're judgmental and emotionally fragile.

If you're like most people, you label the negative person a pessimist and think that if only they would change, things would be better. This is a victim reaction to something you have difficulty handling. The problem isn't that the person is pessimistic; the problem is that you have a negative reaction to the person's pessimistic attitude.

Action plan: When someone acts or talks in a way that upsets you, try to comprehend how things look from his or her point of view. The ability to understand ways of acting, thinking, and living that you disagree with is a high-level skill. This doesn't mean that you agree with or approve of the other person's views or actions. It only means that you comprehend.

Think of a difficult person as your teacher. This person says and does things that you don't like. You can learn and gain strength from this person through curiosity and empathy. Stop blaming them. Ask yourself what payoffs these people get from talking and acting as they do.

Expecting Good Outcomes

Resilient people expect things to work out well. They anticipate handling challenges in a way that leads to the best possible outcome. They adjust their actions to ensure success. They have a high tolerance for ambiguity and uncertainty. In personal conflicts, resilient people look for resolutions that have all sides winning. This synergistic motivation allows everything to work better.

Action plan: When posed with a challenging situation, ask yourself how you can interact with it so that things turn out well for everyone, including yourself. Then work in a gently persistent way to make it so.

Siebert stresses that resilient personalities are not without disadvantages:

> *They sometimes feel like misfits, seldom understood by others. They are expected to always be strong and not have to ask others for emotional help or support. They are so hardy and persistent they may not give up when they should. When they counter-balance optimistic thinking by anticipating what might go wrong, they can be mistakenly labeled by a group as a negative person.*

Despite these disadvantages, Siebert believes that the resilient personality will most likely be the norm generations from now:

> *In past decades children were trained by parents and teachers to dress, act, talk, and think as told. The "good child" training included instructions to never be selfish, not brag, don't talk back, don't be unhappy, don't cause trouble, and cooperate. In today's rapidly changing world, however, people trying to act like good five-year-olds do not adapt or cope as well as people who have more inner resiliency. The highly resilient person has a competitive advantage in today's world. I believe that this will be the "normal" or average person a few generations from now. Profound changes in our world are forcing people to break free from cultural prohibitions that have suppressed the development of their inner strengths.*

Managing Stress

A big part of developing emotional resiliency so that you can master change more easily is keeping your stress level down. Stress is an internal feeling we experience—often as a result of our perceptions of outside forces. We can get so caught up in routinely feeling everyday stress that we don't realize the toll it takes on us both mentally and physically. Strive to keep your stress level down by regularly taking care of yourself physically and emotionally. The following sections offer some useful strategies to keep stress in check.

> ## Carmen, Age 34
>
> Ten years ago Carmen and her husband had the opportunity to purchase the lease on a franchise business. They took the opportunity, and for the first year it looked as though business success was theirs. Unfortunately, a year later, the franchise was shut down for improvements at the option of the franchiser. "We were forced to pay our fixed costs," Carmen says. "The only option available at the time was acquiring debt. That instance was only the first in a succession of occurrences in which we were forced by the franchiser to carry the burden of debt for their ideas. It was our error not to realize in the beginning that the lease was not to our benefit."
>
> Eventually it became painfully clear that it was time to sell the business, even though the result would not recoup their investment. "We decided to stop fighting the current and flow with it," Carmen says, "with hope that we would sail to a better place. After all, when you know your local tax collector on a first-name basis, it's time to admit that things aren't going well. Change was frightening at first. This was a time when our faith was tested. We were rewarded with a stronger sense of family and a strong marital relationship. I'm not saying that financially we were in a great place or that we smiled cheerfully when the bills came in. But people came forward and told us of similar experiences in their lives that we were unaware they had survived. Support came from unexpected sources on a regular basis. Fortunately, what we had done to support ourselves financially for the past 10 years did not define our souls, so when our business was lost, our souls remained. We were left with an experience that gave us more empathy for others and a deeper understanding of faith. We were given what we needed, not the financial success for which we had prayed. We are truly blessed."

Eating Properly

Make sure you eat properly and drink plenty of water. Don't stock the kitchen with junk food. Have on hand nutritious snacks and lunches that keep you energized throughout the day. A healthy sandwich and carrot sticks might not be as exciting as a bag of chips and a candy bar, but it will satisfy you longer.

Diet can also affect your energy levels and moods, which can have a definite impact on your work performance. A good resource on this topic is Elizabeth Somer's *Food and Mood: The Complete Guide to Eating Well and Feeling Your Best* (published by Henry Holt & Co.).

Exercising

Exercise is an excellent form of stress release. "I try to go to the gym four days per week," says Paula, a college student. "I think my workouts really help with stress." Don't get so caught up in your job search that you neglect this wonderful outlet that offers numerous health benefits and can add years to your life. Whether it's jogs, walks, or trips to the local pool or gym, you can't afford not to do it.

If you're currently unemployed, being in job search mode allows you the flexibility to exercise while others are working, so take advantage by plugging it in as a mandatory part of your week. Your mind and body will thank you and undoubtedly pay you back in terms of productivity.

Sleeping

"When I haven't had enough sleep, the next day I'm fuzzy-minded, crabby, and hungry all day," says Lynn, a former bookkeeper. It's hard to be enthusiastic or productive when you're lacking sleep. Make sure you get plenty of rest. If you have difficulty sleeping at night, take brief afternoon naps to give yourself a boost.

If you have a tendency to lie awake worrying at night, write down all your worries in a worry log before you go to bed. Then you can relax and count sheep, knowing that everything is accounted for. If you consistently have insomnia, do more exercise during the day to tire yourself out. Also, eat an adequate meal each night for dinner, and allow at least 2 hours for digestion before you go to bed. If your insomnia persists, see a doctor.

Being Physically Comfortable

Take brief time-outs from repetitive tasks by standing, stretching, and walking around the room at least once every 45 minutes. If you're tense, take some deep breaths and roll your head from side to side, with your eyes closed. Ask your partner or one of your children for a quick shoulder and neck massage.

During an intense job search, you might be working at a computer all day. Reduce your stress by taking care of your wrists, neck, and back. If your wrists or fingers feel sore, take short breaks and wiggle your fingers.

Choose furniture and equipment that's ergonomically correct, which provides physical and psychological comfort tailored to your needs. You can use padded wrist rests, a footstool, and pillows for additional relief and comfort. An excellent book on relieving pain and tension quickly is Eva Shaw's *60-Second Shiatzu: The Natural Way to Energize, Ease Pain, and Conquer Tension in One Minute* (published by Henry Holt & Co.).

Taking Time Out for Yourself

Be sure to carve out some personal time for you. Involve yourself in creative projects outside your job search activities for relaxation such as gardening, cooking, writing, or various crafts. Treat yourself to something relaxing such as a massage, a bath, or a good book. "I like to read while I take a bath," says Pat, the mother of four young kids. "I probably take one a week. I make everybody leave me alone for an hour. Of course, the kids always want to take a bath with me, and I have to fight them off." Spoil yourself a bit—searching for a job is no easy task, so you deserve it.

When you feel stressed, try playing a musical instrument, singing, listening to music, working in the yard, going to the beach, going to church, sewing, or watching a video. Try the Internet. "I'll get on the Internet and read my personal e-mail for a while," says Liz, an aspiring computer programmer. "That relieves my stress."

Spending Time with Your Family

Make a habit of spending one-on-one time with your children. Take a break and have a tea party, dance to music, or play a computer game together. "My stress release is my daughter," says Val, who recently started a home-based business working as a travel agent. "She comes and hugs me, and says, 'Mommy, I love you,' and the stress is all gone."

Treat your family to a surprise such as a brief excursion, the purchase of a big item, or a special dinner out when you experience success. "I have myself on a little incentive program," says Beth, a former nurse who changed directions and decided to be an accountant. "After I land my dream job, I'm taking my family on a Caribbean cruise in December."

Using Humor and Optimism to Lighten Things Up

Research suggests that those who use humor regularly suffer less fatigue, tension, anger, depression, and confusion in response to stress. Whenever a stressful event occurs, try using humor and optimism to ease the tension. When Fran, a new real estate agent, gets yelled at by someone she cold calls, she hangs up the phone, laughs, and moves on to the next prospect.

Learning to Say No

Defining your physical and psychological boundaries and sticking to them in an assertive fashion helps minimize stress. Establish your priorities and learn to say no to requests that take away from what matters to you. Time is your most valuable resource, and other people will waste yours if you let them.

Talking About Stressful Events

Before you reach a breaking point, talk about your upsets and frustrations with a friend or loved one. Crying can also help release pent-up feelings. If you need additional help, consult a mental health professional.

Exploring Relaxation Techniques

Relaxation techniques and self-hypnosis can do wonders for relieving tension and feelings of anxiety. Some people have a natural ability to concentrate deeply and place themselves in a relaxed state of consciousness. You can learn these techniques by attending a class or reading a book on the subject. Shakti Gawain's *Big Book of Relaxation: Simple Techniques to Control the Excess Stress in Your Life* (published by Relaxation Co.) is one good resource.

Practicing Spirituality

Call on your belief system in times of stress. This is an excellent strategy for coping with daily hassles or crises. Ann starts her job search workday by praying on the phone with a fellow job searcher. "My friend Barbara is also looking for a job," she says. "Every morning we pray together. It's become a ritual that we rely on and look forward to."

Using the Four-Step Approach to Reducing Stress

In *The Wellness Book* (published by Simon & Schuster), Herbert Benson, MD, and Eileen M. Stuart, RN, MS, introduce a four-step approach to reducing stress, which is also effective in breaking the habit of automatic negative self-talk:

1. *Stop:* Each time you encounter a stressful event, say "Stop!" to yourself before your thoughts begin to escalate into the worst possible scenarios.
2. *Breathe:* After you stop, breathe deeply to release physical tension and break the negative stress cycle.
3. *Reflect:* After you've stopped the automatic cycle of negative thoughts and taken a deep breath, reflect on the cause of your stress.
4. *Choose:* After you've stopped the process of responding automatically, taken a deep breath, and reflected on the cause of your stress, take a moment to choose how to deal with the stress.

Valuing Your Uniqueness

The topic of mastering change is highly subjective. How each person releases one trapeze bar and "hurtles through the void" to grab the next is as unique as the individual. It's important that you identify and use the strategies that work best for you in creating your new life chapter.

CHAPTER 12

BENEFITING FROM LESSONS LEARNED

"Sharing a part of ourselves is a gift we can pass along every day."

In honor of our uniqueness in how we master career and life transitions, I'm devoting this chapter to the inspirational stories of others who were kind enough to share their experiences. It is my hope and the hope of my contributors that you will not only see yourself in these stories, but that you'll benefit from the lessons learned.

Cindy Crew, Age 44, Elementary School Teacher

The first several months at home with my new daughter were a time of great joy and transition for me. Although I enjoyed every moment I spent with my beautiful daughter, I felt somewhat lonely and isolated. I'd been used to the fast pace of working full time, and I found that I missed not only the demands of working for a growing corporation, but also the paycheck that reminded me of my worth and the daily interaction with adults. I certainly believed that staying home with my daughter was important, but these other things kept nagging at me, occasionally stealing the pleasure I should have been feeling about being home with Katrina.

My girlfriend Susan and I had worked together for several years, had our first babies at the same time, and left the working world only a few weeks apart. After our girls were born, we would get together occasionally and share news, reminisce, and compare notes about our babies. When the girls were about 6 months old, finances dictated that Susan return to work, leaving her daughter in a local day care facility. Part of me felt sorry for Susan, but (you guessed it) part of me was excited for her. Over the next few months, Susan and I kept in touch and continued to compare notes about the girls.

One evening I called Susan to catch up. During our conversation, I told her that Katrina had recently turned her first somersault. It was really just a sideways roll, but I thought it was the most beautiful somersault I had ever seen and was really quite excited about this first. Susan shared with me that her daughter had recently turned a somersault also. The reason she knew about it was because the caregiver at day care had scolded Kerry for doing somersaults in her living room. Apparently, that was against the rules.

As I hung up the phone, I thought about how differently our daughters' firsts had been received. I remembered that I had clapped and cheered at that first somersault. I had called my husband at work to tell him about it. Katrina and I spent quite a bit of time that afternoon perfecting her somersaults and rollovers. Her daddy came home that night full of smiles and hugs, asking to see a "Katrina somersault." I couldn't help but compare the circumstances of Katrina's accomplishment with the circumstances of Kerrie's accomplishment.

I realized that evening that I wanted my children to be surrounded daily by a parent who would cheer them through each of their accomplishments. I wanted them to be applauded each time there was a first. Furthermore, I wanted either my husband or myself to be there to experience those firsts. I realized that staying home was extremely important to my babies' future growth. How much better it is to get a cheer rather than a scolding upon learning something new!

A few years later, my husband and I moved with our two children (Rob was born 2½ years after Katrina) to a new community. At that time, I did have to return to work. However, we never lost sight of our commitment to be at home with our children. We learned to juggle our time at work so that one of us was usually at home when the children were there. When neither of us could be at home, our wonderful parents and other relatives offered help and loving care when we needed it. As a result, Katrina and Rob (now 20 and 17 years old) have continued to have cheerleaders for all their firsts.

Stephanie Davis, Age 38, Corporate Trainer and Consultant

It's easy to get so caught up in roles and goals that you confuse them with the purpose of living. I had a wake-up call while I was living in southeast Asia. One day, I was driving through the jungle on my way to teach a sales course, and I noticed the people in kampong villages; they were sitting at the edges of their huts, swinging their legs, and had peace, pleasantry, and plenty on their faces—yet they had no electricity, running water, or books to teach them how to think and grow rich!

I was dumbstruck. I placed high value on knowledge, learning, and success, yet these people seemed satisfied with family, friends, and Mother Nature. "Who's right?" I wondered. "Is life supposed to be like mine, or like theirs?" That night at dinner, I was informed that deep in the Borneo Jungle, there were tribes of people living in trees, eating bugs, and still practicing headhunting!

The idea that we were all from the same human species, living on the same planet during the same century, within a 30-mile radius of one another, boggled my mind! How could the content of our lives be so different? I wanted to fulfill my purpose, but I couldn't decide if I should go back to the United States to help people "succeed," remain in beautiful Kuala Lumpur, or abandon my belongings and climb a tree!

The experience really put things into perspective. I realized that my purpose had nothing to do with my job. It's about loving and growing personally and spiritually—because I can do that crunching on a cockroach or coping with corporate downsizing. I shifted the entire focus of my seminars from teaching people to do things to freeing them to be fully human and fully alive.

Stephanie Davis is the creator of FrameWorking—a technology for shifting limiting beliefs. She is president of Leapfrog Performance Systems, Inc., in Carlsbad, California (phone 760-438-4333 or 888-LEAPFROG, e-mail leapfrog@email.com).

LeAnna DeAngelo, Age 36, University Lecturer and Researcher

I never made good grades in high school or the early years of college. When I went to have my eyes checked during high school, the optometrist said that I needed to wear glasses if I was going to attend college because I would read more throughout life. In the small town where I lived, nothing was a secret. The optometrist was married to my high school counselor. They did some pillow talk, and the counselor said that with my grades I would never go to college, so I didn't need glasses.

I dropped out of high school at 15 and only returned to school when told I would go to juvenile hall if I didn't. I got kicked out of the first college I attended my freshman year due to poor grades. Then, as I have learned, shift happens! Once I found the right school, I was making A's again. I graduated with honors from Pepperdine University and got a scholarship to attend graduate school.

After earning my master's degree, I worked as a psychotherapist, which had always been my dream. After a few years of practicing psychotherapy, I became burned out and realized that there were other talents I wasn't using. Teaching college sounded interesting. One day, in the middle of a therapy session with a very low-functioning schizophrenic, he prophetically said, "You are meant to be a teacher." I certainly hadn't told him I was thinking about this. I took it as a sign. Within a few weeks, I started calling various colleges to find an adjunct position. The dean at a well-respected private liberal arts college said, "I've been desperately trying to find someone to teach psychology. Your call is a gift from God!"

I quit my full-time job and taught part time at two different colleges. This was financial suicide, but good for my soul. I enjoyed the freedom and the genuineness of teaching so much that rather than go back to working full time in a job I didn't like, I went through bankruptcy. I was teaching at a well-respected school but collecting food stamps. I knew that the way to financial security, and to keep my career intrinsically motivating, was to earn a PhD. But low GRE scores and lack of research experience kept me from being accepted into a PhD program.

Unfortunately, around this time, my brother, who had AIDS, died—he hanged himself from a tree. Two days before his death, I spoke to him. He asked me if I was going to earn my PhD, and I said yes, I wanted to. He said, "I really want you to earn your PhD." I felt very motivated to earn my degree because this was the last conversation he had in life. Finally, I found a graduate school and earned my PhD with a large scholarship.

The moral of the story is to never take no for an answer. I didn't always listen when told no. If I can do it, so can you. People respect me when they hear this story. They respect me because I had the integrity to respect myself.

Tina Egge, Age 39, Writer

When I was 5 months pregnant with my first child, Nicole, I vividly remember having lunch with my manager and quietly stating that I was expecting. My manager's first question, as any good manager's would be, was what I would do after the baby was born. I emphatically told him that I was not the stay-at-home type and that I planned to return to work after an 8-week maternity leave. I did just that. My first day back to work was with 8-week-old Nicole (and husband in tow) on an airplane, headed across the country for the annual sales meeting. I was the "supermom" of the '90s. But life has changed.

After a year of juggling three nannies—one great, one acceptable, and one who had a prescription drug problem—I decided to leave my job and seek less demanding work. My maternal instincts had conflicted too greatly with my 70% travel schedule. Plus, juggling a two-career family was difficult. But leaving a paycheck and career status was very frightening. I had spent 4 years in graduate school and numerous more years working 70-hour weeks to get to my position as regional manager for a medical manufacturer. Why would I give all that up? Although I thought I would jump right into a less stressful (non-travel) job, what really happened was that I had a chance to breathe and think and realize what an impact I had staying at home. There were sacrifices, but I also quickly learned I could live without the things my paycheck bought.

I have since worked at home publishing a magazine, doing freelance writing, and doing some marketing consulting—all new careers. Plus, I have found time to serve on the board of a local charity. If I had never taken the risk and jumped off the career track for my children, I would never have gotten to experience all these new adventures. Now I think, "What is the worst thing that can happen? If it doesn't work out, change it." My motto is "you get what you expect." What I expect now is that my children will grow, and I have the power to balance work and children as best fits my family's needs.

Ralene Friend and Karen Friend, Ages 53 and 30, Founders of Friend Communications and 100 Voices

The idea to start Friend Communications and 100 Voices came to us one evening when we were sitting on the floor together, reading an article about a recently held Marketing to Women conference. It was a huge event, attended by representatives of many of the Fortune 500 companies. The keynote speaker was business guru Tom Peters. Our first question was "What in the world is Tom Peters doing talking about women?" He called women "business opportunity No. 1" as he beseeched corporations to actively focus on the women's market. We looked at each other and said "Hello! Who better to assist businesses in reaching today's female consumer than a couple of today's women—especially a Gen Xer and a Baby Boomer? We *are* the market!"

As we started to develop our ideas, women began to share their consumer experiences with us. They told stories about being ignored by salespeople or being told to "go get your husband, and we'll work up a deal." Tom Peters was right—women were absolutely not being taken seriously as primary buyers. We realized that women needed a place to share their stories. It became obvious that many industries needed to change the way they did business. Again, who better to develop strategies for improving customer relations with women than women themselves?

Along the way, we created a project we had not originally envisioned. We built a Web site dedicated to providing a voice for today's female consumer—a place for women to share their consumer experiences. They could go there to recommend female-friendly businesses to other women and get consumer information. Without those voices talking to us, we might not have stayed with our idea. Women wanted to share their consumer stories—they wanted someone to listen—and they wanted things to change. We wanted to be instrumental in causing the changes. This became our mission.

Starting our business meant lots of changes for both of us. We had to continue working as we developed the business. We didn't have the financial backing to jump in full time right away. Maintaining a balance between working and keeping our business alive wasn't an easy task. Our day jobs continued to devour our time and energy. We were forced to learn to prioritize, to say no, and to remember what was important to each of us.

Probably the biggest blessing of working together as a mother–daughter team has been that Baby Boomer mom notices how different things are for women today and can remind daughter that it hasn't always been this way for women. Generation Xer daughter, on the other hand, gently reminds mom that it isn't "that way" anymore. It keeps us both focused on and excited about the future. Women should intermingle with each other across generations as much as possible. We learn from each other's experience and each other's reality every day.

Ralene Friend and Karen Friend are the owners and founders of Friend Communications and 100 Voices: Understanding Today's Female Consumer. They offer cutting-edge presentations, educational curriculum, customized staff development, personalized consulting, market research, and professional site reviews. You can reach them at 760-941-5445 and info@rfriend.com. Or check out their informative Web site at www.100voices.com.

Andrea Susan Glass, Age 52, Professional Writer and Editor

Fifty loomed. My half-century mark. A time of reflection or resentment? For years, every January 1, I promised myself this would be the year I'd leave the drudgery of my bookkeeping business and commence a full-time writing career. The mental repetitiveness of bookkeeping couldn't have been more divergent from the creativity of writing. Yet as each January passed, my momentum waned. Apparently I'd lacked the courage, not to mention the financial resources, to take the plunge.

Turning 50 was the shove I needed. After thwarting my dream all those years, I couldn't face another year never knowing my capacity to succeed in my chosen passion. On January 1 of the year I would become 50 years young, I gave notice to my bookkeeping clients, some of whom I'd been indispensable to for more than 10 years. I was not without apprehension, but one of my favorite sayings from the book of the same name, *Feel the Fear and Do It Anyway*, has sustained me through many ventures. Few of us who take on challenges are fearless; however, experience has taught us that when we act in spite of fear, the fear almost always abates.

Faith also helped me through this trying transition. Although I believed in my ability to succeed as a writer and had been building networks for years, I'd experienced the writer's share of rejection. However, I chose not to focus on the past, but to create the future with my every waking thought. Praying to God, repeating affirmations, writing out my goals and marketing plan, joining business and writing groups, and working with a Small Business Administration (SBA) counselor all provided the support I needed to survive and thrive.

The financially lean periods were discouraging, but instead of giving up, I occasionally took part-time jobs. Yet the joys of finally working at what I love to do and of growing as a writer and entrepreneur far exceed the trying times. I've become a champion for "going for your dreams!"

Candace Pittenger, Age 38, Founder of GenAMERICA

I was 28 years old, earning good wages in the challenging field of architectural engineering, 1 of 2 women on a 50-man team of engineers—a woman's dream! Yet something was wrong with this picture. Something was missing, and I didn't know what it was.

Several years later, during a Christmas holiday, I invited a few friends to visit the frail elderly residents of a local nursing home. The door was partially open, as I knocked on a particular resident's door. The name on her door was Winifred. I peered into her room. She sat in her wheelchair gazing out the window. I asked, "Would you like to have a visitor today?" There was no answer. I thought to myself, "Maybe she can't hear me." As I walked into her room, she saw me and reached out to me. I took her cold hands and placed them both in the warmth of mine.

While I leaned over, and gently hugged her, she held onto me for a brief moment. When it was time for me to go, I walked toward the door. All of a sudden there was a wailing yell from inside the room. "Wait! Come back! Don't go!" I was completely astonished! I turned around to face Winifred, and she sweetly looked up at me. I knew that the wail had come from within her. There was no one in the room besides the two of us. As I walked over to her, I expected her to speak aloud. She looked at me and reached out her hand.

An angel had spoken to me in that moment. It was her way of letting me know that Winifred was deeply touched by me and by my love. Later, I was told that Winifred had no family or friends to spend time with her. She needed my nurturing and caring. Her angelic exclamation was my miracle that day. For Winifred, it was the only way she could communicate her need to be loved by me.

(Adapted from Ribbons of Wisdom, How to Communicate with Our Elderly *by Candace Pittenger.)*

Throughout hundreds of nursing homes, I have witnessed thousands of lonely, depressed elderly people like Winifred with no visitors. Most have given up on life. Through these experiences, God touched me in a way that changed my life forever, and I found my true passion—the missing link in my life. I knew that I would come to serve the elderly in a much bigger way than I had ever imagined.

In 1994 I founded GenAMERICA, Generations of Americans Serving the Elderly, whose mission is to bring volunteers to visit with the elderly and affect their daily quality of life. In 1997, using the knowledge that our frail elderly have shared with me, I wrote my first book, *Ribbons of Wisdom, How to Communicate with Our Elderly.*

Today, in 1999, I am known as "The Voice of America's Elderly." Traveling across the United States, I give presentations about relating to the elderly. Through improved loving communication, using simple techniques in touch, loving, and caring, we can make a remarkable difference in the quality of life of our elderly, especially the frail and institutionalized.

I know my work is not yet complete; it is still unfolding before me. My story is one of commitment and love for our elderly, stemming from my own grandmother helping to raise me as a little girl and then years later, from Grandma being admitted to a nursing facility. The most precious gift you can give the elderly is the gift of the human spirit. God bless you.

For more information regarding GenAMERICA, write to PO Box 601203, San Diego, CA 92160, or call 888-875-3533.

Jackie Quinn, Age 46, Psychology Doctoral Student

I graduated from a college preparatory high school in 1970, and at that time the only career path available to me (I thought) was either as wife and mother, secretary, nurse, or teacher. I quickly decided that I didn't want to get married until my late 20s, I didn't want to be a nurse, and I didn't want to be a teacher. That left "getting a job." I never gave much thought to choosing a career. I just wanted to get a job in order to pay my bills, go out and have fun, buy lots of clothes, and then get married someday.

My mother was unusual because she was a working mom while I was growing up in the '50s and '60s. There was no such thing as day care, and I wasn't even allowed to stay at my grade school during the lunch hour because I lived a block from school. My family was lucky because my aunt lived nearby and I was able to spend my lunch hour and after-school time with my cousins at their home.

I was raised to be independent, which is probably why I didn't fall into the category of so many women in my city—getting married and raising a family immediately after high school. Although I was raised this way, I wasn't encouraged to go to college or pursue a career. Even though my mother had always worked, and at the time I graduated high school had a great job as an Avon manager managing 150 women, she didn't encourage me to think of a career. It was always assumed that I'd just get a job, get married someday, have children, and let my husband take care of me.

It wasn't until I turned 30 and decided that I still wasn't in a hurry to get married that I seriously started thinking about my future and what role *I* could play in it. One day, when I was complaining that it seemed like I needed a college degree to get ahead in the dead-end jobs that I'd been working, my boyfriend at the time said that he though I should go to school because I was intelligent, not because I needed to for a job.

This was a turning point for me. I realized that I had choices and that I didn't have to let life happen to me. I could actually work toward something for my future. I started attending school on a part-time basis and am, at midlife, within a year of obtaining my PhD in clinical psychology. I'm still not sure "what I want to be when I grow up," but I have learned that life is more about the journey than about the destination.

Eva Shaw, Age 51, Writer and University Instructor

We learn lessons, good and bad, from our mothers. The counsel we are bombarded with as children is there, no matter who we become. Trust me on this. So although I've stopped myself from repeating her favorite clichés, Mama's words are still in me. They've taken me through her young death and the death of too many loved ones, personal potholes rivaling the Grand Canyon, and career changes that only the stalwart of heart could have accomplished. (Or the extremely stupid and naïve could have smiled through—and I've been both.)

"Talk is cheap."

"The road to hell is paved with good intentions."

"Penny smart, pound foolish."

"Sleep with dogs, and get up with fleas."

"Here today, gone tomorrow."

These were a few of Mama's favorites, although given the situation, I can hear Mama's voice repeating more. New Englanders have a knack for coming up with the icing on the cake, and she was a cliché sharpshooter from the old school. Mama started her own career as a secretary for $2.50 a week during the Depression; life was tough, and deprivation was tolerated like a soggy wool overcoat. I believe that these adages helped make sense of senseless loss and frustration to those who lived in the '30s and in a way we cannot even conceive.

Today, I apply the traditional wisdom in a time of high-tech you-name-it, when every idea, ethic, and philosophy seems to have been discarded. The clichés are corny, I'll grant you that, but I've modeled my writing career and personal values around the "horse sense" on which I was raised. I have never forgotten that "a fool and her money are soon parted." I know that you "get as good as you give," and that "every cloud has a silver lining." Next time life throws you a curve ball, apply these clichés!

If you didn't have the opportunity to cut the apron strings with advice that's as American as apple pie, you can share my mother's. Mama would be happy to hear you. So before coveting a colleague's business expertise, accounts, or perfect home (or husband or toddler), be aware that Mama would tell you "the grass always looks greener on the other side of the fence." Next time you hear someone complain about a coworker, you can quote her: "People who live in glass houses shouldn't throw stones." And if you need a boatload of business savvy to share, Mama would tell you, "Don't take any wooden nickels."

Someday in our technological future, perhaps someone will look back on my work and say, Eva did "an honest day's work for an honest day's pay." That would be right as rain for me.

Eva Shaw, PhD, is the author of more than 40 books, including For the Love of Children *(published by Health Communications, Inc.) and* Writing the Nonfiction Book *(published by Rodgers & Nelsen) and more than 1,000 magazine articles, columns, and features. She teaches writing at universities and conferences, and is currently working on 5 books at the same time because "if you want to get something done, give it to a busy person."*

CHAPTER 13

RECOMMENDED RESOURCES

"Seek help, and you will receive it."

SANDY ANDERSON, PhD

Ｎew information on life and career transition is popping up daily, in the form of books, magazines, and newsletters. Help is available from a vast array of organizations, agencies, and online services. This chapter lists a multitude of resources relevant to topics covered in each chapter.

Chapter 1, "Where Are You Now?" and Chapter 2, "Where Do You Want to Be?"

Books

100 Best Careers for the 21st Century, by Shelly Field, Prentice Hall, 1996.

Breaking Out of 9 to 5, by Maria LaQueur and Donna Dickinson, Peterson Publishers, 1994.

Do What You Are: Discover the Perfect Career for You Through the Secrets of Personality Type, by Paul Tieger and Barbara Barron-Tieger, Little, Brown and Company, 1995.

Do What You Love, The Money Will Follow: Discovering Your Right Livelihood, by Marsha Sinetar, Paulist Press, 1987.

The Enhanced Occupational Outlook Handbook, JIST Works (Ed.), 1998.

Finding the Hat That Fits: How to Turn Your Heart's Desire into Your Life's Work, by John Caple, Plume, 1993.

Finding Your Perfect Work: The New Career Guide to Making a Living, Creating a Life, by Paul and Sarah Edwards, Jeremy P. Tarcher/Putnam, 1995.

The Guide for Occupational Exploration, JIST Works (Ed.), 1993.

How to Choose the Right Career, by Linda Schrank, VGM Career Horizons, 1992.

I Could Do Anything if I Only Knew What It Was, by Barbara Sher, Delacorte Press, 1994.

LifeLaunch: A Passionate Guide to the Rest of Your Life, by Frederic Hudson and Pamela McLean, The Hudson Institute Press, 1995.

Making a Living Without a Job: Winning Ways for Creating Work That You Love, by Barbara Winter, Bantam, 1993.

Occupational Outlook Handbook, JIST Works (Ed.), 1998.

Shifting Gears: How to Master Career Change and Find Work That's Right for You, by Carole Hyatt, Simon & Schuster, 1990.

Starting Out, Starting Over: Finding the Work That's Waiting for You, by Linda Peterson, Davies-Black Publishing, 1995.

To Build the Life You Want, Create the Work You Love, by Marsha Sinetar, St. Martin's Press, 1995.

What Color Is Your Parachute? by Richard Bolles, Ten Speed Press, 1995.

Web Sites

Career Advice, www.careeradvice.com.

Career Talk, www.careertalk.com.

Career Magazine, www.careermag.com.

The Career Doctor, www.rpi.edu/dept/cdc/homepage.html.

Careers & Jobs, www.starthere.com/jobs.

Career Mosaic, www.careermosaic.com.

CareerBuilder, www.careerbuilder.com.

CareerPath, www.careerpath.com.

Chapter 3, "Choosing a Suitable Work Arrangement"

Books

199 Great Home Businesses You Can Start (and Succeed in) for Under $1,000, by Tyler Hicks, Prima Publishing, 1991.

1001 Businesses You Can Start from Home, by Daryl Hall, John Wiley & Sons, 1992.

The Best Home Businesses for the '90s, by Paul and Sarah Edwards, Jeremy P. Tarcher/Putnam, 1994.

The Complete Guide to Being an Independent Contractor, by Herman Holtz, Upstart Publishing Company, 1995.

The Complete Guide to Buying a Business, by Richard Snowden, Amacom, 1994.

Create the Job You Love: More Than 550 Ways to Escape the 8 to 5 Grind, by Barbara Johnson Witcher, Prima Publishing, 1997.

Franchises You Can Run from Home, by Lynie Arden, John Wiley & Sons, 1990.

Going Part-Time: The Insider's Guide for Professional Women Who Want a Career and a Life, by Cindy Tolliver and Nancy Chambers, Avon Books, 1997.

How to Buy and Manage a Franchise: The Definitive Resource Guide if You're Thinking of Purchasing a Franchise or Turning Your Business into One, by Joseph Mancuso and Donald Boroian, Fireside, 1992.

How to Form Your Own Corporation, by Anthony Mancuso, Nolo Press, 1993.

How to Start a Service Business: The Essential Tools for Success in the Fastest Growing Industry of the Future, by Ben Chant and Melissa Morgan, Avon, 1994.

Inc. Your Dreams: For Any Woman Who Is Thinking About Her Own Business, by Rebecca Maddox, Viking, 1995.

Jobshift, by William Bridges, Addison-Wesley, 1994.

Making It on Your Own: Surviving and Thriving the Ups and Downs of Being Your Own Boss, by Sarah and Paul Edwards, Jeremy P. Tarcher/Putnam, 1991.

MLM Magic: How an Ordinary Person Can Build an Extra-Ordinary Networking Business from Scratch, by Venus Andrecht, Ranson Hill Press, 1993.

On Your Own, by Lionel Fisher, Prentice Hall, 1995.

Scams, Swindles and Rip-Offs: How to Recognize and Avoid, by Graham Mott, Golden Shadows Press, 1994.

Telecommute! by Lisa Shaw, John Wiley & Sons, 1996.

Teleworking Explained, by Mike Gray, Noel Hodson, and Gil Gordon, John Wiley & Sons, 1993.

The Temp Survival Guide, by Brian Hassett, Carol Publishing Group, 1997.

Tips and Traps When Buying a Franchise, by Mary Tomzack, McGraw-Hill, 1994.

Wave 3: The New Era in Network Marketing, by Richard Poe, Prima Publishing, 1995.

The Work-at-Home Balancing Act: The Professional Resource Guide for Managing Yourself, Your Work, and Your Family at Home, by Sandy Anderson, Avon, 1998.

The Work-at-Home Sourcebook, by Lynie Arden, Live Oak Publications, 1999.

Work of Her Own, by Susan Wittig Albert, Jeremy P. Tarcher/Putnam, 1992.

Newsletters and Magazines

Bootstrappin' Entrepreneur, Suite B261-ND, 8726 S. Sepulveda Boulevard, Los Angeles, CA 90045-4082.

Business Start-Ups, 2392 Morse Avenue, Irvine, CA 92714, 800-274-8333.

Home-Based Business News: Bimonthly Newspaper for the Home-Business Entrepreneur, 0424 SW Pendleton, Portland, OR 97201, 503-246-3452.

Home Office Computing magazine, PO Box 2511, Boulder, CO 80302, 800-678-0118.

Inc.: The Magazine for Growing Companies, PO Box 54129, Boulder, CO 80322, 800-234-0999.

SOHO (Small Office/Home Office) Journal, 200 E. Thirty-seventh Street, Suite 400, New York, NY 10016, 212-683-1830.

Success: The Magazine for Today's Entrepreneurial Mind, PO Box 3038, Harlan, IA 51537, 800-234-7324.

Telecommuting Review, Gil Gordon & Associates, 10 Donner Court, Monmouth Junction, NJ 08852, 908-329-2266.

Working Solo, Portico Press, PO Box 190, New Paltz, NY 12561, 914-255-7165.

Agencies, Associations, and Organizations

American Association of Home-Based Businesses, PO Box 10023, Rockville, MD 20849, 800-447-9710.

American Home Business Association, 4505 S. Wasatch Boulevard, Salt Lake City, UT 84124, 801-272-3500.

Direct Selling Association, 1666 K Street, NW, Suite 1010, Washington, DC 20006, 202-293-5760. (Provides written guidelines on how to evaluate multi-level marketing organizations.)

Entrepreneurial Mothers Association, 375 E. Elliott, Suite Z, Chandler AZ 85225, 602-892-1464.

Home-Based Working Moms, Box 500164, Austin, TX 78750, workhommom@aol.com, www.hbwm.com, 512-266-0900.

Internal Revenue Service, Washington, DC 20224, 800-829-3676.

International Association of Home-Based Businesses, 8333 Ralston Road, Suite 4, Arvada, CO 80002, 800-414-2422.

International Franchise Association, 1350 New York Avenue NW, Suite 900, Washington, DC 20005, 202-628-8000.

Mothers' Home Business Network, PO Box 423, East Meadow, NY 11554, www.mhbn.com, 516-997-7394.

National Fraud Information Center, Box 65868, Washington, DC 20035, 800-876-7060, www.fraud.com.

National Home Office Association, 1828 L Street NW, Suite 402, Washington, DC 20036, 800-664-6462.

SCORE (Service Corps of Retired Executives), 1441 L Street NW, Room 100, Washington, DC 20416, 800-634-0245.

Web Sites

Business at Home: Making a Life While Making a Living, www.gohome.com.

Family Friendly Flexible Work Practices, www.wa.gov.au/gov/doplar/w%26f/ffwp/fam4.html.

Gil Gordon's Web Page (Telecommuting), www.gilgordon.com.

Small Office/Home Office (SOHO) Central, www.hoaa.com.

Small Office Site Work & Family Area, www.smalloffice.com/cooler/keep.htm.

Chapter 4, "Evaluating Your Training and Educational Needs"

Books

Barron's Guide to Distance Learning: Degrees, Certificates, Courses, Barron's Educational Series (Ed.), 1999.

The Best Distance Learning Graduate Schools 1999: Earning Your Degree Without Leaving Home, by Vicky Phillips and Cindy Yager, Princeton Review, 1999.

Careers for Women Without College Degrees, by Beatryce Nivens, McGraw-Hill, 1988.

Careers Without College Series: Health Care, Cars, Computers, Fashion, Fitness, Music, by Peggy Schmidt, Kristin & Schmidt, 1992.

The Fiske Guide to Colleges (15th ed.), by Edward Fiske, Times Books, 1998.

Going Back to School: College Survival Strategies for Adult Students, by Frank Bruno, ARCO Publishing, 1995.

The Insider's Guide to the Colleges: 1999 (25th ed.), by Yale Daily News, Griffin Trade Paperback, 1999.

Peterson's Colleges with Programs for Students with Learning Disabilities or Attention Deficit Disorders (5th ed.), Peterson's Guides, 1997.

Peterson's Guide to Distance Learning Programs (3rd ed.), Peterson's Guides, 1998.

Agencies

American Council on Education, The Center for Adult Learning and Educational Credentials, One Dupont Circle NW, Suite 1B-20, Washington, DC 20036.

College Level Examination Program (CLEP), Box 6601, Princeton, NJ 08541, clep@ets.org, 215-750-8420.

Council for Adult and Experiential Learning (CAEL) National Headquarters, 223 W. Jackson Boulevard, Suite 510, Chicago, IL 60606.

Educational Testing Service, Publication Order Services (TO-1) CN6736, Princeton, NJ 08541-6736.

U.S. Department of Education, 400 Maryland Avenue SW, Washington, DC 20202, 800-USA-LEARN.

Web Sites

Internet Scholarship Search Service, www.finaid.org.

Southwestern College Library College and Financial Aid Links, www.swc.cc.ca.us/CampusResources/Library/aid.htm.

University of Wisconsin-Extension's Distance Education Clearinghouse, www.uwex.edu/disted/home.html.

Accredited distance-learning degree programs, www.accrediteddldegrees.com.

Chapter 5, "Expanding Your Comfort Zone"
Books

The Artist's Way: A Spiritual Path to Higher Creativity, by Julia Cameron and Mark Bryan, Jeremy P. Tarcher/Putnam, 1995.

Attracting Terrific People: How to Find, and Keep, the People Who Bring Your Life Joy, by Lillian Glass, St. Martin's Press, 1997.

Being the Best, by Dennis Waitley, Pocket Books, 1987.

The Confidence Course: Seven Steps to Self-Fulfillment, by Walter Anderson, HarperCollins, 1997.

Creativity: Flow and the Psychology of Discovery and Invention, by Mihaly Csikszentimihalyi, HarperCollins, 1997.

Embracing Your Inner Critic, by Hal Stone and Sidra Stone, Harper San Francisco, 1993.

Feel the Fear and Do It Anyway, by Susan Jeffers, Fawcett Columbine, 1992.

Homecoming: Reclaiming and Championing Your Inner Child, by John Bradshaw, Bantam, 1992.

How to Win Friends and Influence People, by Dale Carnegie, Simon & Schuster, 1981.

Life Skills: Taking Charge of Your Personal and Professional Growth, by Richard Leider, Pfeiffer & Company, 1994.

Maximum Achievement, by Brian Tracy, Simon & Schuster, 1995.

The New Dynamics of Winning, by Denis Waitley, William Morrow and Co., 1993.

The Power of Optimism, by Alan McGinnis, HarperCollins, 1990.

Presentations Plus, by David Peoples, John Wiley & Sons, 1992.

Toxic People: Ten Ways of Dealing with People Who Make Your Life Miserable, by Lillian Glass, Simon & Schuster, 1995.

Unlimited Power, by Anthony Robbins, Ballantine, 1987.

Winning People Over: 14 Days to Power and Confidence, by Burton Kaplan, Prentice Hall, 1996.

Audiotapes

Powertalk! On Creating Extraordinary Relationships, by Anthony Robbins, Audio Renaissance, 1996.

Psychology of Winning, by Denis Waitley, Simon & Schuster, 1995.

The Science of Self-Confidence, by Brian Tracy, Nightingale-Conant, 1991.

Chapter 6, "Getting Your Support Systems in Place"
Books

The Babysitting Co-op Guidebook, by Patricia McManus, ordering address: 915 N. Fourth Street, Philadelphia, PA 19123.

The Complete Guide to Choosing Child Care, by Judith Berezin, Random House, 1991.

The Complete Guide to the Best Summer Camp for Your Child, by Richard Kennedy and Michael Kimball, Times Books, 1994.

Dinntertime Dilemma, The National Potato Board. Send a SASE to 5101 East Forty-first Avenue, Dept MH, Denver, CO 80216.

Encyclopedia of Associations, Gale Research (Ed.), 1999.

Handbook of Child and Elder Care Resources, National Technical Information Service (NTIS), 1995. U.S. Department of Commerce, Springfield, VA 22161, 703-487-4650.

Home-Based Employment and Family Life, edited by Ramona Heck, Alma Owen, and Barbara Rowe, Auburn House, 1995.

How to Avoid Housework: Tips, Hints, and Secrets on How to Have a Spotless Home, by Paula Jhung, Simon & Schuster, 1995.

Kitchen Express, by Dee Wolk with Marsha Palmer, Kitchen Express Publishers.

Mr. Food's Quick and Easy Side Dishes, by Art Ginsburg, William Morrow and Co., 1995.

Nathalie Dupree Cooks Quick Meals for Busy Days, by Nathalie Dupree, Clarkson Potter, 1996.

Once-a-Month-Cooking, by Mimi Wilson and Mary Beth Lagerborg, Focus on the Family Publishing, Colorado Springs, CO 80995.

Ribbons of Wisdom, How to Communicate with Our Elderly, by Candace Pittenger.

Smart Crockery Cooking, by Carol Munson, Sterling Publishing, 1996.

Weekdays Are Quick Meals: From Speedy Stir-Fries to Soups to Skillet Dishes and Thirty Minute Stews, Time-Life Books (Ed.), 1996.

The Working Parents Help Book: Practical Advice for Dealing with the Day-to-Day Challenges of Kids and Careers, by Susan Crites Price and Tom Price, Peterson Publishers, 1996.

Magazines and Newsletters

At-Home Dad newsletter, 61 Brightwood Avenue, North Andover, MA 01845-1702, www.parentsplace.com/readroom/athomedad.

Child magazine, PO Box 3167, Harlan, IA 51593, 800-777-0222.

Nanny News, Childcare News Network Corp., 137 Wood Avenue, Stratford, CT 06497, 800-ME-4-NANNY.

Parents magazine, PO Box 3042, Harlan, IA 51537, 800-727-3682.

Working Mother and *Working Woman* magazines, 230 Park Avenue, New York, NY 10169, 800-234-9675.

Agencies, Associations, and Organizations

American Camping Association, 5000 SR 67 N., Martinsville, IN 46151-7902, 800-777-2267.

The American Council of Nanny Schools, Delta College, University Center, MI 48710, 517-686-9417.

Child Care Aware, 1319 F Street NW, Suite 810, Washington, DC 20004, 800-424-2246.

Families and Work Institute, 330 Seventh Avenue, 14th Floor, New York, NY 10001, www.familiesandwork.org, 212-465-2044.

GenAMERICA, PO Box 601203, San Diego, CA 92160, 888-875-3533.

International Nanny Association, 125 S. Fourth Street, Norfolk, NE 68701-5200, 402-691-9628.

NannyTax Inc., 50 E. Forty-second Street, Suite 2108, New York, NY 10017, 212-867-1776.

National Association of Child Care Resource & Referral Agencies, 1319 F Street, Suite 810, Washington, DC 20004, 202-393-5501.

100 Voices, Friend Communications: Understanding Today's Female Consumer, 760-941-5445, info@rfriend.com, www.100voices.com.

Safe Sitter, 1500 N. Ritter Avenue, Indianapolis, IN 46219, 800-255-4089.

YMCA Child Care Resource Service, 101 N. Wacker Drive, Chicago, IL 60606, 312-977-0031.

Child Care and Elder Care Referral Service, 1160 Battery, 4th Floor, San Francisco, CA 94111, www.careguide.net, 415-474-1278.

Chapter 7, "Creating Winning Résumés and Cover Letters"

Books

Every Woman's Essential Job Hunting & Résumé Book, by Laura Morin, Bob Adams, Inc., 1994.

The Résumé Kit, by Richard Beaty, John Wiley & Sons, 1991.

Résumés in Cyberspace: Your Complete Guide to a Computerized Job Search, by Pat Criscito, Pat Criscito Publisher, 1997.

Résumés That Knock 'Em Dead, by Martin Yate, Adams Media, 1994.

Valut Reports Guide to Résumés, Cover Letters and Interviews, edited by Matt Johnson, Houghton Mifflin Company, 1997.

Newsletters

The Résumé Resources Review by Julia Bauer, julia@bauer.org, www.bauer.org, 650-571-1153.

Organizations

Résumé Resources, julia@bauer.org, www.bauer.org, 650-571-1153.

Chapter 8, "Exploring Your Options"

Books

Occupational Outlook Handbook, JIST Works (Ed.), 1998.

Chapter 9, "Finding the Work You Love"

Books

101 Secrets to Living an Organized Life, by Janet Taylor, ordering address: PO Box 54091, Philadelphia, PA, 19105-4091, 215-229-7232, torganized@aol.com.

Boundaries, by Henry Cloud, HarperCollins, 1996.

The Career Coach, by Carol Kleiman, Dearborn Financial Publishing, 1994.

Career Planning and Job Search Catalog, JIST Works, 1997.

Finding a Job on the Internet, by Alfred and Emily Glossbrenner, McGraw Hill, 1995.

The Gentle Art of Communicating with Kids, by Suzette Elgin, John Wiley & Sons, 1996.

Good Behavior Made Easy Handbook: Over 1200 Sensible Solutions to Your Child's Problems from Birth to Age Twelve, by Stephen Garber, Marianne Daniels Garber, and Robyn Freedman Spitzman, Great Pond Publishers, 1992.

How to Survive Your Computer Workstation, by Julia S. Lacey, CRT Services Inc., 1996.

Is Your "Net" Working?: A Complete Guide to Building Contacts and Career Visibility, by Anne Boe and Bettie Youngs, John Wiley & Sons, 1989.

Job-Hunting on the Internet, by Richard Nelson Bolles, Ten Speed Press, 1997.

Job Strategies for People with Disabilities, by Melanie Astaire Witt, Melanie Astaire Witt, 1992.

The JobBank Guide to Employment Services 1998–1999, by Steven Garber (Ed.), Jennifer Pfalzgraf (Ed.), and Andy Richardson, Adams Media Corporation, 1997.

The Loving Parents' Guide to Discipline: How to Teach Your Child to Behave, with Kindness, Understanding, and Respect, by Marilyn Gootman, Berkley Books, 1995.

The New Dynamics of Goal Setting: Flextactics for a Fast Changing World, by Dennis Waitley, William Morrow and Co., 1996.

The Ninety-Minute Hour, by Jay Levinson, E.P. Dutton, 1990.

Notes from a Friend: A Quick and Simple Guide to Taking Charge of Your Life, by Anthony Robbins, Fireside, 1995.

Organize Your Family! by Ronni Eisenberg with Kate Kelly, Hyperion, 1993.

Organize Your Home! by Ronni Eisenberg with Kate Kelly, Hyperion, 1994.

Parent and Child: Getting Through to Each Other, by Lawrence Kutner, William Morrow and Co., 1991.

Parents' Guide to Raising Responsible Kids: Preschool Through Teen Years, by Karyn Feiden, Prentice Hall, 1991.

Positive Discipline, by Jane Nelson, Ballantine, 1996.

Power Networking: 55 Secrets for Personal and Professional Success, by Donna Vilas and Sandy Vilas, Mountain Harbour Publications, 1992.

Stephanie Winston's Best Organizing Tips, by Stephanie Winston, Simon & Schuster, 1995.

Successful Job Search Strategies for the Disabled: Understanding the ADA, by Jeffrey Allen, John Wiley & Sons, 1994.

Time Management for Unmanageable People, by Ann McGee-Cooper with Duane Trammell, Bantam, 1994.

Time Shifting: Creating More Time to Enjoy Your Life, by Stephen Rechtschaffen, Doubleday, 1996.

Timelock: How Life Got So Hectic and What You Can Do About It, by Ralph Keyes, Ballantine, 1993.

The Top Ten Career Strategies for the Year 2000 and Beyond, by Gary Grappo, Berkley Books, 1997.

Winning the Fight Between You and Your Desk, by Jeffrey J. Mayer, Harper Business, 1995.

You Can Find More Time for Yourself Every Day, by Stephanie Culp, Betterway Books, 1994.

Agencies

Better Business Bureau, 4200 Wilson Boulevard, Suite 800, Arlington, VA 22203, 703-276-0100, www.bbb.com.

National Association of Professional Organizers (NAPO), 1033 LaPosada Drive, Austin, TX 78752, 512-206-0151.

The National Institute of Occupational Safety and Health, 200 Independence Avenue SW, Room 715H, Washington, DC 20201, 800-356-4674. (Publishes a newsletter on how to avoid common home-business ailments related to heavy computer usage.)

Audiotapes

Denis Waitley's Psychology of Motivation, by Denis Waitley, Simon & Schuster Audio, 1993.

Videos

How to Organize Your Home: Secrets of a Professional Organizer, by Stephanie Schur, SpaceOrganizers, 1995.

Web Sites

America's Job Bank, www.ajb.dni.us/index.html.

Boldface Jobs, boldfacejobs.com.

Monsterboard, www.monsterboard.com.
Rebecca Smith's eRésumés & Resources, www.eresumes.com.

Computer Online Services

America Online, www.newaol.com, 800-827-6364.
AT&T Worldnet, www.ipservices.att.com/index.html, 800-809-1103.
CompuServe, www.compuserve.com, 8000848-8199.
Delphi, www.delphi.com, 800-695-4005.
Genie, www.genie.com, 800-638-9636.
Microsoft Network, www.msn.com, 800-426-9400.
Prodigy, www.prodigy.com, 800-822-6922.

Chapter 10, "The Art of Job Interviews"

The 90-Minute Interview Prep Book, by Peggy Schmidt, Peterson's, 1996.
ADAMS Interview Almanac, Adams Media Corp. (Ed.), 1996.
Make Your Job Interview a Success, by J. Biegeleisen, ARCO Publishing, 1994.
Portfolio Power: The New Way to Showcase All Your Job Skills and Experiences, by Martin Kimeldorf, Peterson's, 1997.
Sweaty Palms: The Neglected Art of Being Interviewed, by H. Anthony Medley, Ten Speed Press, 1993.
Take Charge of Your Career, by Daniel Moreau, Kiplinger/Times Business, 1996.

Chapter 11, "Mastering Change"

Books

60-Second Shiatzu: The Natural Way to Energize, Ease Pain, and Conquer Tension in One Minute, by Eva Shaw, Henry Holt & Co., 1995.
Big Book of Relaxation: Simple Techniques to Control the Excess Stress in Your Life, by Shakti Gawain, Relaxation Co., 1994.
Dancing with Fear: Overcoming Anxiety in a World Full of Stress and Uncertainty, by Paul Foxman, J. Aronson, 1996.
Dr. Nancy Snyderman's Guide to Good Health: What Every Forty-Plus Woman Should Know About Her Changing Body, by Nancy Snyderman, William Morrow and Co., 1996.
Eating Well Is the Best Revenge: Everyday Strategies for Delicious, Healthful Food in 30 Minutes or Less, by Marian Burros, Simon & Schuster, 1995.
Food and Mood: The Complete Guide to Eating Well and Feeling Your Best, by Elizabeth Somer, Henry Holt & Co., 1995.
From Panic to Power: Proven Techniques to Calm Your Anxieties, Conquer Your Fears, and Put You in Control of Your Life, by Lucinda Bassett, HarperCollins, 1995.

Learned Optimism: How to Change Your Mind and Your Life, by Martin Seligman, Pocket Books, 1990.

Mastering the Winds of Change: Peak Performers Reveal How to Stay on Top in Times of Turmoil, by Erik Olesen, HarperBusiness, 1993.

The Pleasure Prescription: To Love, to Work, to Play—Life in the Balance, by Paul Pearsall, Hunter House Publishers, 1996.

The Stress Solution: An Action Plan to Manage the Stress in Your Life, by Lyle Miller and Alma Smith, with Larry Rothstein, Pocket Books, 1993.

Success 2000: Moving into the Millennium with Purpose, Power, and Prosperity, by Vicki Spina, Wiley, 1997.

The Survivor Personality, by Al Siebert, Practical Psychology Press, 1996.

Transitions: Making Sense of Life's Changes, by William Bridges, Addison-Wesley, 1980.

The Wellness Book, by Herbert Benson and Eileen Stuart, Fireside, 1992.

You Can Excel in Times of Change, by Shad Helmstetter, Pocket Books, 1991.

REFERENCES

Anderson, S. *The Work-at-Home Balancing Act: The Professional Resource Guide for Managing Yourself, Your Work, and Your Family at Home.* New York: Avon Books, 1998.

Anderson, S., and Anderson, B. *Willpower: How to Gain It and Maintain It.* San Diego, CA: California Dream Publications, 1987.

Bittel, L. *Right on Time!* New York: McGraw-Hill, 1990.

Bauer, J., Résumé Resources, personal communication, February 1999.

Bridges, W. *Transitions: Making Sense of Life's Changes.* Menlo Park, CA: Addison-Wesley Publishing Company, 1980.

Bruno, F. *Going Back to School: College Survival Strategies for Adult Students.* Indianapolis, IN: ARCO Publishing, 1995.

Csikszentimihalyi, M. *Creativity: Flow and the Psychology of Discovery and Invention.* New York: HarperCollins, 1997.

Family Friendly Flexible Work Practices: Job Sharing [World Wide Web, March 28, 1998]. Available at www.wa.gov.au/gov/doplar/w%26f/ffwp/fam4.html.

Fisher, L. *On Your Own.* Englewood Cliffs, NJ: Prentice Hall, 1995.

Friend, R., and Friend, K., Friend Communications, personal communication, February 1999.

The Guide for Occupational Exploration. Indianapolis, IN: JIST Works (Ed.), 1993.

Hassett, B. *The Temp Survival Guide.* Secaucus, NJ: Carol Publishing Group, 1997.

Helmstetter, S. *You Can Excel in Times of Change.* New York: Pocket Books, 1991.

Holland, J. *Making Vocational Choices: A Theory of Careers.* Englewood Cliffs, NJ: Prentice Hall, 1973.

Holtz, H. *The Complete Guide to Being an Independent Contractor.* Chicago: Upstart Publishing Company, 1995.

Hudson, F. *LifeLaunch.* Santa Barbara, CA: Hudson Institute Press, 1995.

Interconnectivity: Email, Listserv Lists and News Groups [World Wide Web, March 3, 1997]. Available at kuhttp.cc.ukans.edu/history/history-dept/internet/ch5.html.

Johnson, M., Elliott, R., Hamadeh, S., Oldman, M., and Hamaden, H. *Valut Reports Guide to Résumés, Cover Letters and Interviews.* Boston, MA: Houghton Mifflin, 1997.

Juline, K. "Peak Experience and Creative Flow." *Science of the Mind*, September 1997, pages 41–51.

Kerka, S. "Distance Learning, the Internet, and the World Wide Web." *ERIC Digest* No. 168, 1996.

Kleiman, C. *The Career Coach.* Chicago: Dearborn Financial Publishing, 1994.

Lankard, B. "Job Training Versus Career Development: What Is Voc Ed's Role?" *ERIC Digest* No. 171, 1996.

Maslow, A. *Motivation and Personality.* New York: Harper & Row, 1954.

McCoy, Doris. *Megatraits: 12 Traits of Successful People.* Plano, TX: Wordware Publishers, 1992.

Michelozzi, B. *Coming Alive from Nine to Five.* Mountain View, CA: Mayfield Publishing Company, 1992.

Morin, L. *Every Woman's Essential Job Hunting and Résumé Book.* Holbrook, MA: Bob Adams, 1994.

"Jobs on Display," *North County Times,* April 29, 1997.

Peoples, D. *Presentations Plus.* New York: John Wiley & Sons, 1992.

Price, S., and Price, T. *The Working Parents' Help Book.* Princeton, NJ: Peterson's, 1994.

Rigdon, J. "Ace That Job Interview." *Reader's Digest,* July 1995, pages 133–134.

"Employment Extra: How to Make Your Career Take Off," *San Diego Union Tribune,* September 23, 1997.

"Employment Extra: Searching for the Perfect Job?" *San Diego Union Tribune,* February 17, 1998.

Shaw, L. *Telecommute!* New York: John Wiley & Sons, 1996.

Siebert, A. *The Survivor Personality.* New York: Berkley Publishing Group, 1996.

Schrank, L. *How to Choose the Right Career.* Lincolnwood, IL: VGM Career Horizons, 1992.

Stahl, N. *Job Search Strategies.* Fallbrook, CA: Fallbrook Career Management Services, 1997.

Stahl, N. *Your Résumé in the Electronic Age.* Fallbrook, CA: Fallbrook Career Management Services, 1997.

Szekely, E. *Gospel of the Essenes.* Lanham, MD: National Book Network, 1986.

Tolliver, C., and Chambers, N. *Going Part-Time.* New York: Avon Books, 1997.

United Way. *Surviving Unemployment.* San Diego, CA: United Way, 1996.

Career Services University of Waterloo. *Career Development Manual* [World Wide Web, February 22, 1999]. Available at www.adm.uwaterloo.ca/infocecs/CRC.

Waitley, D. *Being the Best.* New York: Pocket Books, 1987.

U.S. Department of Labor Women's Bureau. *Facts on Working Women.* Washington, DC: author, 1998.

U.S. Department of Labor Women's Bureau. *Women and Work Factsheet.* Washington, DC: author, 1996.

U.S. Department of Labor Women's Bureau. *Women Workers: Trends & Issues.* Washington, DC: author, 1993.

Yossem, E. *How to Get a Financial Plan.* Santa Barbara, CA: E. David Yossem, 1997.

Young Women's Christian Association, *San Diego Women's Business Directory and Resource Guide,* San Diego, CA: author, 1998.